Cascading
Style Sheets:
A Beginner's Guide

James H. Pence

McGraw-Hill/Osborne

New York   Chicago   San Francisco
Lisbon   London   Madrid   Mexico City   Milan
New Delhi   San Juan   Seoul   Singapore   Sydney   Toronto

McGraw-Hill/Osborne
2600 Tenth Street
Berkeley, California 94710
U.S.A.

To arrange bulk purchase discounts for sales promotions, premiums, or fund-raisers, please contact McGraw-Hill/Osborne at the above address. For information on translations or book distributors outside the U.S.A., please see the International Contact Information page immediately following the index of this book.

Cascading Style Sheets: A Beginner's Guide

1234567890 FGR FGR 0198765432

ISBN 0-07-219295-X

Publisher   Brandon A. Nordin

Vice President & Associate Publisher   Scott Rogers

Acquisitions Editor   Jim Schacterle

Project Editor   Julie M. Smith

Acquisitions Coordinators   Emma Acker, Tim Madrid

Technical Editor   Merlyn Holmes

Copy Editor   Carl Wikander

Proofreader   Carroll Proffitt

Indexer   Jack Lewis

Computer Designer   Carie Abrew

Illustrators   Michael Mueller, Lyssa Wald

Series Design   Gary Corrigan

Cover Series Design   Greg Scott

Cover Illustration   Kevin Curry

This book was composed with Corel VENTURA™ Publisher.

Cascading Style Sheets:

A Beginner's Guide

This book is lovingly dedicated to:
My Lord and Savior, Jesus Christ.
Because he lives, I have hope for the future
(Titus 2:13-14).

Chris and Charlene,
Thanks for being patient while Daddy
was closeted in his study for such long hours.

About the Author

James H. Pence and his wife Laurel live near Dallas, Texas, where he directs Tuppence Creative Ministries, an outreach that promotes excellence in the arts for the glory of God. James turned to writing as a helpful means of expression after the death of his infant daughter, Michelle. Nearly 10 years later, "A Road not Chosen," James's narrative account of his and Laurel's experience was published in Dallas Theological Seminary's *Kindred Spirit* magazine.

A full-time freelance writer with a broad diversity of writing experience, James strives for excellence in all his work. He is the author of *How to Do Everything with HTML* (Osborne/McGraw-Hill). Also a fiction writer, James's suspense-thriller novel, *The Osmosis Project*, will be released by Tyndale House Publishers in the spring of 2003. James has also contributed op-ed pieces to the *Dallas Morning News*, and has been published in *The Writer* magazine and the 2001 edition of *The Writer's Handbook*.

James trained in creative writing and journalism at Dallas Theological Seminary. He is an accomplished speaker and teacher, having served as an ordained minister for more than 20 years. James is also a gospel chalk artist and vocalist. He uses these talents in reaching out to inmates in the Texas prison system.

For more information on James's writing and ministries, visit his Web sites: www.tuppence.org and www.jamespence.com, or email him at jim@tuppence.org.

Contents at a Glance

Contents

PART 2

Exploring the CSS Toolbox

Acknowledgements

Writing a book such as this is a team effort. I may provide the ideas and write the text, but without the help and hard work of a lot of other people my hard work would be fruitless.

Thanks to Jim, Emma, Tim, Julie, and Carl for all your hard work in crafting and producing a quality product.

A special thanks to Merlyn Holmes, my tech editor. Thank you for sharing your experience with me and putting your own stamp on my book. It's been a joy working with you.

My agent, Michael Rosenberg deserves credit for negotiating a great contract. Thanks again to the best agent on the planet.

Finally, thank you, Laurel, for encouraging me through the entire process. I'd have never made it without you.

Introduction

Several months ago, I was online, browsing through the posts in an HTML discussion group. One member had asked a question about how to create a simple visual effect on a Web page. Several people had responded, suggesting that the questioner try using CSS to create the effect he wanted. His response was a panicked, "Please! No CSS. I can understand HTML, but CSS is just too difficult."

Unfortunately, many beginners share this man's opinion. They shy away from CSS because they think it is difficult. After all, it has a strange syntax, strange terms (selectors, properties, and so on), and it seems altogether foreign. However, Cascading Style Sheets are easy to learn and use. If you have a basic understanding of how HTML works, you can be up and running with CSS in no time at all.

If that's true, why are many beginners afraid of CSS?

Who Should Read this Book

CSS isn't difficult, it's *different*. If you have been working with HTML for any time at all, you've become acquainted with *elements*, *attributes*, and *values*. Then, when you try to use CSS for the first time, you are confronted with *selectors*, *properties*, and a host of other strange things such as *pseudo-classes* and *pseudo-elements*. Add to that the weird syntax that CSS uses, and many beginners are ready to throw up their hands in frustration. They've just gotten used to HTML, and to use CSS they have to learn an entirely different language. If you count yourself among the frustrated, *CSS: A Beginner's Guide* is the book for you. However, even if you've not experienced any frustration, and are just looking for a good "entry-level" book on CSS, you'll find this book to be helpful.

You don't need to be an expert in HTML to work through this book, but it does help to have a basic understanding of how HTML works. A familiarity with basic HTML syntax, how to create a simple Web page, the concepts of elements, attributes, and values, and so on, will provide the foundation for learning CSS. If you want to brush up on your HTML while you are learning CSS, you might consider getting a copy of my book, *How to Do Everything with HTML*, or Wendy Willard's excellent text, *HTML: A Beginner's Guide*. Beyond that, all you need is the patience and discipline to work through this book's modules and exercises. It won't be long before you are routinely doing style sheets for all your Web pages.

What this Book Covers

CSS: A Beginner's Guide is divided into three sections: A Painless Introduction to CSS, Exploring the CSS Toolbox, and Designing with CSS.

Part, 1 "A Painless Introduction to CSS" introduces you to Cascading Style Sheets with a minimum of trauma and confusion. The essential concepts of CSS are covered in the five modules that make up this section, laying a foundation for a more complete understanding of CSS later in the book.

● **Module 1, "HTML and CSS: Focus on the Similarities"** gets you off to a good start by showing you that HTML and CSS have more in common than you might think. The terminology may be different, but many of the concepts are the same. As you learn to associate new concepts with ones you are already familiar with, your transition into CSS is made much easier.

● **Module 2, "Understanding and Using Selectors"** helps you understand selectors, one of the most important concepts in CSS. This module begins with simple "type" selectors and moves all the way through the concept of pseudo-classes and pseudo-elements.

● **Module 3, "Surveying CSS Properties"** gives you a quick introduction to the five most commonly used types of "properties," used in CSS. You will learn to understand text, font, color/background, box, and descriptive properties as you work through this module.

● **Module 4, "Applying Values"** introduces you to the basic value types that can be used in CSS. In this module you will learn how to use percentage values, measurement units, color values, and much more.

● **Module 5, "Understanding Cascade and Inheritance"** helps you understand why Cascading Style Sheets are called "cascading." In this module you will learn the concept of "the cascade," that is, how different styles and style sheets are prioritized by a browser. You will also learn how to give the styles you choose an extra "edge," in a browser's priority rankings.

Part 2, "Exploring the CSS Toolbox" moves you to the next level in your introduction to Cascading Style Sheets. In this section you will learn in detail about the different kinds of properties you can use in applying style to your Web pages.

● **Module 6, "Working with Font Properties"** shows you how to choose font families, set font size, create italic and bold text and much more.

● **Module 7, "Work with Text Properties"** will teach you how to adjust word and letter spacing, line spacing, create indents, and add special effects like "small caps."

● **Module 8, "Applying Color and Background Properties"** shows you how to control color on your page. You will learn how to set background and foreground (text) colors, add background images with CSS instead of HTML, even learn how to control how background images "tile."

● **Module 9, "Using Box Properties"** will show you how to create borders around virtually any HTML element. You can also manipulate margins and add "padding" inside each element. Most important, the box properties are fundamental to working with CSS layout. As you learn how to use these properties, you will be developing a foundation for designing pages with CSS.

● **Module 10, "Applying the Descriptive Properties"** tackles the often confusing subject of descriptive or "classification" properties. In this module you will learn about the function of the descriptive properties, and how you can use them to influence the behavior of any HTML element.

Part 3, "Designing with CSS" puts all the pieces of the puzzle together by showing you how to use CSS in designing your own Web site. This section also covers CSS 2 selectors and properties, giving you a sampling of some of the new CSS capabilities that are on the horizon.

● **Module 11, "The Visual Model"** acquaints you with different positioning schemes, and shows you how you can use the "box" concept to create attractive Web pages. Difficult subjects such as absolute and relative positioning are explained in simple terms and with practical projects.

● **Module 12, "CSS Visual Effects,"** demonstrates how to create special effects with Cascading Style Sheets. In this module you will learn how to work with the overflow, clipping, z-index, and visibility properties, and you will even get a chance to use CSS to create some simple DHTML (Dynamic HTML) effects.

● **Module 13, "CSS and Site Design"** covers the essentials for designing a Web site with CSS. Beginning with general Web design principles and moving into style sheet design and layout, this Module will give you the information you need to begin constructing a Web site and designing style sheets for it. It also covers the important issue of cross-browser compatibility, and how to design your style sheets for maximum compatibility.

● **Module 14, "Advanced CSS"** explores the world of CSS 2, covering advanced selectors, aural (audio) style sheets, CSS for paged media, and much more. Because many of these properties are not yet supported by browsers, this module gives you a survey of some of the neat things in store for you as a Web page designer in the next few years.

In Part 4, the "Appendixes," you'll find reference material that will complement your reading of the rest of the book.

- Appendix A, "**Answers to Mastery Checks**" provides the answers to the Mastery Check quizzes at the end of each module.

- Appendix B, "**CSS 1 Quick Reference**," is a series of charts covering selectors and properties from CSS 1, and some of the more commonly used (and better supported) selectors and properties from CSS 2. As you begin working with CSS, this will provide you with an easy reference while you are designing your style sheets.

How to Read this Book

This book is designed so that you can read through it from cover to cover, or just work through a particular module, as needed. If you are a beginner, it is recommended that you work through the modules in order, because the content of each module builds on the previous one.

Each module has at least one project for you to complete. You will find that your grasp of the material will increase significantly if you take the time to do the projects. It's one thing to read about CSS; it's another thing altogether to work with it.

Special Features

Throughout this book you will find *Hints*, *Tips*, and *Notes* that will provide you with extra information, or helpful ways to improve your grasp of certain points. You will also find detailed *code listings*, often containing both the HTML and CSS code. The code listings are set apart in gray boxes, and often will include special boxes that highlight key features of the code. *1-Minute Drills* are scattered throughout each module, giving you the opportunity for a quick "check-up" on your comprehension of the material. *Ask the Expert* sections provide added information in an easy to follow, question and answer format. Every module ends with a *Mastery Check* section that gives you the chance to test your knowledge of the subject matter thus far. You will find the ends to the Mastery Checks in Appendix A.

All of the code from this book may be downloaded from Osborne's Web site (www.osborne.com), and it may be accessed online at the author's Web site, (www.jamespence.com).

That's all you need to know to get started. So, fasten your seat belt and prepare to launch into a whole new world in Web design. I guarantee, when you see how easy CSS is to learn and work with, you'll wonder why you waited so long to learn it.

Part I

A Painless Introduction to CSS

Module 1

HTML and CSS: Focus on the Similarities

The Goals of this Module

- Understand how the limitations of HTML created the need for CSS
- Review HTML terminology and page structure
- Create a CSS test page
- Compare HTML and CSS terminology
- Create inline, embedded, and external style sheets

HTML revolutionized the World Wide Web. Now, Cascading Style Sheets are revolutionizing HTML. In the past, Web authors would painstakingly design page layouts, only to see those layouts mangled by different browsers, monitors, and screen resolutions. Accustomed to the precise control available in the print media, Web designers were horrified to discover that they had virtually *no* control over the appearance of their pages once they were posted on the Internet. A resourceful lot, those designers came up with a number of "workarounds" to solve the problem. Over time, HTML was also "extended" to include elements that governed presentation and appearance. Unfortunately, none of the solutions worked perfectly.

Enter Cascading Style Sheets. As defined by the World Wide Web Consortium (W3C), "Cascading Style Sheets (CSS) is a simple mechanism for adding style (e.g. fonts, colors, spacing) to Web documents." With CSS, a Web author's ability to control the appearance of a page has taken a quantum leap forward. However, many beginning Web authors don't seem to find CSS all that simple. They find it confusing and intimidating. Perhaps you find yourself among those who have skipped over the sections on CSS in your favorite HTML books. You decided to concentrate on learning HTML and worry about style sheets later on. Now that you've picked up this book, "later on" has arrived, and you're ready to learn how to use CSS.

At its most basic level, CSS is surprisingly easy to learn. In fact, by the time you have finished this module, you'll be using style sheets and probably wondering what you were afraid of. However, before you begin to explore CSS and learn how to create your first style sheets, you may find it helpful to get a little HTML and CSS history under your belt. How, exactly, did CSS develop? And why are style sheets so important?

Ask the Expert

Question: What is the W3C?

Answer: W3C stands for *World Wide Web Consortium*. It is an international group that establishes standards for HTML, CSS, and just about anything else related to the World Wide Web. The stated goal of the W3C is to "lead the Web to its full potential." You can visit their Web site and find a wealth of information on CSS and many other topics: **www.w3.org**.

A Brief History of HTML and CSS

If you know anything about the Internet, you know that the vast majority of Web pages are written in *Hypertext Markup Language* (HTML). What you may not know is that HTML was not designed to handle the flashy, graphics-heavy pages that are so common on the Web today. It was designed originally to display material with no more visual pizzazz than your average college research paper.

HTML's Documentary Origins

HTML was developed in the late 1980s at the European Laboratory for Particle Physics (CERN) as a means for scientists to exchange research information over a network of computers. Tim Berners-Lee, the creator of the World Wide Web, wanted to develop a cross-platform system that would enable documents to be linked together through the use of *hypertext*. To accomplish his goal, he used a complex language called *Standard Generalized Markup Language* (SGML).

SGML is a *meta language*. In other words, it can be used as sort of a "parent" language for designing other languages. Berners-Lee used SGML to create Hypertext Markup Language, a language that would enable scientists and researchers to define the structure of their documents and link them together. Remember, nothing particularly fancy was needed. All the scientists required was the ability to identify different levels of headings, lists, paragraphs, and so on, along with the ability to weave documents together by means of links. A little later on, the concept of tables was added to make it easier to display "tabular" data. Thus, HTML was born. It was a "no frills" markup language that facilitated the exchange of documentary information. And it was more than adequate—until the Web took the world by storm.

HTML's Inherent Limitations

Because HTML was designed for a very specific purpose, the World Wide Web's explosive growth created a problem. As long as HTML remained in the domain of scientists and researchers, its capabilities were not stretched beyond its limits. Even in the very early days of the Web, when everyone used simple text-based browsers such as Lynx, HTML could keep up with the demands being placed upon it. However, once graphical browsers were introduced, bringing pictures and colors into the mix, something had to change.

Ask the Expert

Question: What exactly is "hypertext?"

Answer: Simply put, hypertext is a *non-linear* way of linking documents. For example, consider one of the many CD-ROM encyclopedias, such as Microsoft's Encarta. If you look up a topic, astronomy perhaps, you will not only find an article on astronomy, you will also find links that lead you to other related material. Perhaps a portion of the article that deals with the Moon will have a link to an article on Apollo 11, which may have a link to a photo of Neil Armstrong, which may have a link to an audio clip of his famous "one small step for man" quote. The material is "non-linear" because you don't need to wade, page-by-page through an entire document to find what you want. You can jump from topic to topic and document to document by means of links.

Question: What is a markup language?

Answer: A markup language uses *tags* to "mark up" a document, indicating how the various elements of the document should be structured. The tags do this by identifying different *elements* of the document. For example, in HTML the <h1> </h1> tags identify the beginning and ending of a level one heading element. Thus, to set something apart as a level one heading in HTML, you would enclose it in <h1> tags, like this:

```
<h1>Level One Heading</h1>.
```

Question: Does SGML have any other "children?"

Answer: SGML has "spawned" many other markup languages. One that you'll be hearing a lot about in the future is *Extensible Markup Language* (XML). Extensible Markup Language is the heir-apparent to HTML and another good reason to learn how to use style sheets (XML requires them).

For a comparison, consider what happened to radio when television came along. In the glory days of radio, entertainment programs had to worry primarily about content. Granted, they still needed good actors and actresses, and good

1

musicians and sound effects people, but the main issue in a radio drama like *Gunsmoke* or *The Shadow* was its content. There was no need for make-up, costumes, sets, or anything of a visual nature. However, when TV became the dominant force, the whole paradigm behind production had to change. No longer could actors just stand at a microphone, holding their scripts; they had to perform in front of a camera. Now, they couldn't just sound right for the part; they had to *look* right for the part. Of course, studios also had to create sets, props, wardrobes, and many other things they didn't need when the medium was only radio. In other words, content and structure were no longer the only considerations. Producers also had to deal with visual presentation. That's essentially what has happened with HTML. It was designed to reflect *content* and *structure;* it came to be used to control *presentation.*

Workarounds and Extensions

With the advent of graphical browsers and the explosive growth of the Web, HTML was stretched beyond its limits. To compensate for HTML's design weaknesses, Web authors began to develop "workarounds." For example, to display large fonts, they would use the six different sizes of heading elements (<h1>, <h2>, and so on), even though that element was never intended to govern font size. To control layout, designers began to use tables, even though tables were intended to work like spreadsheets, not to be page layout devices. Complicating the whole process was the ongoing competition between Netscape and Microsoft.

Note

Netscape's *Navigator* browser came on the scene in 1994, challenging NCSA's *Mosaic* and quickly garnering an overwhelming percentage of market share. Microsoft's *Internet Explorer*, introduced in 1995, quickly became a strong competitor. To this day, these two browsers dominate the market.

Attempting to attract greater market shares for their browsers, these two companies added "proprietary" extensions to HTML (Netscape's <blink> element, and Microsoft's <marquee> element, for example). Some of these extensions (<font>, for example) were eventually incorporated into the HTML standard; others were not. Thus, the problem of presentation only worsened. Now, depending on how Web designers write their code, their pages might look good when viewed on Netscape, while looking terrible on Internet Explorer, or vice versa.

CSS Develops Alongside of HTML

As the browser wars were raging, the idea of developing a system of style sheets to control a Web page's presentation was gaining in popularity. The concept of style sheets for Web pages was not a new one by any means. In fact, it had been around from the inception of the Web and HTML, but there were many issues that needed to be ironed out. For example, who should have final control over how a Web page appears: the designer or the user? Another issue was whether style sheets should be written as separate documents, independent from browsers, or whether the styles should be embedded in the browsers themselves. Plus, a number of different style sheet languages were developing simultaneously.

However, in 1996 the World Wide Web Consortium (W3C) finally adopted Cascading Style Sheets Level 1, developed by CERN researcher Håkon Wium Lie and mathematician, Bert Bos, as its official recommendation. Since that time, CSS2 has been adopted as the new recommendation (1999), and CSS3 is currently under development. Ideally, the W3C would like to see Web authors use CSS to style their documents while using HTML or XHTML to structure them. In fact, with the adoption of XHTML as the official recommendation for page authoring, the W3C has taken a giant step toward restoring HTML to its original function: defining structure.

Ask the Expert

Question: What is XHTML?

Answer: The *Extensible Hypertext Markup Language* (XHTML) is a transitional language that is intended to move the Web from HTML to XML. In its strictest form, XHTML will completely separate structure from style. It is based in XML and follows XML's stricter rules, yet it uses the markup (tags, elements, attributes, and so on) that you have become familiar with in HTML. However, XHTML *transitional* still allows for the use of some "presentational" markup. Don't worry too much about XHTML at this point. Most of the important details will be covered in Module 13.

What does all this mean for you as a Web author? It means that the W3C wants you to develop the practice of separating style from content and structure in your Web pages. You should use HTML to define the structure of your pages and CSS to design the style. That's what this book is all about. As you progress through each of the modules and work through the projects, you will learn how to construct your pages in HTML and style them with CSS.

1-Minute Drill

● Who invented HTML?

● Why was it created?

Why CSS Seems Difficult

You may be saying to yourself at this point, "But I've *tried* to learn CSS, and I just can't seem to understand it." You're not alone in that frustration. Often, beginning Web authors get their first introduction to CSS is in a chapter of a book on HTML. They've been reading along, spending quite a bit of effort becoming acquainted with elements, tags, attributes, and HTML syntax. Then, just when they're becoming comfortable with HTML, the author introduces Cascading Style Sheets. Suddenly, the readers are confronted with selectors, properties, classes, pseudo-classes, and an *entirely* different syntax. No wonder many readers just skip over that chapter, hoping to come back to it some other time. After all, you don't really *need* style sheets to make your Web pages work, so why bother learning how to create them?

Reasons to Learn CSS

The fact that you are reading this book demonstrates that you are at least curious about CSS, and maybe deep down you really do want to learn how to use them. Unfortunately, it's easy to become comfortable using the old HTML workarounds, the <font> element, for example, or the "bgcolor" and "align" attributes. If you are in the habit of using HTML to govern your presentation,

---

● Tim Berners-Lee of CERN
● To enable scientists and researchers to exchange information and link documents via hypertext

you may still need a little convincing about why you should learn to use CSS instead. Consider some of the following reasons:

- **CSS gives you "global" format control**   If you create a single style sheet and link the pages in your site to it, you can change the appearance of every page just by modifying the style sheet. In the long run it will save you time.

- **CSS allows for precise positioning**   If you've designed a few Web pages, you've already experienced the difficulties inherent in using HTML to arrange objects on your pages. This is why many Web designers rely on tables to create their layouts. CSS addresses that problem by enabling you to precisely position, and even overlap, elements on your page.

- **CSS enables you to "customize" HTML**   By learning how to use class selectors and ID selectors you can, in a sense, customize HTML elements to suit your own needs. For example, you could use class selectors to design a handful of different <p> elements, each with its own distinct size, color, spacing, positioning, and background. The possibilities are limited only by your own imagination.

- **CSS gives you the freedom to be creative**   At its best, HTML is a poor design tool. You are limited with regard to font sizes, positioning, decoration, and just about anything else that is related to design. On the other hand, design is CSS's forté. Once you begin to use it, and experience the freedom it gives you, you won't want to go back to "the old way" of creating pages.

- **CSS will eventually become a necessity**   Whether you like it or not, this is where the Web is headed. If, as many expect, XML eventually becomes the primary language for Web authoring, you won't have a choice. An XML page won't even display properly without some kind of style sheet.

- **Deprecated elements will no longer be supported**   In its program to separate structure from style, the W3C has begun "deprecating" many presentational elements and attributes, such as <font> and "bgcolor." While you can still use these elements, as browsers become more CSS-compliant, they will eventually stop supporting the deprecated HTML elements and attributes. If you have not been using CSS your pages could lose most of their formatting when displayed in these browsers. Granted, this probably won't happen any time soon, but sooner or later it will.

1

The preceding list offers only a few of the reasons you should learn to use Cascading Style Sheets. Many more could be suggested. However, perhaps the best reason, if not the most important, is that they're fun to use.

Review HTML Terms and Page Structure

The first step in learning how to use CSS is to make sure you have a good command of HTML terms. As you'll see in the next section, many of the concepts behind style sheets are easier to understand if you use HTML as a point of reference.

Basic HTML Building Blocks

Although some aspects of HTML (frames, for instance) can become quite complex, the foundational parts of a Web page are really very simple. The markup in every HTML document is simply an arrangement of *elements, attributes,* and *values.* The elements you choose, the attributes you modify, and the values you assign work together with your content to create your Web page. Even if you've been doing Web pages for a while, it will be helpful to quickly review the basic building blocks of HTML.

- **Elements**   An *element* works like a container. Whatever you put into that container is identified with the container's characteristics. For example, to identify a paragraph, you use the paragraph <p> </p> element. An ordered (numbered) list goes inside the ordered list <ol> </ol> element. Each list item goes inside a list item element <li> </li>

- **Tags**   An element is (generally) made up of an opening tag <tag> and a closing tag </tag>. There are certain elements that don't use closing tags. These are called *empty elements* and should include the slash from the closing tag within the opening tag, thus combining the two. They look like this: <emptyelement />.

Tip

Don't confuse tags with elements. The terms are not interchangeable, although they are often used that way. An *element* is made up of *tags,* but tags are not elements.

Note

An element that does not take a closing tag is called an "empty" element because it does not "contain" anything. For instance, the horizontal rule <hr /> element is considered empty because you don't place any content in it. When you place the <hr /> element on a page, the browser draws the rule for you.

- **Attributes** An *attribute* names a characteristic of an element. For example, if <automobile> was an element, possible attributes might include color, horse-power, engine-type, and so on. Likewise, in HTML, the <table> element could have a number of possible attributes added to it, such as <table width, border, cellpadding, and cellspacing >. However, just adding attributes won't provide any useful information. An attribute must be paired with a *value*.

- **Values** A value simply describes the attribute to which it is attached. Going back to the preceding example, you might have <automobile color="red" horsepower="325" enginetype="V8">. To modify the <table> element, you might add values such as the following: <table width="90%" border="0" cellpadding="5" cellspacing="5">. These values would mean that you set the table to take up 90% of the browser window (horizontally), to have no border, to add 5 pixels worth of padding inside each cell, and to space the cells 5 pixels apart.

Tip

Always enclose values in quotation marks, as in the following: attribute="value".

Essentially, then, in creating an HTML document all you are doing is using elements to identify what you want on the page (heading, table, list, image, form, and so on). Then, as you need to, you specify one or more attributes (characteristics) of the elements and add the appropriate values: <element attribute="value">content goes here</element>. Once you understand the concept behind elements, tags, attributes, and values, you're ready to assemble an HTML document.

Basic HTML Document Structure

A simple HTML document uses four elements: <html>, <head>, <title>, and <body>. Although technically you could get away with omitting some of these elements, your page would not be *well formed.* In other words, it would not be properly written according to HTML syntax. Although browsers are pretty forgiving where syntax errors are concerned, eventually they will interpret your code according to a strict standard. Therefore, anticipate the future as you write your code and don't take any shortcuts.

The structure of the document is simple to follow. It begins and ends with <html> tags. Thus, all of the rest of the document is contained inside the <html> element. Then, the document divides into two main sections, marked off by the <head> and the <body> elements. The <title> element, which identifies the document and displays on the browser's title bar, is inserted in the <head>. Your basic HTML document should look like the following:

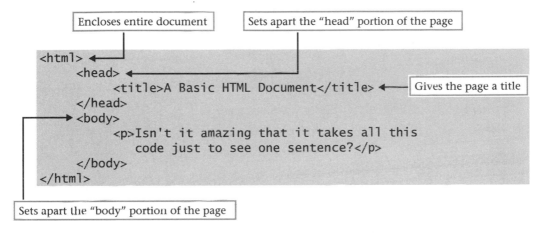

Encloses entire document

Sets apart the "head" portion of the page

Gives the page a title

Sets apart the "body" portion of the page

```
<html>
    <head>
        <title>A Basic HTML Document</title>
    </head>
    <body>
        <p>Isn't it amazing that it takes all this
            code just to see one sentence?</p>
    </body>
</html>
```

Save the page as basichtmldoc.htm and view it in your browser. It should look like the illustration that follows

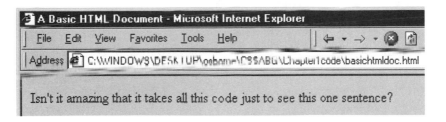

As you can see, an "unstyled" page doesn't look like much. Realistically, though, you didn't really add any content beyond a simple text line. To get a feel for unstyled HTML, as well as to have a tool for working with when you learn how to use style sheets, you need to create a style sheet test page.

Project 1-1: Create an HTML Sampler Page

In this project, you will create a page that offers a sampler of different HTML elements. In addition to providing a good HTML refresher for you, it will also give you a tool you can use throughout this book and in the future. When you create a style sheet, you will be able to see how it looks by simply linking this page to it. When you've finished it, be sure to notice how plain HTML does not really address style at all.

Step-by-Step

1. Open a simple text editor such as Windows Notepad or an HTML editor and choose File | New.

2. If you are using an HTML editor, the basic structural elements will probably be supplied for you. If not, you will need to use the following elements to structure your document: <html>, <head>, <title>, and <body>, as in the preceding code listing.

3. Add the phrase "HTML Sample Page" in between the <title> </title> tags.

4. Using the <h1>, <h2>, and <h3> elements, add three levels of heading text (as in <h1>Heading 1</h1>, and so on).

5. Insert the horizontal rule element <hr /> to add a dividing line.

6. Add a small four-celled table to the page by inserting the following code:

```
<table border="1"  width="25%">
  <tr>
    <td>Row 1 Col 1</td>
    <td>Row 1 Col 2</td>
  </tr>
  <tr>
    <td>Row 2 Col 1</td>
    <td>Row 2 Col 2</td>
  </tr>
</table>
```

7. Add another horizontal rule, <hr />, then add the following code to create a sample unordered list:

```
<hr />
<ul>
```

```
<lh>Sample Unordered List</lh>
    <li>Item one</li>
    <li>Item two</li>
    <li>Item three</li>
</ul>
```

8. Add a sample paragraph, like this:

```
<hr />
<p>This is a line of sample text.</p>
```

9. Add a second paragraph, and this time also insert a sample link between the paragraph tags:

```
<p>This is another line of sample text.
<a href="http://www.nolink.com">Sample Link</a></p>
```

10. Save the document as htmltestpage.htm, then display it in your browser. Compare it with Figure 1-1.

```
<html>
<head>
<title>HTML Test Page</title>
</head>
<body>
<!-- Heading samples -->
<h1>Heading 1</h1> <h2>Heading 2</h2> <h3>Heading 3</h3>
<!-- Horizontal Rule -->
<hr />
<!-- Sample Table -->
<table border="1"  width="50%">
  <tr>
    <td>Row 1 Col 1</td>
    <td>Row 1 Col 2</td>
  </tr>
  <tr>
    <td>Row 2 Col 1</td>
    <td>Row 2 Col 2</td>
  </tr>
</table>
<hr />
```

```
<!-- Sample Unordered List -->
<ul>
<lh>Sample Unordered List</lh>
    <li>Item one</li>
    <li>Item two</li>
    <li>Item three</li>
</ul>
<hr />
<!-- Sample text and link -->
<p>This is a line of sample text.</p>
<p>This is another line of sample text.
<a href="http://www.nolink.com">Sample Link</a></p>
<hr />
</body>
</html>
```

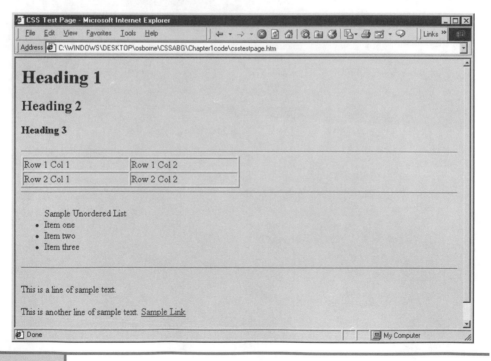

Figure 1-1 CSS Test Page

Project Summary

When you display the test page on your browser, you will see that all of the various elements on the page are simply placed one after another. The only real formatting that goes on is with each individual element. In other words, a table is formatted as a table, a list as a list, and so forth. As you begin to use style sheets, you will see how you can work with the elements on that page, rearranging and styling them any way you wish.

1-Minute Drill

● What are the four basic elements in an HTML page?

● If your HTML is syntactically correct, what is it considered to be?

CSS and HTML: Focus on the Similarities

Now that you have covered the basics of using HTML markup, you will see that style sheets, though different, operate on much the same principle. The terms may be different and the syntax unfamiliar, but the basic concepts are very similar. With HTML you learned to work with elements, attributes, and values; with CSS you will work with *selectors*, *properties*, and *values*.

Basic CSS Terminology

Many beginning Web authors find CSS intimidating simply because the terms seem foreign. However, if you compare them (CSS and HTML terms) one by one, you'll discover that the terms are not confusing at all. The terms that follow are the basic ones you need to know as you begin working with CSS. There are others, but those will be introduced later.

● **Selector**　You'll find the term *selector* easier to understand if you compare it with "element." A selector corresponds to an HTML element and is nothing more than an element that you have *selected* to modify. Although this is a simplification of what a selector is and does, it provides a good foundation for understanding the term. For example, if you want to

---

● <html>, <head>, <title>, and <body>
● Well formed

modify the <table> element, you use the "table" selector. To add style to the <h1> element, you use the "h1" selector. Any element in HTML can be modified or stylized this way.

● **Property** A *property* in CSS corresponds loosely to an "attribute" in HTML. Remember that an attribute names a characteristic of an element. Likewise, a property names a characteristic of a selector. For example, with the <table> element you can set the width with the "width" attribute, the border with the "border" attribute, and so on. In CSS, you use a property to accomplish the same thing. To stylize a table by adding a background color, you would use the "background-color" property with the "table" selector. If you wanted to adjust the size of the font used for the <h1> element, you would use the "h1" selector with the "font-size" property.

● **Value** A *value*, of course, works about the same way as it does in HTML. The value describes how you want to modify a particular property. For instance, to modify a selector (element) to display with a 36 point font, you simply add that value to the font-size property: *value* font-size: 36pt.

● **Declaration** A *declaration* is another of those unfamiliar terms that newcomers to CSS sometimes find confusing. A declaration is nothing more than a combination of a property and a value. In the preceding paragraph, "font-size: 36pt" is a declaration. You are, in effect, *declaring* the font size for a selector.

● **Rule** A *rule* is a complete statement, combining selectors, properties, and values. It can be simple, as in h1 {font-size: 36pt;}, or it can be complex, including more than one selector and many property-value declarations. A style sheet is made up of one or more "rules."

1-Minute Drill

● What does a CSS selector correspond to in HTML?

● What does a style declaration contain?

● How is a declaration different from a rule?

● A CSS selector corresponds to an element in HTML.
● Style declarations contain one or more property-value combinations.
● A declaration is like an incomplete sentence, having only a property and value. A rule must also include a selector.

Once you have a handle on the basic terms common to CSS, you are almost ready to create your first style sheet. However, you need to learn a little bit about CSS syntax first. Syntax, of course, is the "grammar and punctuation" that you must follow if you want your style sheet to work.

Basic CSS Syntax

For those who are not programmers and who have worked only with HTML, problems of syntax have probably not been a major concern. After all, browsers are fairly tolerant of errors in HTML code. However, as you venture into the world of CSS, you'll discover that you need to pay close attention to how you write your style sheet code. Fortunately, there's not a great deal of syntax that you need to know at this point. The principles in the following list should be sufficient to get you started:

- In a style rule the selector is named first.

- Declarations must be enclosed in curly braces:

```
selector      {property:value}
```

- Properties and values are separated by a colon.

- Multiple declarations must be separated by semicolons:

```
selector    {property:value; property:value; property:value;}
```

- Declarations can be placed all on one line, as in the preceding, or on separate lines:

```
selector      {property:value;
               property:value;
               property:value;}
```

- If the name of a property or value has more than one word, the words must be hyphenated, as in background-color, font-size, Times-New-Roman, and so on.

Tip

It's easier to read and edit your style sheet if you place declarations on separate lines, rather than alongside one another.

There is a lot more to learn about CSS syntax, but this will be enough to get you started working with style sheets. However, before you begin to add styles to your test page, you need to know how to attach a style sheet to an HTML document.

Attaching Style Sheets

There are essentially three ways to attach a style sheet to an HTML document. Style sheets can be *inline*, *embedded*, or *linked*. As you'll learn in Module 5, how a style sheet is attached to a document will determine whether its styles take priority or are superseded by other kinds of style sheets. This is partly what is meant by the term *cascade*. The following list describes the basics of attaching style sheets:

- **Inline Style Sheet** An inline style sheet is the easiest for a beginner to create, since it actually functions as an attribute within an HTML element. To add an inline style, you insert the "style" attribute into the element you want to modify, then add your declaration. A style added to an <h1> element would look like this: <h1 style="font-size: 36pt; color: blue;">. One important difference in syntax here is that the declaration must be enclosed in quotation marks rather than curly braces. An inline style takes priority over both embedded and linked style sheets. You would generally use a linked style sheet for "spot" styling, that is, adjusting styles for only specific items on a particular page rather than throughout the Web site.

- **Embedded Style Sheet** An embedded style sheet is placed in the <style> element, in the <head> portion of the HTML document. For example, to set the background color for an entire document, you could add a style that looks like this:

```
<head> <style type="text/css"> body    {background-color: white;} </style> </head>
```

An embedded style sheet takes priority over a linked style sheet, but not over an inline style. Embedded styles might be used when you want to have a page that differs in style from the rest of your site.

- **Linked (or External) Style Sheet** A linked style sheet is a separate text document, saved with a ".css" extension and linked to the page by means

1

of the <link /> element. This is the most useful of the ways to attach style sheets, because you can control an entire site with just one document. For example, say you want the text for all the pages on your site to display in maroon. You would create a blank text document in your text editor, then write: body {color: maroon;}. You would then save it as something like styles.css. To link to the style sheet, you would then insert the <link /> element within the <head> </head> element. Your link would look something like this: <head><link rel="stylesheet" type="text/css" href="styles.css" /></head>. When you load your Web page, the browser will look for the style sheet, and tailor the page to your specifications. Both embedded and inline style sheets take precedence over an external style sheet.

Note

A style sheet can also be imported using a slightly different syntax. Placed in the head of a document, it would go inside the <style> element and would look like this: <style type="text/css" @import url(style.css)> </style>. This means of attaching a style sheet is attractive because it can actually be placed inside an external style sheet, enabling you to link to multiple style sheets at the same time. Unfortunately, support of this rule is spotty, so you're better off using the <link /> element for the present.

Ask the Expert

Question: What do the "rel," "type," and "href" attributes do in the <link /> element?

Answer: The "rel" attribute describes the relationship between the Web page and the item that is being linked to it. In this case, it is a style sheet, so that is the value. The "type" attribute identifies the format (MIME type) of the sheet, so the browser knows how to read it. The proper value there should be "text/css." The "href" attribute tells the browser where to look for the style sheet.

Project 1-2: Create Style Sheets

You have covered the basics of style sheet terminology and syntax, and you know how to apply styles to an HTML document. In this project, you will get to see style sheets at work by adding an inline, embedded, and external style sheet to the CSS test page you created in Project 1-1. Although this project will give you just a tiny sampling of the power of style sheets, you will quickly see the potential.

Step-by-Step

1. Open htmltestpage.htm in a text editor and save it as csstestpage.htm

2. Add an inline style to the first line of sample text near the bottom of the page. Set the font-family property to "arial" and the color to "blue," as in the following:

```
<p style="font-family: arial; color: blue;">This is a line of
sample text.</p>
```

- Embed a style in the page by adding the <style> element to the <head> portion of the page. Set the table's background-color property to "cyan," its text color to "red," font-size to "12pt," and font-weight to "bold," as in the following:

```
<style type="text/css">table {background-color:cyan;
                              font-size:12pt;
                              font-weight:bold;
                              color:red;}</style>
```

3. Create a blank text file in Notepad or another text editor and save it as csstestpage.css.

4. Add a style rule to give your page a white background, change the color of <h1> to navy, and the alignment of all headings to center. To do this, you will use the "body" selector with the "background-color" property, the "h1" selector with the "color" property, and the "h1, h2, and h3" selectors with the text-align property. Your code should look like this:

```
body {background-color: white;}
h1   {color: navy;}
h1,h2,h3 {text-align: center}
```

5. To link the CSS test page to your style sheet, add the <link> element to the <head /> portion of the page like this:

```
<link: rel="stylesheet" type="text/css" href="csstestpage.css" />.
```

6. Save the updated csstestpage.htm and view it in your browser. The page should look very different now. Hopefully, it will resemble the one in the following illustration:

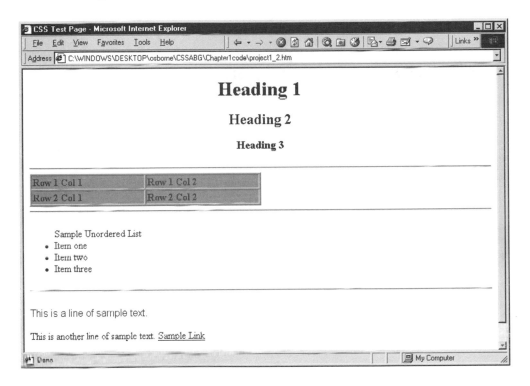

☑ *Mastery Check*

1. According to the W3C, HTML markup should be used to define a Web page's:

   A. Accessibility

   B. Presentation

   C. Structure

   D. None of the above.

2. An HTML element functions like a:

   A. Container

   B. Property

   C. Attribute

   D. Class

3. In CSS, the concept of properties and values corresponds to HTML's:

   A. Elements and attributes

   B. Elements and selectors

   C. Attributes and values

   D. Selectors and properties

4. CSS properties and values must always be separated by:

   A. A period

   B. A colon

   C. A hyphen

   D. Curly braces

☑ Mastery Check

5. Of the four types of style sheets listed below, which one would have the priority over all the others?

   A. Inline

   B. Embedded

   C. Linked (External)

   D. Imported

6. Which of the four style rules below is *correctly* written?

   A. body {color="blue"}

   B. h1 {font size: 12pt}

   C. <h1 style="color: red;">

   D. table {background color: yellow;}

Module 2

Understanding and Using Selectors

The Goals of this Module

- Understand What Selectors Do
- Learn How to Apply "Type" Selectors
- Understand and Use Descendent (Contextual) Selectors
- Create Class and ID Selectors
- Use Pseudo-Classes and Pseudo-Elements

The basic concept behind style sheets is that you can take a plain "unstyled" HTML document and write a description of how the page should look when it is displayed. You'll see as you progress through this book that CSS can take you far beyond that point, enabling you to specify how Web pages should be formatted for printing, how they should "display" in non-visual (aural or Braille) browsers, and much more. However, in order to apply any kind of style to a Web page, you must have a means for identifying exactly which part of the page you want the style to affect. This is where selectors enter the picture. Selectors provide the mechanism for pinpointing which elements of a page you want to "stylize."

How Selectors Work

Selectors enable you to "select" all or part of a document a number of different ways, ranging from simple to very complex. For instance, *type* (element) selectors simply are HTML elements, such as <body>, <p>, <table>, and so on. The only difference is that in CSS you don't put the "less than" and "greater than" marks around the element. On the other end of the spectrum, with CSS II it is possible to create an incredibly precise selector based on the attributes and values an element contains, which element it is a "descendent" of, and so on. This way it is possible to focus your selections in a document with pinpoint accuracy. Incidentally, don't worry too much about these complex selectors. They'll be covered in Module 14; however, you probably will not find it necessary to use them for simple sites, so don't worry about them right now.

Types of Selectors

Selectors fall into four basic categories: *type, descendent, attribute,* and *pseudo-classes and elements.* Sorting them out is not difficult if you keep in mind what you learned in Module 1: When you hear "selector," think "element." All selectors, except pseudo-classes and pseudo-elements, are somehow or other based in an element. Pseudo-classes and pseudo-elements address special conditions, as you will see later in this section. The following list briefly summarizes the different categories of selectors and how they work:

- **Type**   Type selectors apply style directly to an element.
- **Descendent**   Descendent selectors apply style based on an element's relation to other elements in the document.

- **Attribute**   Attribute selectors apply style based upon attributes contained in an element.

- **Pseudo-class/Pseudo-element**   This is a special category of selectors that apply style based on conditions that exist within the document itself.

Understand Type Selectors

These are the easiest selectors to understand and use, as they are simply HTML elements without the tag markers. Any HTML element can be used as a type selector, and, depending on which elements you choose, the style can affect all or only part of your document. For example, if you decided to apply a background color to the <body> element, you would be setting the background color for the entire page. To set a red background for a page you would write:

```
body {background-color: red;}
```

The effect would be the same as if you had written in HTML: <body bgcolor="red">. However, where CSS shines is in giving you the ability to add a background color to any element you choose. For instance, if you want to emphasize all your large headings, you could write a style rule that reads:

```
h1 {background-color: red;}
```

Now, every instance of the <h1> element will have a red background. If you want to see how this works, the following HTML code will create a page that has a page with a blue background, a headline with a red background, and the headline letters will be white:

```
<html><head><title>Red Headlines</title>
<style> h1 {background-color: red; color: white;}
        body {background-color: blue;}</style></head>
<body><h1>Happy Fourth of July!!!!!</h1></body></html>
```

Understand Descendent Selectors

These used to be called "contextual selectors," but "descendent" is actually a better descriptive term. With a descendent selector, you are selecting an element *based upon its relation to other elements* in the document. To understand how this works, think about HTML and the practice of nesting elements. In a well-formed HTML document, all of the elements are properly nested within one another. When one element, <body> for instance, is nested inside another element, in this case <html>, the first element is called a "child" element. In other words, the <body> element is a *descendent* of the <html> element. With descendent selectors, you can add style to an element on the basis of how it occurs in the document. For instance, perhaps you have used the bold <b></b> element to create boldface type in a list item:

```
<li>This is a <b>very</b> important point</li>.
```

You've also used the bold element in some paragraphs and even in a table. As you work on design, perhaps you decide that you would like the bold type in the list item element, <li>, to also display in blue. You would then write a style rule using a descendent selector, like this:

```
li b {color: blue;}
```

When the page is displayed, any <b> element that is nested inside a <li> element will be blue, but the rest of the <b> elements in the document will be unaffected. You can see why these were originally called "contextual" selectors. In the preceding listing, the <b> element is given the color blue when it occurs in the *context* of an <li> element.

Ask the Expert

Question: I'm not clear on the concept of "nesting." Could you explain further?

Answer: If you are unsure of what nesting means, think of a joke many children like to play on their parents at Christmas. They buy a tiny gift and wrap it in a small box. Then, they place the small box in a slightly larger one and wrap that one. The two wrapped boxes go into a third, even larger, box, and so on, until the final package looks as though it could hold a grand piano. That's nesting. One inside another, inside another, inside another.

2

Question: So, how does nesting work in HTML?

Answer: All elements in HTML should be properly contained (nested) within other elements, with no overlapping. For example, the main (or root) element of an HTML document is the <html> </html> element. Nested inside this element are the <head> and <body> elements, like this:

```
<html> <head></head> <body></body> </html>
```

The <title> element is nested inside the <head>:

```
<html> <head> <title></title> </head> <body></body> </html>
```

The important thing to notice is that properly nested tags *never* overlap. That is, you never see this pattern:

```
<a> <b> </a> </b>.
```

Understand Attribute Selectors

This type of selector focuses on an attribute contained within an element. In Module 1, you already saw an example of an attribute selector. An inline style is applied through the use of the "style" attribute. For instance, suppose you want to emphasize one certain paragraph in your document by enlarging the font size to fourteen points and coloring it green. You could use the style attribute to create an inline style such as this:

```
<p style="font-size: 14pt; color: green;">This displays in 14pt
green type</p>
```

Other attribute selectors, such as class and id actually allow you to define your own selectors. For instance, if you wanted to, you could create five different paragraph selectors, named "green," "14ptgold," "vanillaicecream," or whatever else you want to name them. This greatly increases the range of options you have, because you are not limited to using only HTML elements. Class and id selectors and their syntax will be covered later in this module.

Advanced attribute selectors actually allow you to target certain attributes that already exist in an HTML document. For example, suppose someone wants you to write a style sheet for a Web page, but does not want the HTML code rewritten. You can read the code for the page and then assign styles based on certain attributes that are already present. For example, you might change the color of every element that contains the attribute align="center". This makes CSS flexible enough to adjust to complicated documents without requiring a total reconstruction of the HTML code. Advanced attribute selectors will be covered in detail in Module 14.

Tip

Within certain parameters, you can name your classes whatever you like, but you'll find it helpful if you give them short, descriptive names. It will aid you and anyone else who edits your style sheet and Web pages down the line. For more on naming classes, see the section in this module titled "Create Class and id Selectors."

Understand Pseudo-Classes and Pseudo-Elements

By their very names, pseudo-classes and pseudo-elements tell you that they are somehow different from other selectors. This category of selectors was created to address special situations that are not reflected in HTML code. For example, one of the more popular effects in Web design is the "mouseover." That's when a button or some other part of a page changes color when the mouse passes over it. Usually these effects require the use of a scripting language such as JavaScript to make them work. However, you can create the effect with the "hover" pseudo class. To do this, all you do is write a style rule that looks like this:

```
a:hover      {background-color: yellow;}
```

You don't need to make any changes to your HTML code at all. Whenever the page displays, every link will be highlighted in yellow when someone "mouses over" it. That's the idea of a pseudo-class. It doesn't represent an actual part of your HTML code, but rather addresses a "condition" that occurs (hover, in this case) when the page is actually displayed.

2

Pseudo-elements are similar, but they deal with certain conditions that occur within an element. For example, if you want to emphasize the first line of a paragraph by having it display in uppercase, but want the rest of the paragraph to remain unchanged, you would use the "first-line" pseudo element to write a style rule like this:

```
p:first-line      {text-transform: uppercase;}
```

If you were to incorporate this style into a page, the first line of every paragraph element would display in uppercase letters. Of course, that might be overdoing things, as far as your design is concerned. Instead you might decide to combine this pseudo-element with a class selector for a more specific style rule, such as the following:

```
p.special:first-line      {text-transform: uppercase;}
```

Now, only paragraph elements that have the class="special" attribute will be affected by that style rule. As you can see, it is this ability to combine selectors that enables you to focus your styles rather than painting everything with a broad brush. As you work through the rest of this module, you will learn how to combine selectors and tailor them to your specific needs. However, before you do that, you need to create a document to work with.

1-Minute Drill

● On what basis do descendent selectors apply style?

● What must be true of an element if it is to be considered a "descendent" of another element?

Project 2-1: Create an Unstyled Web Page

In this project you will create a Web page with HTML alone. The reason for this is to get you into the habit of using HTML to properly structure your page. The more acquainted you become with style sheets, the more important this will be. You see, with the selectors listed above and the properties you will learn

---

● On the basis of an element's relation to other elements in the document
● It must be "nested" within the other element's tags, either directly or indirectly

about in later modules, you could take a simple paragraph <p> element and style it so that it looks and functions like a heading <h1> element. Thus, it is possible with style sheets to defeat the entire purpose of HTML: structuring documents. With this project, then, you will create a simple Web page, giving attention to creating its structure with HTML. Then, in the rest of this module, you will learn how to use the different types of selectors to add style to the page.

For the purposes of this project, imagine that you are a schoolteacher and you want your class to learn the Preamble to the United States Constitution. You have decided that a creative way to help them learn is by creating a Web page that displays the Preamble. In the steps that follow, you will create your Constitution Web page.

Step by Step

1. Open your text editor and create a new file, saving it as constitution.htm.

2. Add the basic HTML elements to the document, as in the following listing.

```
<html>
   <head>
     <title> </title>
   </head>
   <body>
   </body>
</html>
```

3. Insert a title in between the <title> </title> tags.

```
<title>The Preamble to the U.S. Constitution</title>
```

4. Inside the <body> </body> tags, use the <h1> element to give the page a heading.

```
<h1>The Constitution of the United States of America</h1>
```

5. Add a second-level heading with the <h2> element, and use the italics element, <i>, to cause the word "preamble" to appear in italicized text.

```
<h2>The <i>Preamble</i> to the Constitution</h2>
```

6. Below the heading, add a paragraph with the <p> element and insert the Preamble in between the text tags, using the line break element, <br />, to insert line breaks where you want them.

```
<p>We the People of the United States<br />
in Order to form a more perfect Union, establish<br />
Justice, insure domestic Tranquility, provide for<br />
the common defence, promote the general Welfare<br />
and secure the Blessings of Liberty to ourselves<br />
and our Posterity, do ordain and establish<br />
this Constitution for the United States of America.</p>
```

7. Insert another level-two heading <h2> that advises your visitors to access some related resource links. Use the underline element, <u>, to underscore the word "online".

```
<h2>Visit some <u>online</u> Constitution Resources</h2>
```

8. Add a patriotic image with the image <img /> element. Use the "align" attribute to set it for left alignment. Don't forget to specify a pixel size with the "height" and "width" attributes, and use the "alt" attribute to add alternate text for non-visual and text-based browsers.

```
<img align="left" src="constitution.gif" height="200"
width="250" alt="Patriotic image"/>
```

9. Using the <p> and <a> elements, add a few links to other Constitution resources.

```
<p><a href="http://www.house.gov/Constitution/
Constitution.html">ConstitutionOnline</a></p>
<p><a href="http://memory.loc.gov/const/
abt_contst.html">About the Constitution</a></p>
```

10. Save constitution.htm and view it in your browser. It should resemble Figure 2-1.

Tip

You can download the code and images for this project and all of the projects in this book by visiting Osborne's Web site: **www.osborne.com**. You can also see the author's version of the projects by visiting **www.jamespence.com**.

```
<html>
<head>
<title>The Preamble to the U.S. Constitution</title>
</head>
```

```
<body>
<h1>The Constitution of the United States of America</h1>
<h2>The <i>Preamble</i> to the Constitution</h2>
<p><i>We the People</i> of the United States<br />
in Order to form a more perfect Union, establish<br />
Justice, insure domestic Tranquility, provide for<br />
the common defence, promote the general Welfare<br />
and secure the Blessings of Liberty to ourselves<br />
and our Posterity, do ordain and establish<br />
this Constitution for the United States of America.</p>
<img align="left" src="constitution.gif"
height="200" width="250" alt="Patriotic image"/>
<h2>Visit some <u>online</u> Constitution Resources</h2>
<p><a href="http://www.house.gov/Constitution/
Constitution.html">Constitution Online</a></p>
<p><a href="http://memory.loc.gov/const/
abt_contst.html">About the Constitution</a></p>
</body>
</html>
```

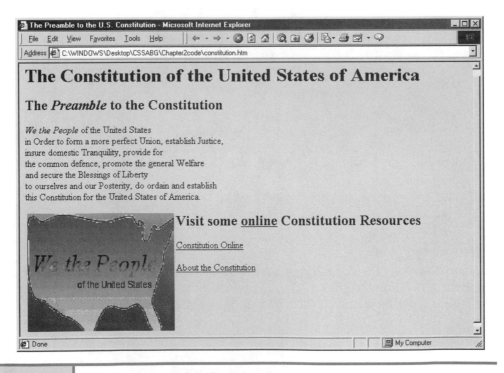

Figure 2-1   A Page Structured with HTML

2

Project Summary

In this project you have created a simple Web page, structuring it with HTML. You used <h1> and <h2> to indicate headings, <p> to set off paragraphs, and <img /> and <a href=" "> to add an image and create some links. Although it doesn't look *bad*, it certainly lacks something in the area of style. As you progress through the rest of this module, you will learn how to apply various CSS selectors to this page to make it more appealing to the eye.

Work with Type Selectors

Because they are easy to use and closely parallel what you are familiar with in HTML, "type" selectors are the place to begin when you are learning to work with style sheets. To apply a style to a type selector, you simply list the element or elements you wish to modify and then write your style declarations.

A List of Type Selectors

Since type selectors are simply HTML elements, it's fairly easy to come up with a list to work from. Although technically a style can be applied to *any* HTML element, realistically there are certain elements, <meta> for instance, that do not affect the appearance of a page and thus are unlikely candidates for style selectors. Table 2-1 provides the selectors you are most likely to want to use in styling your pages:

Selector	Description	Selector	Description
a	anchor element	img	embedded image
acronym	designates an acronym	input	form control
abbr	abbreviation	ins	inserted text
address	information about author	kbd	text to be entered by user
b	bold text	label	form field label text
big	large text	legend	fieldset legend
blockquote	extended quotation	li	list item
body	body of HTML document	noframes	alternate content for non frame–based browsers

Table 2-1   Type (or Element) Selectors

Selector	Description	Selector	Description
br	line break	noscript	alternate content for non script–based browsers
button	push button	object	generic embedded object
caption	table caption	ol	ordered list
citation	citation or short quote	optgroup	option group
code	computer code snippet	p	paragraph
col	table column	pre	preformatted text
colgroup	table column group	q	short inline quotation
dd	definition description	small	small text style
del	deleted text	span	generic container
dfn	instance definition	strong	strong emphasis (bold)
div	generic container	sub	subscript
dl	definition list	sup	superscript
dt	definition term	table	table
em	emphasis	tbody	table body
fieldset	form control group	td	table data cell
form	interactive form	tfoot	table footer
frame	subwindow	th	table header
frameset	window subdivision	tr	table row
h1-h6	heading levels 1 through 6	tt	monospaced text (teletype)
hr	horizontal rule	u	unordered list
i	italics	var	instance of a variable
iframe	inline frame		

Table 2-1 Type (or Element) Selectors (*continued*)

Basic Type Selector Syntax

You don't need to absorb a lot of rules for applying type selectors. In fact, the basic syntax has been demonstrated several times in this module already. All that is necessary for using a type selector is that you supply the name of the element you want to "stylize."

Apply Style to a Single Element

As you have already seen in preceding examples, using a type selector to apply style to an element is very easy. You simply choose the element you want to stylize, then add one or more properties and values to specify the style. A properly written style rule for a single element (selector) would look like this:

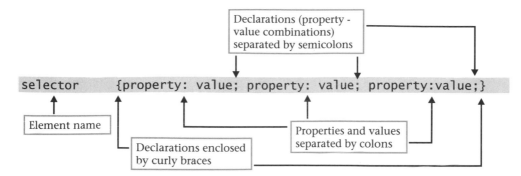

For example, if you want the <h2> element in the Constitution page to display in red text, you would use the "h2" selector along with the "color" property and the "red" value, as in the following line:

```
h2      {color: red;}
```

Add Style to Multiple Selectors

What if you want to apply the same style to several different selectors? For instance, you have decided that all the headings in your document should be in an Arial font and colored maroon instead of black. You only plan on using three levels of headings, so you will need only the h1, h2, and h3 selectors. You could write the style this way:

```
h1      {font-family: Arial; color: maroon;}
h2      {font-family: Arial; color: maroon;}
h3      {font-family: Arial; color: maroon;}
```

The preceding listing would apply your style to the selectors you have specified, but you had to write the style rule three times to accomplish your goal. However, since all three rules are identical except for the selectors, you can streamline the process (not to mention reducing the size of your file) by writing it this way:

```
h1, h2, h3      {font-family: Arial; color: maroon;}
```

All you need to do is list the selectors you want to affect and make sure they are separated by commas. Writing your style rules this way will enable you to save a lot of time in the long run.

Tip

As a rule, the spacing between selectors and declarations (property-value combinations) is a matter of personal taste. CSS generally disregards extra "white space." Thus, you should arrange your selectors and declarations in a way that will make it easiest for you (and others) to read your style sheet later.

1-Minute Drill

● Type selectors are based directly on HTML _____.

● If you want the same style to apply to multiple selectors, how should you list them?

Work with Descendent Selectors

Remember that descendent (or contextual) selectors work by applying style to an element based upon its relationship to other elements in the document. To understand how this works, you might find it helpful to view an HTML document as a "tree." When you view a page this way, you can easily see what is meant by "descendent."

Understand the HTML Document Tree

At first glance, it would seem that the "tree" analogy falls short, as this particular tree branches *down* rather than up. However, don't think of a "tree" in the sense of bark, leaves, and summertime shade; think of a document tree

---

● Elements
● List them side by side, separated by commas

as a genealogy—a *family* tree. When you create an HTML document tree, you are writing down the genealogy of all the elements in one particular document. With this in mind, you can begin to understand some important concepts for using descendent selectors.

Parent and Child Elements

An element that is nested within another element is said to be the *child* of the first element. For example, the main (root) element of every HTML page is <html> </html>. Nested inside the <html> element are the <head> and <body> elements. Therefore, as the following illustration shows, <head> and <body> are child elements or *descendents* of the <html> element. Also, since <head> and <body> are both immediate descendents of the <html> element, they are called *siblings*. Logically, the elements from which other elements descend are called *parents* or *ancestors*.

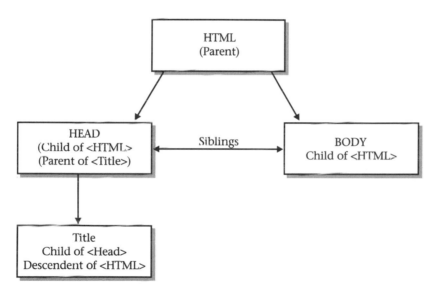

Obviously, the larger the document, the more complex the tree. However, no matter how complex it becomes, the basic idea is the same. Consider the

Constitution page you created in Project 2-1. If that page were laid out on a chart, it would look something like the following illustration:

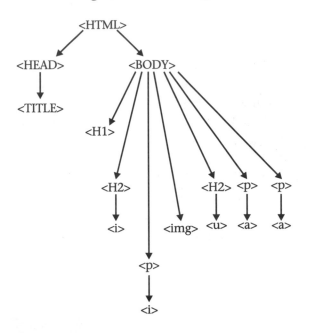

The Concept of Descendency

If you're still fuzzy on the idea of descendency, look at the preceding document tree again. You may notice that the <p> elements are listed as siblings of the <h1> and <h2> elements, not as descendents. That might seem confusing, because in an outline the content of the <p> elements would naturally fall under the various heading elements. However, remember that in HTML an element is a descendent only if it is actually "nested" in between another element's tags. Thus, in the preceding document tree the two anchor <a> elements are considered descendents of the <p> element. On the other hand, the <p> elements are siblings of the <h1> and <h2> elements because they are all nested inside the <body> tags. Why is the idea of descendency important? Because you can use it to focus your style sheet selectors.

Using Descendent Selectors

With a descendent selector, you can apply your style rules with more precision than is possible with type selectors. For example, in the Constitution page you created for Project 2-1, you used the italics element, <i>, to add special emphasis to part of your first <h2> heading. However, you also used the <i> element to italicize the phrase "We the people" in the Preamble. What if you want to make "We the people" also display in bold text, but you don't want to affect the text of your heading? You can use a descendent selector to focus your style rule exactly where you want. You could add a rule to the document head, like this:

```
<style> p i      {font-weight: bold;} </style>
```

By listing the "p" selector first, then the "i" selector, you are telling the browser to apply the style to all "i" elements that are descendents of "p" elements. All other occurrences of the <i> element will be ignored unless they fit the pattern you set down.

Note

It is important to keep in mind that a descendent selector applies to all the descendents, no matter how many "generations" are involved. Therefore, in the preceding example, an "i" element will be affected by the style, even if it is a "great-grandchild" of a "p" element. If you want to restrict your focus only to the actual "child" element, you would use a "direct child" selector. Advanced Selectors will be covered in Module 14.

Descendent Selector Syntax

Descendent selectors are not difficult to write as long as you keep a few basic rules in mind:

- The selectors should *not* be separated by any punctuation. Remember, selectors that are separated by commas are interpreted to be multiple selectors. Descendent selectors should be written as in the following listing.

```
selector selector selector  {property: value;}
```

- List the selectors in order of their "generations." That is, list the parent first, then child, grandchild, and so on.

```
parent child grandchild great-grandchild {property: value;}
h1 em i u {color: blue;}
```

┤Caution

Netscape 4.* seems to have some difficulty with very specific descendent selectors, as in the preceding listing.

1-Minute Drill

● What are the two primary "children" of the <html> element?

● How do descendent selectors apply style to an element?

● What punctuation should separate descendent selectors?

Project 2-2: Apply Type and Descendent Selectors

This project will give you some practice in applying style to an HTML document with type and descendent selectors. You will begin to "stylize" the constitution.htm page you created in Project 2-1. You will also create an external style sheet for this page. As you work through this project, keep in mind that you will need to save your HTML document and style sheet *every time* you make a change to either one. Otherwise you won't see your changes reflected in your page's display.

┤Tip

If you're working with Windows, you can make things easier by opening your HTML document in Notepad and your CSS document in Wordpad, or vice-versa. If you decide to use a word processor, such as Word or WordPerfect, be sure you save the file as text only. Otherwise, the word processing program will add some of its own codes to your document.

Step-by-Step

1. Open Notepad or your favorite text editor and save a file as constitution.css. Be sure to save it in the same directory as constitution.htm.

2. Open constitution.htm in your Web browser. You'll find it helpful to toggle back and forth between your style sheet and browser as you make adjustments

---

● The <head> and <body> elements
● On the basis of an element's descendency from other elements
● No punctuation should separate descendent selectors

to the style. That way you can keep tabs on your page's progress and remove or adjust styles you don't like.

3. Link constitution.htm to your HTML document by adding the <link /> element to the <head> portion, as in the following listing:

```
<link rel="stylesheet" type="text/css"
 href="constitution.css" />
```

4. Change the color of the <h1> element to blue by adding the following line to constitution.css :

```
h1      {color: blue;}
```

5. Change the font family of the <h2> elements to Arial by adding the following line to your style sheet:

```
h2      {font-family: arial;}
```

6. Center the Preamble by modifying the <p> element like this:

```
p       {text-align: center;}
```

7. Enlarge the size of the italicized "We the people" phrase by using a descendent selector:

```
p i      {font-size: 24pt;}
```

8. If you haven't already, save constitution.css.

9. Open your browser and load constitution.htm. If you already have that page loaded, simply click the "refresh" or "reload" button on the browser toolbar.

Project Summary

As the following illustration demonstrates, your new Constitution page, with style applied, will look very different from the page you created earlier in this module. What is most important to remember, though, is that you made all these changes without having to change a single line of code on the HTML document itself. All the changes were made by means of the style sheet. Compare the illustration that follows with Figure 2-1 and note the changes.

Note

Obviously, since the illustrations throughout this book are in gray scale, you won't be able to see the colors without doing the project yourself. Remember that all the pages designed for this book can be downloaded from Osborne's Web site: **www.osborne.com**, or you can view them by visiting the author's "EZ HTML Workshop" Web site: **www.jamespence.com**.

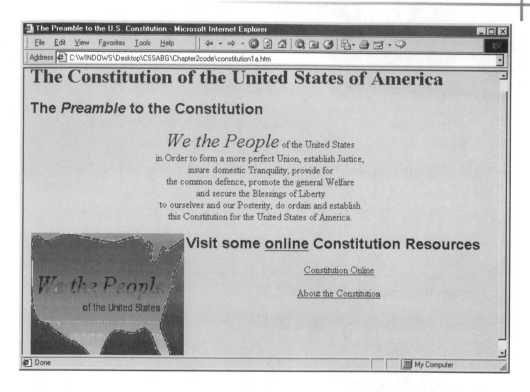

```
h1 {color: blue;}
h2 {font-family: arial}
p  {text-align: center}
p i {font-size: 24pt;}
```

Note

There are other, more complicated descendent selectors that you can use. Module 14 will cover some of these.

Work with Attribute Selectors

The third general category of selectors that was specified earlier in this module was that of "attribute" selectors. Attribute selectors apply style to an element on the basis of an attribute that element contains. The good news for people just learning CSS is that the simplest attribute selectors to use are also among the most powerful.

Class Selectors

A class selector is essentially a tailor-made selector that you design yourself, then apply to an element via HTML's class attribute. When creating a class selector, instead of creating an element name, you create a name of your own choosing for your style rule. The class selector is identified by a period before the class name you give it.

How Class Selectors Work

Class selectors can enable you to create very powerful and broad-sweeping selectors. In fact, this aspect of CSS virtually allows you to design your own elements. Say you want to use a class selector to create a special style for bold and red text. You could name it "boldred" and would create it by writing a style rule something like this:

```
.boldred      {font-weight: bold; color: red}
```

Be sure to note that there is a period before the class name "boldred." This is very important, because the period is what actually identifies the selector as a class selector. To apply that style in your document, you simply add the class attribute wherever you want the text to display bold and red. The value you assign to the class attribute would be "boldred."

```
<p class="boldred">This text will display bold and red.</p>
```

That's all there is to creating a simple class selector. However, there are some things you will want to keep in mind about class selector syntax.

Class Selector Syntax

Class selectors may be created with nothing more than a period and a class name, but their versatility comes from the different ways you can construct them. The following list covers some of the different ways you can build class selectors and tailor them to your specific design needs.

- A period followed by a class name creates a non-specific class that can be applied to any element in the document.

```
.classname {property: value;}
```

- A type selector (element) followed by a period and then a class name creates a class that can be applied to one specific type of element. The following style rule will affect any <h1> element that is assigned the value "blueitalic".

```
h1.blueitalic {font-style: italic; color: blue;}
```

- A class selector must contain only letters and numbers. It cannot contain any spaces or symbols, except for hyphens. In other words, blue+italic, blue italic, and !!&&)) are all invalid names for class selectors. However, blue-italic would be acceptable.

- Class selectors are case sensitive. Thus blueitalic and BlueItalic are two different classes.

ID Selectors

An id selector is also a "tailor-made" selector, but it is applied to your HTML document with the id attribute. The primary difference between class and id selectors is that an id selector must be unique in the document. In other words, you can't create one id and apply it to multiple elements, as you can with "class." Just as your fingerprints, DNA, and Social Security number are unique to you, so an id must be unique in the document.

Although *id* selectors are similar to class selectors in their function, their syntax is a bit different. As with class selectors, you can specify whatever you want as an id . However, instead of identifying it with a period, you use the "crosshatch" or "pound sign." Thus, an id can be h1#blue, table#saeif12459,

2

p#myfavoritecolor, or whatever else you wish. You then apply it in the HTML document with the id attribute. For example, to create an h1#blue id and apply it to an element, you might write the style rule and HTML code like this:

```
h1#blue  {color: blue;}
<h1 id="blue">Blue is beautiful!</h1>
```

Hint

The id "blue" could have just as easily been "slkefjl" or "129r57d," but it's good to choose descriptive names when possible. Remember, some day you or someone else may need to "decipher" your styles or HTML code. Clarity may not seem important at the present, but several months or years down the line, you'll be glad you chose easy to understand names for your classes and ids.

ID Selectors Must be Unique

Although id selectors work about the same way as do class selectors, there is one important difference to note. Class selectors don't need to be unique in a document, but id selectors do. In other words, you could choose a name for a class selector—"purplefont," for instance—and apply that class to a number of different elements. The id selectors must be unique in a document. You couldn't have a p#purplefont that specified a 12 point font, a table#purplefont that used a 10 point font, and a h1#purplefont that used a 36 point font, all in the same document. If you want different characteristics to apply with an id selector, you must give each selector a unique name.

Ask the Expert

Question: If class and id selectors are so similar, what's the advantage of one over another?

Answer: The main advantage with id selectors is that, because they are unique, they are considered more "specific" by browsers. That means that if there are conflicting styles applying to the document, the id selector will be more likely to be the style that is displayed. For more on this subject, see Module 5.

Tip

Although technically you could apply a single #purplefont id to different elements, providing the style rules are not changed, it is contrary to the purpose of the id attribute. The ids are intended to be used *once* in a document.

ID Selector Syntax

Most of the syntax rules that apply to class selectors also apply to id selectors. However, id selectors have some quirks unique to themselves. The following list covers these other important aspects of id selector syntax:

● All id selector names begin with the "pound" sign rather than a period.

```
#idname        {property: value;}
```

● If a type selector is attached to the id name, then that style affects only elements of that type that also have the id name. For instance, the following listing will affect only those tables that also have the id="bigfont" attribute included in the opening tag.

```
table#bigfont {font-size: 24pt;}
```

● As with class selectors, id selectors can have numbers and letters, but cannot contain spaces or other characters (except hyphens). In the following listing, the first line would be acceptable, but the second line would not.

```
table#big-font {font-size: 24pt;}
table#big font {font-size: 24pt;}
```

1-Minute Drill

● A class selector is indicated by a _____, while an id selector is indicated by a _____.

● Which type of selector must be unique in a document: class or id?

● Period, Pound Sign
● The id selector must be unique

Work with Pseudo-Classes and Pseudo-Elements

Perhaps the most fascinating of all the selector categories are the pseudo-classes and pseudo-elements. To get an idea of what is being referred to here, you need only remember that the word "pseudo" means "false." So, essentially, we're talking about "false-classes" and "false-elements." What is it that makes them "false"?

Understand Pseudo-Classes and Pseudo-Elements

Pseudo-classes and pseudo-elements are "false," in that they don't actually exist in the HTML code that you are working with. Instead, they represent conditions that can exist on a Web page. For instance, the easiest pseudo-classes to understand are those that pertain to links.

How Pseudo-Classes Work

On most Web pages, when you click on a link, the link will change to a different color. This serves to remind you of what links you have visited. Although the color can be set with HTML, there is nothing in the HTML code that determines whether or not a link has been visited. The browser makes that determination. So, what if you want to use style sheets to control the style of your links? You use the "a" (anchor) pseudo-class, writing it like this:

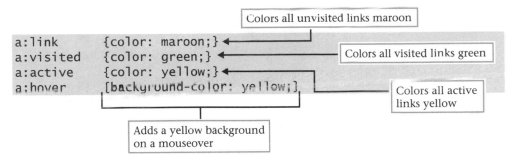

```
a:link        {color: maroon;}
a:visited     {color: green;}
a:active      {color: yellow;}
a:hover       {background-color: yellow;}
```

Colors all unvisited links maroon

Colors all visited links green

Colors all active links yellow

Adds a yellow background on a mouseover

How Pseudo-Elements Work

Pseudo-elements address a somewhat different situation. Perhaps you want to add a "large cap" to the first letter of your document. Although it would be possible to create such an effect by using a class or id selector, you would have to also create some clumsy HTML code, as is demonstrated in the following listing.

```
<style> p#bigcap {font: 200%;}</style>
<p><p id="bigcap">W</p>e the People</p>
```

On the other hand, the *first-letter* pseudo-element enables you to specify a style that will only affect the first letter of an element. You could write a style rule that looks like this:

```
<style> p:first-letter {font-size: 200%;}</style>
<p>We the People</p>
```

Thus, with the first-letter pseudo-element, you are, in effect, adding a "phantom" element to the "We the people" line.

Hint

You (and your visitors) will need Netscape Navigator 6, Internet Explorer 5.5, or Opera 3, 4, or 5 to view this effect.

Pseudo-Class and Pseudo-Element Syntax

The syntax for pseudo-classes and pseudo-elements is essentially the same. The following list gives some things to keep in mind with this special category of selector:

- All pseudo-classes and pseudo-elements are identified by a colon placed after the element, as in the following listing.

  ```
  a:link    {property: value}
  ```

- You can combine pseudo-classes and pseudo-elements with class and id selectors.

  ```
  p#idname:first-line  {property: value;}
  p.classname:first-letter {property: value; }
  ```

● Pseudo-elements and pseudo-classes can only be attached to *block level* elements or elements that have their display properties set to *block*.

Note

In HTML, block level elements are the basic structural elements which go into a Web page: <h#>, <p>, <br />, <hr />, and so on. Pseudo-elements and pseudo-classes can be attached only to that kind of element. With CSS, it is possible to set an element's *display properties* to block, but that procedure is more commonly used with a language like XML, where block and inline elements are not defined for you. You will learn more about setting display properties in Module 10.

Recognizing Pseudo-Classes and Pseudo-Elements

Unlike other categories of selectors, there are only a few pseudo-elements and pseudo-classes to choose from. Unfortunately, the ones that *are* available are not all that strongly supported, except in the newest browsers. So, if you plan on using these selectors you will be well advised to test your pages in a number of different browser versions. The pseudo-classes and pseudo-elements that are currently available in CSS are listed in Tables 2-2 and 2-3.

Note

Some of the pseudo-classes and pseudo-elements may seem strange and unfamiliar, "lang" and "focus" for example. These are part of the CSS 2 (advanced CSS) standard and will be covered in Module 14.

Pseudo-Class	Function
:link	Set styles for hyperlinks
:active	Set styles for active links (or elements)
:visited	Set styles for visited links
:hover	Set styles for links (elements) on mouseover
:focus	Set styles for elements that are the focus of attention
:first-child	Set styles for an element that is the first child of another element

Table 2-2   Pseudo-Classes

Pseudo-Class	Function
:lang(a)	Set styles for an element that is in a specific language
:first	Set styles for the first page of a document
:left	Set styles for the left pages of a document
:right	Set styles for the right pages of a document

Table 2-2 Pseudo-Classes (*continued*)

Project 2-3: Apply Class, ID, and "Pseudo" Selectors to Constitution.htm

If your head is swimming after reading about class, id, and "pseudo" selectors, you can relax. You will learn how to use these selectors in later modules as you work through other aspects of CSS. However, just to get a feel for how they perform, try applying them to your Constitution page by working through this project. In it you will use class, id, and "pseudo" selectors to add some "pizzazz" to your page.

Step-by-Step

1. Open constitution.css in a text editor and constitution.htm in a text editor and browser.

2. Begin modifying your style sheet by setting the background color for constitution.htm to white:

```
body {background-color: white;}
```

There are even fewer pseudo-elements, and the support issue remains the same for them. Always test your styles when using these.

Pseudo-Element	Function
:first-letter	Set styles for the first letter of an element
:first-line	Set styles for the first line of an element
:before	Inserts specially generated content "before" an element
:after	Inserts specially generated content "after" an element

Table 2-3 Pseudo-Elements

2

3. You have already set the color for the <h1> element to blue. Add another declaration that will align the heading in the center of the page:

```
h1      {color: blue; text-align: center;}
```

4. Change the descendent selector "p i" to a bold font rather than 24 points:

```
p i      {font-weight: bold;}
```

5. Add a combination type/id/pseudo-element selector to create a large first letter for the preamble. You would write it like this:

```
p#first:first-letter   {font-size: 200%}
```

6. Add a class selector named "boldred" that can be used to set the font to a bold and red display:

```
.boldred      {font-weight: bold; color: red;}
```

7. Add another class selector that sets the font color to blue:

```
blue {color: blue;}:
```

8. .To have a little fun with the links, use the a:link pseudo- class to set the normal link appearance to red, the a:visited pseudo-class to set the visited link appearance to maroon, the a:active pseudo-class to set the active link to blue with a red background, and use the a:hover pseudo-class to create a reverse of that effect, blue text with a red background, whenever someone "mouses over" a link:

```
a:link {color: red;}
a:visited {color: maroon;}
a:active {color: blue; background-color: red;}
a:hover {color: red; background-color: blue;}
```

9. Save constitution.css and, if you haven't done so already, bring up constitution.htm in a text editor.

10. Change the first <h2> element to read as in the following listing:

```
<h2>The <i class="boldred">Preamble</i> to
the Constitution</h2>
```

11. Add the following class and id attributes to the first line of the Preamble:

```
<p class="blue" id="first"><i class="boldred">We the
People</i> of the United States<br />
```

12. Modify the second <h2> heading by adding the "blue" class attribute to the <u> element:

```
<h2>Visit some <u class="blue">online</u> Constitution
Resources</h2>
```

13. Save constitution.htm and view it in a browser, preferably IE 5 or higher, Netscape 6, or Opera. Your results should resemble the following illustration:

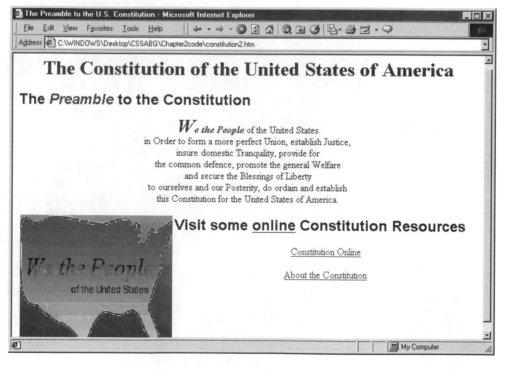

Project Summary

In this project, you took a plain HTML page and added styles with all four major categories of selectors: type, descendent, attribute (class, id), and pseudo. As you work more with CSS in later modules, you'll begin to develop a feel for how to use these selectors, and which ones are best suited for which tasks. However, even more important than working with selectors is the fact that you have begun to see the potential of CSS—and you've only scratched the surface. Get ready. The best is yet to come.

constitution.css

```
body {background-color: white;}
h1 {color: blue; text-align: center;}
h2 {font-family: arial}
p  {text-align: center}
p i {font-weight: bold}
p#first:first-letter    {font-size: 200%;}
.boldred {font-weight:bold; color: red;}
.blue {color: blue;}
a:link {color: red;}
a:active {color: blue; background-color: red;}
a:visited {color: maroon;}
a:hover {background-color: blue; color: red;}
```

constitution.htm

```
<html>
<head>
<title>The Preamble to the U.S. Constitution</title>
<link rel="stylesheet" type="text/css"
href="constitution.css">
</head>
<body>
<h1>The Constitution of the United States of America</h1>
<h2>The <i class="boldred">Preamble</i> to
the Constitution</h2>
<p class="blue" id="first"><i class="boldred">We
the People</i> of the United States<br />
in Order to form a more perfect Union,
establish Justice,<br />
insure domestic Tranquility, provide for<br />
the common defence, promote the general Welfare<br />
and secure the Blessings of Liberty<br />
to ourselves and our Posterity,
do ordain and establish<br />
this Constitution for the United States of America.</p>
```

```
<img align="left" src="constitution.gif"
height="200" width="250" />
<h2>Visit some <u class="blue">online</u> Constitution
Resources</h2>
<p><a href="http://www.house.gov/Constitution/
Constitution.html">Constitution Online</a></p>
<p><a href="http://memory.loc.gov/const/
abt_contst.html">About the Constitution</a></p>
</body>
</html>
```

✓ Mastery Check

1. List the four major categories of selectors.

_____

_____

2. A selector that deals with situations not directly reflected in HTML code is
called a _____-_____ or a _____-_____.

3. What things are wrong with the following style rule?

```
p.yellow+large   (background color:green;)
```

_____

_____

4. The <body> element is a _____ of the <html> element and a
_____ of the <head> element.

_____

_____

5. Which of the following style rules is written correctly?

A. ul /li /li {font-size; 24pt: color; magenta}

B. p.largetext:link {background-color: green;}

C. p em i u {color: purple;}

D. a:visited {font size="24pt"}

2

Module 3

Surveying CSS Properties

The Goals of this Module

- Become Acquainted with the Five Categories of Properties
- Experiment with Text Properties
- Apply Font Properties
- Control Color and Background
- Understand and Use Box Properties
- Understand Descriptive Properties

If you've ever built a house, you know that before construction begins, some blueprints are drawn up. The blueprints give you precise detail about the house's layout as well as the arrangement of the various rooms, windows, doors, and so on. No one will question the fact that a set of well-drawn blueprints is important—if not essential—to properly constructing a house. Yet, if you were to build a house based *solely* on the blueprints, it would be a barren place indeed. The blueprints define a building's structure, but they don't address *style*. They won't tell you what color of carpeting you should have, the pattern for your wallpaper, or the kinds of lighting fixtures you should choose. Those are matters of style and present decisions that you as a homeowner must make. In fact, two people making different style choices could end up with two very different-looking houses from an identical set of blueprints. The same is true with HTML and CSS. HTML gives you the basic structure of a page. However, depending on what style properties you apply and the values you assign to them, you can create a variety of different "looks" from the same basic HTML code—and you do it all with CSS properties.

This module will provide you with a brief introduction to CSS properties. It will not describe everything there is to know about properties or even touch on every one the ones you can use. Rather, you will be introduced to the basic categories of properties and see how they can affect the overall appearance of a Web page. Later, Modules 6 through 10 will provide more extensive coverage of properties and how to use them.

Understand Properties and their Functions

HTML enables you to design a blueprint of a page's structure that a browser constructs and displays as a Web page. CSS properties take you to the next level by providing a means to make style choices. However, with CSS you won't be choosing carpeting, fixtures, and paint colors; you'll be choosing fonts, colors, positions, borders, and much more.

Understand Properties

In Module 2 you learned that selectors enable you to specify what elements of a page you want to apply a style to. You use the "h1" selector to apply style to an <h1> element, "h2" to an <h2> element, and so on. However, once you have identified what part of a page you want to "stylize," you still need some way to tell the browser what kind of style to apply. That's where properties come in. A property identifies the part or parts of a selector's "style" you want to modify. For instance, suppose you have chosen to add styles to the "h1" selector. You might use the font-size property to make the font larger, the text-align property to control alignment, the color property to specify a font color and so on. Properties, in essence, are the "tools" CSS gives you for designing Web pages. Thus, it's important to know up front what tools you have in your toolbox. You may not use all of them, but you definitely should be acquainted with all of them.

3

Five Categories of Properties

An alphabetical list of the properties that are available in CSS I and II presents a rather daunting array of items. Although the functions of many properties are self-explanatory (text-align and font-size, for instance), others seem downright confusing. What, after all, would properties named "azimuth" or "ruby-overhang" control? Thus, the best way to learn how to use CSS properties is by becoming familiar with the five basic categories that properties fall into: Text properties, Font properties, Color/Background Properties, Box Properties, and Classification Properties.

Ask the Expert

Question: What are CSS 1 and CSS 2?

Answer: CSS 1 refers to Cascading Style Sheets, Level 1, which was the first "version" of style sheets that the W3C made an official recommendation. CSS 1 primarily focuses on the visual style of Web pages: fonts, spacing, colors, backgrounds, borders, and so on. CSS 2 is the second (and current) recommendation by the W3C. It extends CSS 1 by adding an expanded range of selectors and properties in existing categories, plus adding style properties for "paged media." In other words, with CSS 2 you can design styles that specify how your Web pages would be formatted when they are printed out. CSS 2 also is designed to increase accessibility to the Web by offering styles for "media," as in aural and Braille styles. This capability will enable

Web authors to create style sheets that can be implemented by "non-visual" browsers.

Question: Should I use CSS 1 or CSS 2?

Answer: Since as of this writing even CSS 1 is not fully supported by the major browsers (Netscape and Internet Explorer), this is almost a moot point. The support for CSS 2 is much weaker. Thus, although you may want to be familiar with the capabilities of CSS 2, you're better off sticking with CSS 1 for now. However, even with CSS 1 you will have to test your pages in multiple browsers and be aware of support problems. In fact, you should probably just assume that some of your visitors will be using browsers that don't fully support CSS, and code your pages accordingly. (For information on how to write CSS pages that will display properly on non-CSS browsers, see Module 13.)

Question: How do I tell the difference between CSS 1 and CSS 2?

Answer: The only way to tell the difference is to learn which properties belong to CSS 1 and which belong to CSS 2. Modules 6 through 10 cover the properties of CSS 1. CSS 2 will be covered in Modules 14 and 15. Also, the CSS reference chart in Appendix B will indicate whether a property belongs to CSS 1 or 2.

Question Will there be a CSS 3?

Answer: CSS 3 is currently under development by the W3C. The newest version of CSS will include properties that aid in designing pages for different languages, new accessibility features, the ability to style scalable vector graphics, and so on. You can review the CSS 3 standard by visiting the W3C's Web site at: **http://www.w3.org/Style/CSS/current-work**.

Text Properties

Text properties are used to control such things as the position of text and the spacing of letters, words, and lines. You do not use text properties to choose fonts or font colors. Those aspects of style are controlled by font properties.

For example, if you want to center your text, you would use the "text-align" property, as in the following listing:

```
h1.new        {text-align: center;}
```

This style rule creates a special class for the <h1> element, named "new." To see how the text-align property works, create a simple HTML page with two <h1> elements, as in the following listing. Add the preceding style rule to the <head> section of the page, using the <style> element, as in the following example:

```
<html>
<head>
<title>Properties Demo</title>
<style> h1.new {text-align: center;}</style>
</head>
<body>
<h1>A boring, unmodified headline</h1>
<h1 class="new">An exciting, stylized headline</h1>
</body>
</html>
```

Hint

Be sure to add the class="new" attribute to the second <h1> or else the style will not be applied.

When you save this page and view it in a browser, the second <h1> element should be centered, as the following illustration demonstrates.

A boring, unmodified headline

An exciting, stylized headline

Note

Although the second headline does not look very "exciting" or "stylized" at this point, watch what happens to it as more styles are applied.

Font Properties

Font properties are intended to replace HTML's <font> element. Whereas the <font> element and its attributes gave you limited control over how fonts displayed, CSS's font properties literally set you free to control size, font family, weight, color, and much more. For example, suppose you want to change the headline above to display at 32 points and also to have it use a more interesting font. You could add a declaration to your "h1.new" selector that specifies a 32-point fantasy font, as in the listing that follows:

```
h1.new      { text-align: center;
             font-size: 32pt;
font-family: fantasy;}
```

As the following illustration demonstrates, when this page is displayed, your browser will use a fantasy font, and it will be sized much larger.

Tip

The fantasy font family is one of five generic fonts that CSS is designed to recognize: serif, sans-serif, cursive, fantasy, and monospace. Although you can specify any font you want in your styles, it is good practice to include one of the generic fonts as an alternative, just in case your visitor's system doesn't have the font you specified.

A boring, unmodified headline

An exciting, stylized headline

Color and Background Properties

HTML gives you the ability to set background colors for entire pages with the "bgcolor" attribute. This attribute can also be used to assign background colors for individual cells in tables. CSS goes far beyond HTML by enabling you to set background colors for virtually any element. You can stylize your elements with background images as well. All of this and more is made possible with the color and background properties.

Just as an example, take the "stylized" headline created in the previous section. What if you added a peach-colored background image and changed the font

3

color to green? You can see the results by adding the following lines to the demonstration page:

```
h1.new        {text-align: center;
               font-size: 32pt;
               font-family: fantasy;
               color: green;
               background-image: url(texture72x72.gif);}
```

Hint

You'll need a background image to make this work. The image used for this illustration can be downloaded from Osborne's Web site, along with the rest of the code from this book. Simply go to **www.osborne.com** and click on the "free code" link at the top of the page. At the free code page, scroll down to the title, *CSS: A Beginner's Guide*, and click on the link. All the code from this book will automatically download to your system as a zip file.

Now, when you save the page and display it in your browser, your "plain" headline has taken on a bit of personality. The headline now displays as green text superimposed upon a tiled background image.

A boring, unmodified headline

An exciting, stylized headline

Note

Obviously, since the illustrations in this book are in gray scale, you will not be able to see the differences in color. However, all of the images created for this book can be downloaded for viewing on your own system by visiting Osborne's Web site: **www.osborne.com**

Box Properties

Thus far, most of the property categories have been self-explanatory. However, the function of box properties may not be so obvious. When you work with CSS, you'll find it helpful to imagine every element of a page as if it were contained in an invisible "box." For instance, if you look at the preceding illustration, you can see the box that "contains" the second headline. The image tiles make the box visible. As you will see in Module 11, the "box" model will enable you to lay out your Web pages in a way you never could with HTML. For now, however, just keep in mind that the box properties also allow you to add borders, margins, padding, and so on to your content.

Consider the properties demo page that has been built in the preceding sections. What if you decided to spruce up your headline by adding an attractive border? One handy "box property" is the *border* property. By adding the following declarations to your "h1.new" style rule, you can put a border around the "box" that contains the h1 element.:

```
h1.new          {font-family: fantasy;
                font-size: 2.1em;
                text-align: center;
                color: green;
                background-image: url(texture72x72.gif);
                border-style: outset;
                border-color: yellow;
                border-width: thick;}
```

As shown in the following illustration, your headline now appears almost as if it were raised up from the rest of the page. As you learn to work with CSS, you'll discover that using box properties enables you to lay out pages, create sidebars and link boxes, and much more. In fact, you will be able to do everything you probably do with tables now—and much more.

A boring, unmodified headline

An exciting, stylized headline

Classification Properties

Classification properties are used to define how the various elements and their "boxes" should behave. For example, you can use the display property to define various elements as "inline," "block," or "list-item." Since browsers treat block elements as separate divisions on a page, changing a block element such as <h1> to display as inline would cause it to behave differently when displayed.

Instead of inserting a line before and after the <h> element, the browser would treat it as any other inline element. For an example, look at what happens when both of the <h1> elements from the preceding example are changed from their natural "block" display to "inline." This is accomplished by adding the following declaration to the style rule:

```
h1.new          {font-family: fantasy;
                 font-size: 2.1em;
                 text-align: center;
                 color: green;
                 background-image: url(texture72x72.gif);
                 border-style: outset;
                 border-color: yellow;
                 border-width: thick;
                 display: inline;}}
h1              {display: inline;}
```

Hint

A *block* element defines a division on a page and is generally preceded and followed by a line break. For instance, the paragraph <p>, heading <h#>, and line break <br /> elements are all block elements. An *inline* element works "in-line" and does not create a division on a page. For example, the image <img /> element is an inline element. A *list item* is an item that displays either as a numbered (ordered) or bulleted list.

As you can see in the following illustration, the <h1> elements behave like inline elements rather than as headings:

A boring, unmodified headline An exciting, stylized headline

Since it is possible with this property to completely alter HTML's basic structure, you should proceed with caution if you decide to use it. Nevertheless, as you will learn in Module 10, *display* and other classification properties, such as *visibility* and *position*, are powerful tools that you may find use for as you begin to style your pages.

1-Minute Drill

● What does a property do?
● What are the five basic categories of CSS properties?

Project 3-1: Construct an HTML Practice Page

Before you begin to experiment with the different categories of properties, you will need a Web page to which to apply the styles. In this project, you will create a page for "Fred's Adventure Tours." Fred is offering a summer special on tours to South America. This particular page offers his visitors a great deal on tours of Machu Pichu, the "lost" city of the Incas.

You will structure this page using header elements, paragraphs, tables, lists, and an image. Remember that you will use the HTML to properly structure your page. Then, in the second half of this module, you will learn how to stylize the page using CSS. One important thing to remember in this process is that you should always structure your page's content in a logical manner. Keep in mind that, if your pages are to be interpreted for non-visual or aural browsers, the structure and content must follow a natural flow in order to ensure that someone using these alternative browsers can correctly interpret your pages.

Tip

Try to write the HTML code on your own by following the step-by-step instructions. If you need help, the completed code for the page is listed after the instructions. Also, all the files and images you will need to complete this project can be downloaded from the Osborne Web site (**www.osborne.com**). You can also view the author's version of it by visiting **www.jamespence.com**.

Step-by-Step

1. Create a blank HTML page and save it as fredstravel.htm. Be sure to include a set of style tags inside the <head> portion of the page and to include a title between the <title> tags.

● A property identifies the part or parts of a selector's "style" you want to modify
● The five basic categories of CSS properties are: Text, Font, Color/Background, Box, and Classification

3

2. Just inside the first <body> tag, add three headings. The first one should be a main <h1> heading for "Fred's Travel," the second an <h2> "Summer Special" heading, and the third an <h3> special heading for the Machu Pichu tour that reads "Machu Pichu: The Lost City of the Incas"

3. On the next line, insert a photo of Machu Pichu with the image <img /> element. Don't forget to specify the image's height and width (to enable the page to load faster), and use the alt attribute to provide a description of the image for those who use non-visual browsers (or have images turned off).

Tip

Notice how the image's name includes its height and width. If you develop the habit of supplying dimensions with all your images, you'll save a lot of time when you need to assign values to the height and width attributes.

4. Use the paragraph, <p>, element and add a brief "teaser" description of the trip. The paragraph should read: "Travel back in time this summer as you visit Peru's Machu Pichu, also known as the "lost" city of the Incas. Complete tour packages as low as $1500.00 per person."

5. Following the teaser, add a table that lists several tour packages and fares. Create a simple, four-row table with one cell in each row. Set the table's border to "1."

6. Just beneath the table, add a bulleted (unordered) list that details what is covered by a customer's tour fee. Use the <ul> element to create the list, the <lh> element to create a heading that reads "All Tours Include:" and the <li> element to add several items to the list. The items could include the following:

   - Round Trip Airfare
   - Meals and Accommodations
   - Transportation and Admission to Attractions
   - Little Mints on Your Pillow Each Night

7. Below the list, use the anchor element to add some links to additional information. Use <a href=" "> </a> to create the hyperlinks. One link should read: "Peru Tour Information," and the other "Other Great Tour Deals."

8. Wrap up the page with another paragraph element, this time containing a "slogan." Make the slogan read "Have the adventure of a lifetime this Summer with Fred's Travel Adventures."

9. Save the page as fredstravel.htm and display it in a browser.

When you save your page and display it in a browser, you should come up with something that resembles Figure 3-1.

Note

The page created with the preceding steps will not display in a single browser window, because HTML arranges page elements in a linear (one after another) fashion. As you apply style to this page throughout the rest of this module, you will rearrange the elements to display in one window.

```html
<html>
<head>
  <title>Fred's Travel Adventures</title>
<!-- Style information  -->
<style>
</style>
</head>
<body>
<!-- Headings -->
<h1>Fred's Travel Adventures</h1>
<h2>Summer Special</h2>
<h3>Machu Pichu: The Lost City of the Incas</h3>
<!-- Image of Machu Pichu -->
<img src="mp250x177.jpg" height="250" width="177"
alt="Picture of Machu Pichu" />
<!-- Teaser -->
<p>Travel back in time this summer as you visit Peru's
Machu Pichu, also known as the "lost" city of the Incas.
Complete tour packages as low as $1500.00 per person.</p>
<!-- Table of Tour Packages and Fees -->
<table border="1">
<tr><th>Tour Package</th><th>Cost Per Person</th></tr>
<tr><td>Deluxe (10 Day)</td><td>$3500</td></tr>
<tr><td>Standard (7 Day)</td><td>$2750</td></tr>
<tr><td>Economy (4 Day)</td><td>$1500</td></tr>
</table>
<!-- List of Included Items -->
<ul>
<lh>All Tours Include:</lh>
    <li>Round Trip Airfare</li>
    <li>Meals and Accommodations</li>
```

```
        <li>Transportation and Admission to Attractions</li>
        <li>Little Mints on Your Pillow Each Night</li>
</ul>
<!-- Related Links -->
<a href="perutour.htm">Peru Tour Information</a>
<a href="othertours.htm">Other Great Tour Deals</a>
<!-- Slogan -->
<p>Have the Adventure of a Lifetime this Summer
with Fred's Travel Adventures.</p>
</body>
</html>
```

3

Project Summary

If you compare the various elements in this HTML document with the page
displayed in Figure 3-1, you'll notice that each element displays in succession:
the three heads, the image, the teaser, the table, the list, the links, and finally

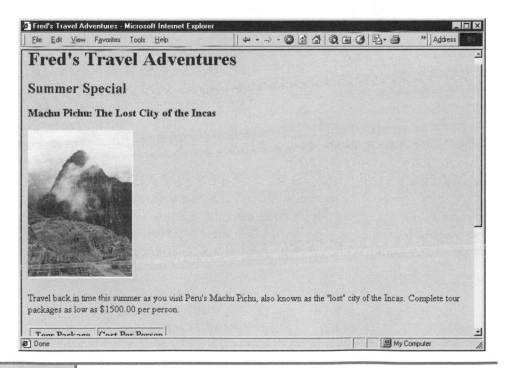

Figure 3-1   A Web page structured with HTML, but with no styles applied

the slogan. Unfortunately, this arrangement also causes much of the page's content to display off the bottom of the screen, making it necessary for a visitor to scroll down to see the rest of the page. Although it would be possible to use some presentational HTML markup (align="left" inserted in the <img /> element) to cause the rest of that page's contents to display to the right of the image, you'll discover in the rest of this module that you can do that and much more with CSS properties.

Working with Properties

Now that you have become acquainted with the five basic categories of CSS, you'll want to get a better idea of what you can do with them. Modules 6 through 10 will cover each of these property categories in detail; however, you'll find it beneficial to experiment with them a bit and see them in action before you begin to explore the fine details. Thus, the following sections will apply various style properties to the page you created in Project 3.1. That way, you can have a little experience with properties before you move on.

Control Text Arrangement with Text Properties

As mentioned earlier in this module, text properties are used to control the position and behavior of text, line spacing, word spacing, and so on. At least with CSS 1, text properties are not concerned with the actual *appearance* of text. However, these properties are important tools for *arranging* the text on your pages.

Survey Text Properties

Table 3-1 lists some of the properties that you can use for arranging text. Although there are more text properties than are listed here, these are among the most common and best-supported properties. Module 7 will provide a complete list of text properties as well as the values each takes and the browsers that support them.

Note

CSS 2 includes some properties, such as "text-shadow," that do affect the appearance of text. However, since these properties aren't supported by *any* browsers as of this writing, it is still accurate to say that text properties do not affect the text's appearance.

To do this:	Use this property:
Center left or right-align text	text-align
Add underlines, overlines, strike-throughs, or make text blink	text-decoration
Indent text	text-indent
Change the case of a block of text	text-transform
Control the vertical alignment of text	vertical-alignment
Control line height (the vertical space between lines of text)	line-height
Add or remove space between letters	letter-spacing

Table 3-1   CSS 1 Text Properties

Working with Text Properties

To see some text properties at work, try modifying Fred's Travel Adventure page by centering all of the headings and adding an indent to the teaser paragraph. To center all three of the heading elements, place the following style rule in between the <style> tags in the <head>portion of the page:

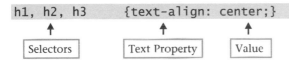

```
h1, h2, h3      {text-align: center;}
```

While you're at it, center the contents of the table cells by adding the following selector to the preceding rule:

```
h1, h2, h3, table      {text-align: center;}
```

Just for fun, use the text-transform property to convert the third heading to all-caps. Top it off by underlining it with the text-decoration property. Because

⎧Hint

The text-decoration property can also be used to *remove* underlines. If you want the links on your page to appear without their default underline, you would use the "text-decoration:none" declaration with the a:link pseudo class selector. However, if you choose this option, you'll need to also do it for the a:active and a:visited selectors. Otherwise, the underlines will return to your links after someone has clicked on them.

it is applying new styles that you do not necessarily want to apply to your other headings, you need to write a separate rule for this one.

```
h3        {text-transform: uppercase; text-decoration: underline;}
```

As the following illustration shows, your headings will now appear in the center of the page, and the third heading will be in capital letters and underlined. The HTML code with the embedded styles follows the illustration.

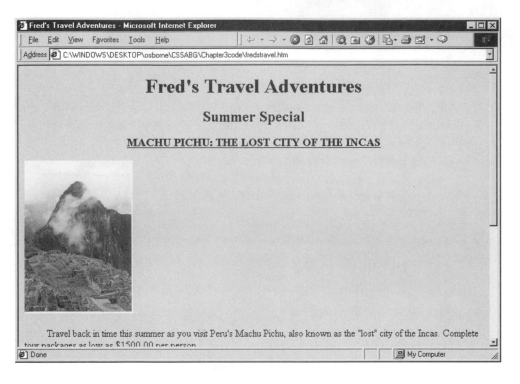

```
<html><head><title>Freds Travel Adventures</title>
<style>
h1, h2, h3, table        {text-align: center;}
h3                       {text-transform: uppercase;
                          text-decoration: underline;}
</head>
```

Once you've finished with the headings, indent the teaser paragraph by 36 pixels:

```
p       {text-indent: 36px;}
```

The value added to the text-indent property calls for the indent to be 36 pixels, which at 72 pixels per inch will create about a ½-inch indent. There are other ways to express that value, which will be covered in Module 4, but for now using pixels is the simplest. When you display the page, the "teaser" paragraph will be indented. However, by indenting the teaser paragraph, you are creating a potential conflict with the slogan paragraph.

Because the <p> element occurs twice on the page, your indent declaration will also affect the slogan paragraph at the bottom of the page. However, a problem arises if you decide to apply any formatting to the slogan. For instance, if you want to have the slogan centered and include a "text-align: center" declaration for the <p> element, the centering instruction will throw off the alignment of your teaser paragraph. The teaser will still retain the indent, but the rest of the paragraph will display as centered text. You can get around this problem by creating a class selector named "p.slogan." You can now apply styles to the slogan paragraph without affecting the other paragraphs on the page.

Hint

Be sure to remember to add the class="slogan" attribute to the first <p> tag of the slogan paragraph. Otherwise the styles will not be applied. The tag should look like this: <p class="slogan">.

```
p.slogan      {text-align: center}
```

Thus far, your style sheet for Fred's Travel Adventures should resemble the following listing:

```
<style>
h1,h2,h3,table      {text-align: center;}
h3                  {text-transform: uppercase;
                     text-decoration: underline;}
p                   {text-indent: 36px;}
p.slogan               {text-align: center;}
</style>
```

1-Minute Drill

● What property would you use to create "strike-through" text?

● What property can create right-aligned text?

● What property would you use to change the case of a text block?

Modify Fonts with Font Properties

The font properties enable you to control the appearance of the fonts on your page, much the same way as HTML's <font> element does. However, once you begin to work with font properties, you'll probably forget about <font> pretty quickly. Whereas <font> gives you limited control over the appearance of text on your Web pages, the font properties sets you free to indulge your creativity.

Survey Font Properties

CSS 1 font properties allow you to describe your fonts in terms of their family, size, style, weight, and variant. However, you cannot set a font's color with font-properties. The color of your text must be controlled with the color property, which will be covered in the next section. Table 3-2 shows what properties you need for modifying your fonts.

To do this:	Use this property:
Choose a font	font-family
Switch between normal and italic fonts	font-style
Switch between normal and small caps	font-variant
Adjust the boldness of a font	font-weight
Specify the size of a font	font-size

Table 3-2   Properties for Controlling Fonts

● Text-decoration
● Text-align
● Text-transform

Work with Fonts

To get a feel for the versatility of the font properties, try making some modifications to the fonts in the Fred's Adventure Tours page. Begin by applying the font-family property to cause the h1 selector to display with a 36 point fantasy font, and the h2 and h3 selectors to use a sans-serif font. In addition, add a rule that makes the h2 selector display in italics. The style rules would look like this:

```
h1      {font-family: fantasy;
          font-size: 36pt;}
h2      {font-style: italic;}
h2, h3 {font-family: sans-serif;}
```

As the following illustration shows, your revised headlines look much different from the ones you started with in Figure 3-1:

Fred's Travel Adventures

Summer Special

MACHU PICHU: THE LOST CITY OF THE INCAS

To give the slogan at the bottom of the page a different look, use the font-variant property to change it to small caps, the font-weight property to cause it to display boldface, and the font-style property to make it display in italics. Your style rule will look like this:

```
p.slogan          {text-align: center;
                  font-variant: small-caps;
                  font-style: italic;
                  font-weight: bold;}
```

You can see in the following illustration how this style rule has changed the appearance of the slogan paragraph.

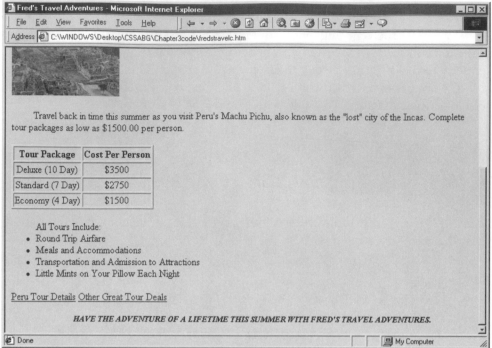

1-Minute Drill

● What property will create small caps?

● What property allows you to create larger fonts?

Add Color with Color/Background Properties

By now, you're probably getting tired of working with a basically "black and white" page and thinking that the whole thing would look a lot better with a little color added. You're absolutely right. It's amazing how drab a colorless Web page can be, and it's even more amazing how many of them you can find out there. As you'll see, adding some color to your page is a breeze with the Color and Background Properties.

● Font-variant
● Font-size

3

Survey Color/Background Properties

As you probably have inferred from the name, these properties control both color *and* background. In essence, they perform much the same function as HTML's "bgcolor," "color," and "background" attributes. However, as you use CSS's color/background properties, you'll discover that they give you design abilities you never had with HTML alone. In fact, you might be amazed at what you can do with these simple tools. Table 3-3 lists the Color/Background properties and their basic functions.

Experiment with Color/Background Properties

Returning to "Fred's Travel Adventures," suppose you want to spruce it up by using green text (to remind your visitors of the jungle) with a yellow-orange "sidebar" graphic (to remind them of beautiful Peruvian sunsets) that runs down the left side of the page. To do this with CSS is a snap. You will use a single graphic (sidebar20x72.gif) and then tell the browser to repeat the image down the left side of the page. To do this, you need:

- **Background-image**   to insert the image

- **Background-repeat**   to instruct the browser to repeat the image

- **Background-position**   to position the image

- **Background-color**   to set a background color for the rest of the page

- **Color**   to set the default text color to green

To do this:	Use this property:
Set text color	color
Select a background color	background-color
Include a background image	background-image
Specify whether a background image should repeat (tile) or not.	background-repeat
Specify whether a background image should scroll with the page or remain fixed	background-attachment
Position a background image	background-position

Table 3-3   Color/Background Properties

Tip

It's a good idea to always specify a background color, even when you are planning to have an image "tile" across the entire background. That way, you have a backup background if for some reason the image should fail to load.

You might be wondering which selector to use for a background image. With CSS, you can place a background image in virtually any element; however, since this is intended to be a background for the entire page, you will want to create your style rules with the <body> element in mind. Thus, you will use the body selector. Your style rule should look something like this:

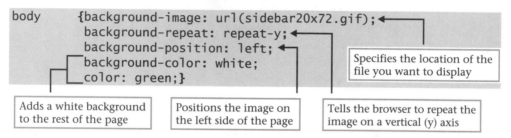

```
body      {background-image: url(sidebar20x72.gif);
           background-repeat: repeat-y;
           background-position: left;
           background-color: white;
           color: green;}
```

Specifies the location of the file you want to display

Adds a white background to the rest of the page

Positions the image on the left side of the page

Tells the browser to repeat the image on a vertical (y) axis

When you save the file and display it in a browser, you should see something that looks like the following illustration:

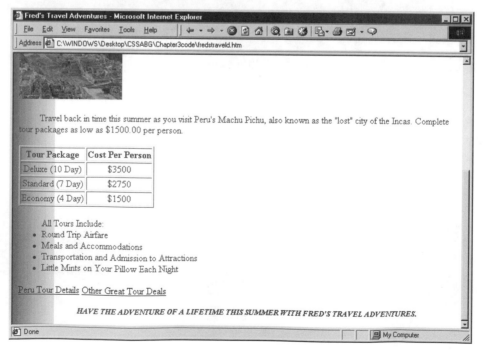

One obvious problem with the Web page in the preceding illustration is that most of the other page elements are now partly overlapping the sidebar image on the left. Needless to say, this makes your page layout look sloppy. Fortunately, you can easily correct the problem with some of the box-properties.

1-Minute Drill

● What property is used for setting text colors?

● The background-repeat property is used for what purpose?

Position Elements with Box Properties

The box properties provide the most extensive array of style "tools" in basic CSS. However, even though the overall category of box properties may seem somewhat confusing, the properties themselves are fairly self-explanatory. The box properties allow you to control things like margins, padding, borders, and so on. The key to working with the box properties is to remember that every element of your document should be viewed as being contained in a "box." As you work with the box properties, you'll see how this will help you.

Survey the Box Properties

The box properties will enable you to position elements on your page with much greater freedom than you had with HTML. If you are familiar with HTML tables, you know that you can add "padding" to individual table cells. Box properties allow you to do this with *any* element. You can also use box properties to set margins. If you're still a bit fuzzy about what, exactly, a "box" is, you can easily make them visible by adding a background color to any selector. As the illustration below demonstrates, most selectors' (elements') "boxes" extend clear across the page. However, notice that the boxes for the table and links do not go beyond their actual dimensions.

● The color property
● To control how a background image is repeated or "tiled."

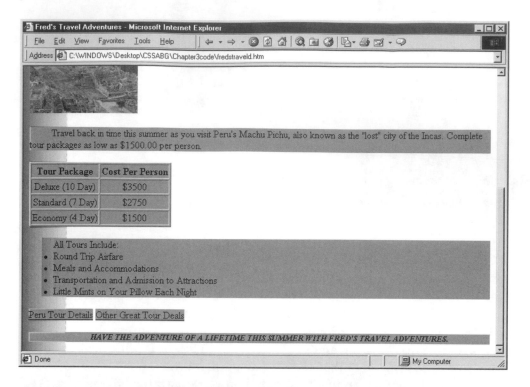

Table 3-4 lists some of the basic box properties.

To do this:	Use this property:
Adjust a margin (spacing outside the "box")	margin
Add padding inside the "box"	padding
Create a border around the "box"	border
Adjust a "box's" height	height
Adjust a "box's" width	width
Cause other elements to "wrap" to one side or another	float
Prevent other elements from being positioned on one side or another	clear

Table 3-4   Box Properties

Work with Box Properties

You can see how some of the box properties work by using them to rearrange the various elements of the Fred's Travel Adventures page. As the page exists now, most of the elements are overlapping the decorative sidebar on the left. You will want to move them over to the right. However, another problem is that a visitor to this page must scroll down to see all of the content. Fred has told you that he wants all the content to be visible on a single screen. Finally, Fred feels that the slogan paragraph is a little drab. He would like you to add a border to jazz it up.

To reposition the various elements, you need to use the margin property. It is possible with this property to adjust a box's margins all the way around or to specify one or more margins. In this case, you only need to adjust the left margin. So, you write a style rule that looks like this:

```
h1, h2, h3, img   {margin-left: .75in}
```

Note

The choice of .75in (3/4 of an inch) is actually not the best way to measure things on a video monitor; however, it is the simplest. In Module 4 you will learn better ways to specify lengths and other kinds of measurements.

Now, to reposition the image, table, list, and links, you will use the *float* and *clear* properties. These work much the same way as the "align" attribute does in HTML. In other words, if you choose float: left, the element is positioned to the left and everything else wraps to the right, and vice-versa. To keep other elements from wrapping, on one side or another, you would use the clear property. The following style rules will rearrange the basic elements of the page and bring them up beside the image;

```
img, table        {float: left;}        ← Causes the table and image to
ul                {float: right;           "wrap" to the left of the list
                   margin-right: 5%;}

a:link            {clear: right;}       ← Causes the list to "wrap" to the
a:visited         {clear: right;}          right of the image and table
a:active          {clear: right;}
```

Causes the table and image to "wrap" to the left of the list

Causes the list to "wrap" to the right of the image and table

Brings the list in 5% from the page's right margin.

Prevents anything from displaying to the right of the links

Finally, to add a little pizzazz to the slogan, add a border by including the following rule in your style sheet:

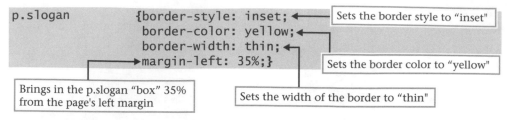

```
p.slogan          {border-style: inset;      ◄—— Sets the border style to "inset"
                   border-color: yellow;     ◄
                   border-width: thin;       ◄
                 ►margin-left: 35%;}
```

Sets the border color to "yellow"

Brings in the p.slogan "box" 35% from the page's left margin

Sets the width of the border to "thin"

Now that you have repositioned the elements for Fred's Travel Adventures Web page, it should look something like the following illustration:

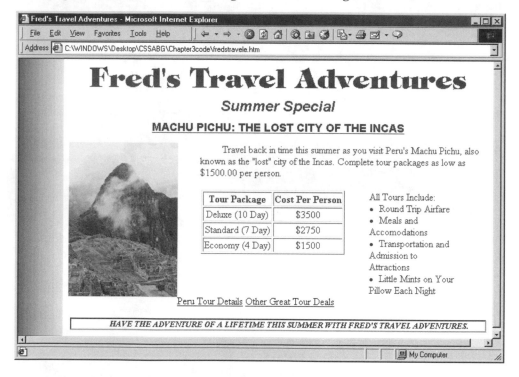

Control Display with Classification Properties

As mentioned earlier in this module, the classification or "descriptive" properties govern how certain elements are displayed. In basic CSS (CSS 1), these properties include those controlling the display of list items, white-space, and element classification (block, inline, and so on). Although these properties might not be high on your list of favorite CSS tools, they do have important functions.

Survey of Classification Properties

If you are familiar with HTML, you know that there are a number of ways to display lists and list items. Although it is possible to control the display of lists with HTML elements and attributes, you can also use CSS and the classification properties. You can also use classification properties to cause text to display *exactly* as you formatted it, mimicking the effect of HTML's preformatted text, <pre>, element. Also, as has been covered earlier in this module, you can redefine an element's basic display characteristics from block, to inline, list item, and even to "none." Table 3-5 lists the classification properties and their basic functions.

Experiment with Classification Properties

Just to get a feel for how to use the classification properties, modify the Fred's Travel Page document by changing the bulleted list's display from disc to square. You would do that by adding the following rule to your style sheet:

```
ul      {list-style-type: square;}
```

Once you have saved your page, display it in a browser. The list bullets should now be squares, as in the following illustration:

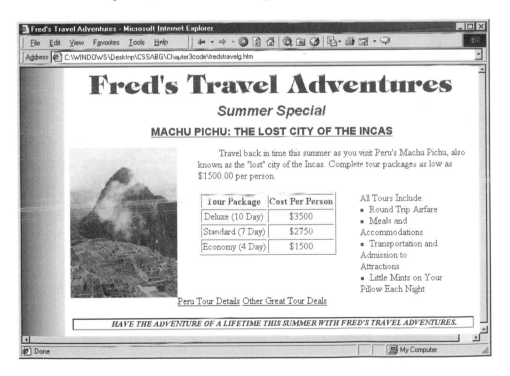

To do this:	Use this property:
Change an element's display properties from block to inline or vice-versa.	display
Preserve your text formatting. It's also used to control the extra spacing within text and the wrapping of lines.	white-space
Choose how a list displays (disc, circle, square, and so on).	list-style-type
Use a graphic image for list bullets.	list-style-image
Position the bullets on a list.	list-style-position

Table 3-5 The Classification Properties

1-Minute Drill

- What does the float property do?
- The white-space property functions like what HTML element?

Project 3-2: Add More Style to Fred's Travel Adventures

After you showed your stylized page to your client (Fred), he came back with some suggestions for improvement. In this project, you will incorporate Fred's suggestions and further modify the existing style sheet. All of the changes can be made using what you have learned in this chapter.

Step-by-Step

1. Open fredstravel.htm, the HTML document you created in Project 3-1.

2. If you haven't done so already, add the styles created in the preceding section. You can embed them by using the <style> element in the <head> portion of the document, or you can create a separate style sheet, named fredstravel.css. If you decide to use a separate style sheet, be sure to save

---

- It positions an element on the page and causes other elements to "wrap" to one side or another
- It controls extra "white-space" within text as well as line wrapping and can be used to preserve your text formatting

it in the same directory as the HTML document, then insert the following line in between the <head> tags:

```
<link rel="stylesheet" type="text/css" href="fredstravel.css" />
```

3. Once you have added the styles from the preceding section, add a *thin, green, inset* border around the picture of Machu Pichu. You will need to modify the img selector and use the border-width, border-color, and border-style properties. The values you will use are the italicized words in the first sentence of this paragraph.

4. Reposition the links so that they are not right up against the picture. To do this, you will need to enclose the links in the <div> element, as in the following listing. The <div> element serves as a generic "block level" element that you can use for applying styles. To use <div> to center the links, you will need to write a style rule that sets the text-align property for <div> to "center," as in the following rule:

```
div     {text-align: center;}
```

```
<div>
<a href="perutour.htm">Click for More Information</a>
<a href="othertours.htm">Click for Other Great Deals</a>
</div>
```

5. Give the table a green background, and make the text display white. For this, you will use the background-color and color properties.

6. Reduce the size of the text in the list and the table, setting it to .75em. (*Ems* are a unit of measurement based on the default font size. These will be covered in Module 4.) You will need to add the font-size property to the table and ul selectors.

7. Resizing the text should have thrown off the position of your slogan. Reposition it by adding a "clear: right" declaration to the p.slogan selector.

8. Save your file as fredstravel2.htm and display it in a Web browser. If you have any problems, the stylesheet and HTML code for this project follow the illustration. The page should look something like the following illustration.

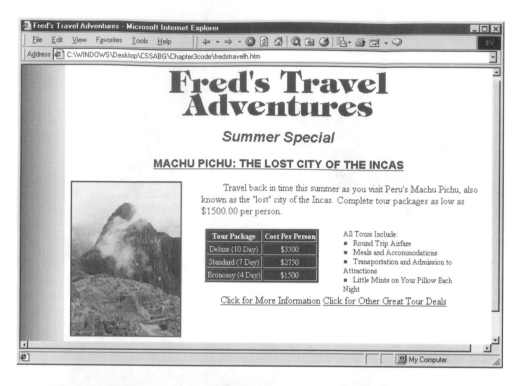

```
<html>
<head>
<title>Fred's Travel Adventures</title>
</head>
<style>
body              {background-image: url(sidebar20x72.gif);
                   background-repeat: repeat-y;
                   background-position: left;
                   background-color: white;
                   color: green;}
h1, h2, h3, img   {margin-left: .75in}
h1,h2,h3,table    {text-align: center;
                   color: green;}
h1                {font-family: fantasy; font-size: 36pt;}
h2,h3             {font-family: sans-serif;}
h2                {font-style: italic;}
h3                {text-transform: uppercase;
                   text-decoration: underline;}
p                 {text-indent: 36px;
                   margin-left: 38%;}
```

```
p.slogan            {text-align: center;
                    font-variant: small-caps;
                    font-style: italic;
                    font-weight: bold;
                    border-style: inset;
                    border-color: yellow;
                    border-width: thin;
                    margin-left: 10%;
                    clear: left;}
img                 {float: left;
                    border-style:inset;
                    border-color: green;
                    border-width:thin;}
table               {float: left;
                    margin-left: 5%;
                    color: white;
                      background-color: green;
                      font-size: .75em;}
ul                  {float: right;
                    margin-right: 5%;
                      list-style-type: square;
                    font-size: .75em;}
a:link              {clear: right;}
a:visited           {clear: right;}
a:active            {clear: right;}
div                 {text-align: center;}
</style>
<body>
<h1>Fred's Travel Adventures</h1>
<h2>Summer Special</h2>
<h3>Machu Pichu: The Lost City of the Incas</h3>
<img src="mp250x177.jpg" height="250" width="177"
alt="Picture of Machu Pichu" />
<p>Travel back in time this summer as you visit Peru's
Machu Pichu, also known as the "lost" city of the Incas
Complete tour packages as low as $1500.00 per person.</p>
<table border="1">
<tr><th>Tour Package</th><th>Cost Per Person</th></tr>
<tr><td>Deluxe (10 Day)</td><td>$3500</td></tr>
<tr><td>Standard (7 Day)</td><td>$2750</td></tr>
<tr><td>Economy (4 Day)</td><td>$1500</td></tr>
</table>
<ul>
<lh>All Tours Include:</lh>
```

```
    <li>Round Trip Airfare</li>
    <li>Meals and Accommodations</li>
    <li>Transportation and Admission to Attractions</li>
    <li>Little Mints on Your Pillow Each Night</li>
</ul>
<div>
<a href="perutour.htm">Click for More Information</a>
<a href="othertours.htm">Click for Other Great
Tour Deals</a>
</div>
<p class="slogan">Have the Adventure of a Lifetime this
Summer with Fred's Travel Adventures.</p>
</body>
</html>
```

Project Summary

In this project, you have changed the appearance of the Fred's Travel Adventures page by modifying an existing style sheet. If you were to experiment further by changing the values in the various style rules, you could develop a number of different variations on this theme. Simply changing background and text colors can dramatically change the appearance of the page. Before you move on to Module 4, take some time to play with the design and discover what new combinations you can come up with.

☑ *Mastery Check*

1. List the five basic categories of properties.

_____

_____

2. To convert a block of text to small caps, you would use:

    A. text-transform

    B. font-convert

    C. convert-case

    D. font-variant

3. Write a style rule for the <h1> element that sets the text color to red, the background color to white, and adds a thin, inset, blue border.

_____

_____

4. To change the bullet on an unordered list, what property would you use?

_____

_____

5. Write a style rule that sets the default text for a page to a 12 point, blue font.

_____

_____

3

Module 4

Applying Values

The Goals of This Module

- Understand the Importance of Values
- Learn the Basic Types of Values
- Understand CSS Measurement Units
- Learn How to Specify Colors in CSS
- Understand the Simplest Measurement Units

S uppose that just before you leave on vacation—in a flash of creative inspiration—you decide to have your house painted. You hire a contractor to do the work, and you tell him that you want your entire house painted by the time you return. In a desperate rush, you hang up the phone and then leave for a two-week vacation in the Bahamas, confident that you will return to a beautiful, freshly painted house. However, when you pull into your driveway you are furious to discover that the contractor has painted your house hot pink. When you call to complain, he quietly responds, "You never told me what color to paint it, so I just chose my favorite color." As silly as that may seem, it provides at least some illustration of the importance of "values" in CSS. If you don't specify them, someone or some*thing* else will.

Understand Values and Their Importance

In the two preceding modules, you learned the basics of using selectors and properties and about the amazing control they can give you over the appearance of your HTML documents. However, without "values," selectors and properties are powerless. Selectors identify which parts of a document you want to apply styles to (heading, paragraph, tables, lists, and so on); properties identify which styles you wish to apply (font, background color, margins, and so forth). Values supply the details.

Values tell a browser whether you want large text or small text; red, white, blue, or chartreuse backgrounds; big margins or small; and much more. In essence, values are where you get to exercise a measure of personal control over the appearance of your page. Keep in mind that your control is never absolute, because there are many other factors that influence how your Web pages look. For instance, it is possible for people who visit your Web site to define their own style sheets, which can override yours. Also, browsers have their own *default* style sheets built in, which they will try to apply to your pages. This happens most often when your pages are displayed in browsers that don't support CSS. Finally, CSS itself has its own hierarchy in which styles are applied through *inheritance* and the *cascade*. Thus, if you are using a style sheet and do not take cascade and inheritance into account, CSS may end up supplying styles where you may not have wanted them. With all these possible values, you can begin to see why it is important for you to specify the styles you want in your document. If you don't, someone else will. So, how do you know which values to use? The way to start is by learning about the different kinds of values resident in your CSS "toolbox."

Ask the Expert

Question: What is "inheritance?"

Answer: *Inheritance* is the mechanism in CSS whereby styles applied to a "parent" element are transferred to its "children." For example, in Project 3-2 all <h1> elements are set to green by an embedded style sheet. In writing your HTML document, you may decide to use the italics text element, <i>, inside the <h1> element to add emphasis to a certain word, like this: <h1>This is an <i>italicized</i> word</h1>. The word inside the <i> tags will be green, even though you never specified that color for it. Why? Because in this case the <i> element is the "child" of the <h1> element. Thus, it inherits its parent's green color. As with the cascade, inheritance can become more complicated, but this is basically the idea behind it. For more about inheritance and the cascade, see Module 5.

Question: What do you mean by "cascade"?

Answer: The *cascade* is the means by which a browser determines which styles to use when conflicting style sheets apply to the same selector. A basic illustration of the cascade is in the relationship between linked, embedded, and inline styles. Suppose you have a page where a linked style specifies that all <h1> elements should be red, but embedded in the <head> portion of the page is a style that specifies all green <h1> elements. Also, the first <h1> on the page has an inline style, specifying that it should be blue. Which style applies? By the rules of the cascade, the <h1> element with the inline style will be blue; all others will be green. This is because inline styles take precedence over both embedded and linked styles. The rest of the <h1> elements will be green, because embedded styles have priority over linked. It gets a bit more complex than this, but you don't need to worry about it in this module. For more information on the cascade, check out Module 5.

Different Value Types

Because there are so many different properties, there are necessarily many different kinds of values. So many, in fact, that memorizing them all would be a difficult (though not impossible) task. However, it isn't necessary to know all the different CSS values "by heart." In fact, if you think about values first in terms of categories, you'll find them fairly easy to keep sorted out. The basic categories of CSS values are

- Specific Values
- URL Values
- Color Values
- Measurement Units

Specific Values

Some properties take very specific values. Consider the "border-style" property. When designing a border for a selector, you use this property to specify the kind of border you want to display. Your value options for the border-style property are dotted, dashed, solid, double, groove, ridge, inset, and outset. Another property like this is the "font-variant" property. Your choices here are limited to either normal or small-caps. Many of the properties in CSS take specific values, and the only way to become familiar with these is to learn them property by property. In Modules 6 through 10, you will learn what these values are and see how they work. As you learn them, keep in mind that a major consideration with these "specific" values is whether or not they are supported by the major browsers (Internet Explorer and Netscape).

Because even CSS 1 is not fully supported by the major browsers, you are likely to run into problems with your designs if you fail to consider whether a certain value is supported broadly enough for your purposes. For example, if you choose "dotted" as a value for the border-style property, you need to be aware that it is not supported in Internet Explorer 4 and 5, but it *is* supported in Netscape 6. Thus, if you place a dotted border around a paragraph element and display it in Netscape 6, it will look like the following illustration:

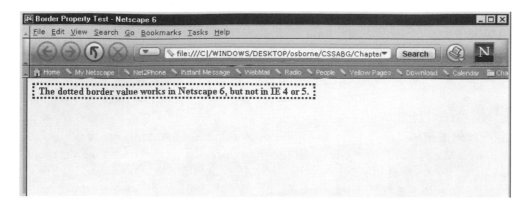

However, if you display the same page in Internet Explorer 5, you'll still get a border, but, as the next illustration shows, it won't be the one you specified:

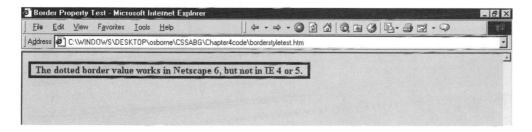

Now, if you are designing pages for a corporate Intranet, and you know that everyone will be using Netscape 6, you have no problem. On the other hand, if you are designing pages for a public Internet site with a broad audience, you'll have people visiting your pages with all sorts of browsers, and your pages may not turn out the way you expect them to.

Thus, the primary issues with specific values are knowing what they are, how well they are supported, and which ones will best suit your needs. You also need to have a good idea of the users who make up your audience and which browsers they are using.

4

Tip

If your Web host provides site statistics, you will generally find a summary of the browsers that are being used to visit your site. As for your audience, you need to analyze them based on the type of site you have, your subject matter, and so on. In other words, you have to do some research and study your audience. However, as you should do this routinely when you are planning a site, most of the work should already be done.

URL Values

A few properties—the background-image property, for example—require you to specify a Web address or "URI" (Uniform Resource Identifier). This requirement is obviously designed to allow the browser to locate the file you wish to use for a background image. Thus, you need to supply a value that points the browser to the image's location. The syntax for this kind of property-value declaration is easy. You simply write the letters **url**, then put the actual address beside it in parentheses, as in the following example:

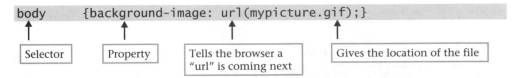

```
body     {background-image: url(mypicture.gif);}
```

| Selector | Property | Tells the browser a "url" is coming next | Gives the location of the file |

Ask the Expert

Question: What is a "URI"?

Answer: You may be more familiar with the term "URL" (Uniform Resource Locator). An url (pronounced "you are el") is the "address" of a file on the Web. For example, the URL of Osborne's Web site is **http://www.osborne.com.** So what's a URI? Don't let the difference in terms throw you. They both mean essentially the same thing. It's just that "Uniform Resource Identifier" is actually a broader term, meant to include more than a URL. It is being used in anticipation of the days in the future when you won't just have URLs, but URNs (Uniform Resource Names) and URCs (Uniform Resource Characteristic). However, when specifying a Web address in CSS, you must still use the acronym URL.

Percentage Values

You might think of a percentage value as sort of a "wild-card" value. Quite a few properties allow you to supply values in terms of percentages rather than with specific details. If you've worked with tables in HTML, you probably have already had some experience with this concept. With HTML tables, you can use percentages in specifying a table's width, thereby creating a variable-width table that will adjust to the size of the browser window. Percentage values in CSS work in basically the same way, but over a much larger range of applications. You are not limited to using percentages for tables and frames; you can use them for almost anything. For example, if you want to set font size and margins and indent the text for the paragraph element, an easy way to do so is with percentages, as in the following style rule:

```
<html><head><title>Percentage Demo</title>
<style> p {text-indent: 5%;
           margin-left: 25%;
           margin-right: 15%;
           font-size: 150%; </style>
<body>
<p>This paragraph's font, margins, and indent have been
set with percentages.</p>
</body>
</html>
```

If you save and display the preceding HTML code, the first line of every block of text enclosed in the <p> element would be indented 5% of the total width of the browser window. Likewise, the margins would be set 25% of the way in from the left side of the browser window and 15% of the way in from the right side. The font will be set at 150% of the default font size. The following illustration demonstrates how the percentage values affect the overall presentation of the material on the page:

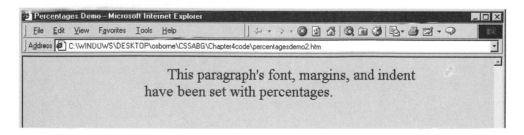

Another interesting characteristic of values is that *sometimes* properties will allow you to apply "negative" values. For instance, as the following illustration shows, if you change the value of the text-indent property to -5%, you will get a "hanging indent."

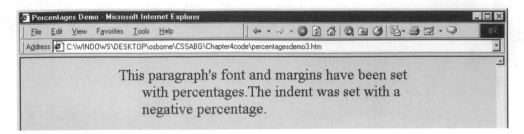

Not all properties will accept a negative value, but the ones that do can enable you to create some interesting designs. As you progress through the rest of the modules of this book, you will learn which properties accept negative values and which do not.

Color Values

If you have worked with HTML, you are probably somewhat familiar with specifying color values. HTML allows you only two options: keywords and hexadecimal code. That is, you can identify a color by name (keyword)—for example: "red," "navy," "maroon," and so on. You can also identify colors with a code that computers will recognize. For example, #ff0000 is the code for red. CSS expands your options for identifying colors from two methods to five: keyword, hexadecimal, abbreviated hexadecimal, decimal, and percentage. If you're not familiar with "technical" terms, don't worry, as they will be explained in this module's section on Simplifying Color Values. For now, Table 4-1 gives you a side by side comparison of sixteen basic colors as they would be specified with each of these different methods:

Measurement Units

When you are specifying font size, margins, word and letter spacing, padding, or virtually anything else that requires a "measurement of distance," you will supply your value using measurement units. Value choices with measurement

Keyword	Hexadecimal	Hex-3	Decimal	Percentage
Aqua	#00ffff	#0ff	rgb(0,255,255)	rgb(0%,100%,100%)
Black	#000000	#000	rgb(0,0,0)	rgb(0%,0%,0%)
Blue	#0000ff	#00f	rgb(0,0,255)	rgb(0%,0%,100%)
Fuchsia	#ff00ff	#f0f	rgb(255,0,255)	rgb(100%,0%,100%)
Gray	#808080	#888	rgb(128,128,128)	rgb(50%,50%,50%)
Green	#008000	#080	rgb(0,128,0)	rgb(0%,50%,0%)
Lime	#00ff00	#0f0	rgb(0,255,0)	rgb(0%,100%,0%)
Maroon	#800000	#800	rgb(128,0,0)	rgb(50%,0%,0%)
Navy	#000080	#008	rgb(0,0,128)	rgb(0%,0%,50%)
Olive	#808000	#880	rgb(128,128,0)	rgb(50%,50%,0%)
Purple	#800080	#808	rgb(128,0,128)	rgb(50%,0%,50%)
Red	#ff0000	#f00	rgb(255,0,0)	rgb(100%,0%,0%)
Silver	#c0c0c0	#ccc	rgb(192,192,192)	rgb(80%,80%,80%)
Teal	#008080	#088	rgb(0,128,128)	rgb(0%,50%,50%)
White	#ffffff	#fff	rgb(255,255,255)	rgb(100%,100%,100%)
Yellow	#ffff00	#ff0	rgb(255,255,0)	rgb(100%,100%,0%)

Table 4-1   The 16 Windows VGA Colors in CSS Color Value Units

units can be confusing, simply because of the number of different measurements you can employ.

- **Standard Measurements**   If you want, you can specify measurements using the same measurements you would use for anything else: inches, centimeters and millimeters. Thus, it would be possible to specify a margin of 1 inch from each side of the screen, a text indent of 1 centimeter, and word spacing of 2 millimeters. However, as you will see, standard measurements are generally not the best choice when working with Web pages.

- **Points and Picas**   These are standard typesetting measurements, with a ratio of 72 points to an inch. If you work with word processing software, you are probably familiar with points. A pica is equivalent to 12 points, and so there are 6 picas to an inch. You may be tempted to use points and picas, simply because you have a better visual concept of their relative sizes. However, again these do not represent the best choice for Web style sheets.

● **Pixels**   This refers to the dots on a computer monitor screen. Using pixels might seem an obvious choice, if you are writing style sheets for Web pages; however keep in mind that there can be a vast difference in video display capabilities, *including* the number of pixels per inch.

● **Ems and Exes**   Traditionally, an *em* is a measurement value calculated in relation to the width of the font's capital *M*. That is, 1.0 em is equal to one *M* width. On the other hand, an *ex* is a measurement value equal to the height of the lowercase letter *x*. In CSS, as a rule, the em simply is regarded as a value equal to the default font size. Because the ex value is more tightly tied to a font's letter *x* it is less reliable as a measurement tool. However, you should become familiar with ems and learn to use them in your style sheets.

● **Percentages**   You can also specify measurements by using percentages. For example, you could set the left and right margins for a page to 10% by writing a style rule like this: body {margin-left: 10%; margin-right: 10%}. Percentages have an advantage as measurement values, because they can *scale* (adjust) in relation to the size of the browser window, display resolution, and so on.

Although it might be tempting to go with the more familiar forms of measurement (inches and points, for example), as you learn how measuring lengths and sizes in CSS works, you'll discover these are not generally the best options. Whenever possible, you want to use *relative* measurements such as percentages and *ems*. The CSS length and size units you can use are listed in Table 4-2:

Measurement Unit	Absolute or Relative	Sample
Inches	absolute	margin-left: 1.5in;
Centimeters	absolute	margin-right: 1.1cm;
Millimeters	absolute	margin-top: 32mm;
Points	absolute	font-size: 24pt
Picas	absolute	word-spacing: 2pc
Pixels	relative	padding-left: 55px
Ems	relative	font-size: 1.2em
Exes	relative	letter-spacing: .3ex
Percentage	relative	margin-left: 15%

Table 4-2   Measurement Units

1-Minute Drill

● What kind of values could you use to describe distance or length measurements?

● What are the five ways you can specify color in CSS?

Absolute vs. Relative Units

In the preceding chart, you will notice that some of the measurements are listed as *absolute*, while others are listed as *relative*. Absolute measurements are easy to understand. For example, inches are absolute. So are millimeters and centimeters. These measurements represent the same thing on a style sheet as they do on a ruler: a fixed length. In other words, an inch is an inch—period. It is not flexible, and it does not adjust to accommodate changes in environment. That is what is meant by an "absolute" measurement.

Note

In practice, an inch may not display precisely as an inch on a video monitor. Many possible variations in display capabilities can affect the actual result. The important thing to remember is that whether your "inch" displays correctly or as 15/16ths of an inch, it is still a fixed measurement.

Absolute measurements can be very useful, particularly with some of the CSS 2 properties that allow you to design style sheets that specify how your pages should look when they are printed out. You are safe using absolute measurements in that type of context, because you *know* the environment in which your page will display, for instance: an 8 1/2" x 11" sheet of paper. However, absolute measurements do not work well in Web design because, as a rule, you do *not* know where your pages will be displaying. It is then that you want to use "relative" measurements.

Relative measurements earned that name because they are made *relative to* something else. They give you a flexibility in your design that you don't get with absolute measurements, because they enable your pages to be "scalable." In other words, they give your pages the ability to adjust to the size of the

---

● You can specify measurements with inches, centimeters, millimeters, points, picas, pixels, ems, exes, or percentages
● You can specify color with keywords, hexadecimal, short or abbreviated hexadecimal, decimal, and percentages

display that they are viewed on. However, when you use relative measurements it's important to know what the measurement is relative *to*. Otherwise, you could end up with some unexpected results. For example, if you are writing a style rule to enlarge the font size for an <h1> element, you might use a relative measurement such as 150%, thinking that you are setting the font size to 1 1/2 times the size of an <h1> font. You might be surprised when your results look like the following:

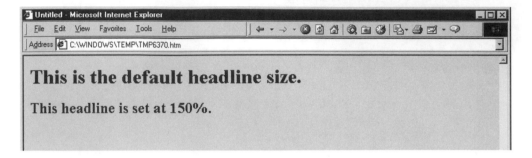

Why is the 150% headline *smaller* than the default <h1>? Because the font-size is not measured against the <h1> element, but rather against its "parent," which in this case would be the <body> element. In other words, you are specifying that the headline be 150% of the "body text" font size. You can see, then, that using relative measurements can be tricky; however, with a little practice, they are not difficult to use.

Simplifying Color Values

If you plan on using only the 16 basic colors in Table 4-1, then you don't really need to worry much about understanding color theory or about how to specify custom colors. However, if you plan on doing much Web design, you will most likely find the 16 basic colors somewhat limiting. Thus, you will need to learn a little about how colors work on Web pages and how you can specify your own.

Understand Additive Color Mixing

If you have ever painted with oils or watercolors, drawn with colored-pencils or crayons, or even finger-painted, you know a little bit about color theory. You probably know that the primary colors are red, yellow, and blue. As for color mixing: yellow and blue make green, red and yellow create orange, and red and blue produce purple. Simple, huh? Unfortunately, when you are mixing colors for the Web all that knowledge gets tossed out the window, because colors work differently when you are mixing them for a video display.

When you mix colors with paints or other pigments, you are doing what is called *subtractive* color mixing. In other words, as you combine the colors, the more color you add the darker your result. If you mix the three primary colors together in equal amounts, you'll eventually wind up with black (actually closer to mud than to true black).

When you mix colors for display on a video monitor, you are not using pigments. You are mixing with light, and all the rules are different. This is called *additive* color mixing: the more color you add, the brighter your result. With additive color mixing, if you mix the three primary colors together in equal amounts (and at full value), you'll end up with white. Also, your primary colors are different. Instead of red, yellow, and blue the primary colors are red, *green*, and blue.

4

Hint

Often the primary colors are referred to as "RGB." In fact, if you'll look again at Table 4-1, you'll see that the letters "RGB" are an important component of decimal and percentage color values. That's because all color is specified in terms of the amounts of red, green, and blue light that are to be mixed.

As for how to mix colors to produce the results you want, almost none of the color mixing rules you have ever used will work. For example, if you mix red and green in full (100%) amounts, the result will be yellow. Try *that* with watercolors. Also, while it is true that if you mix colors in equal amounts you will get a neutral gray, the more color you add, the brighter the result. So you can see that mixing colors for the Web is a different ballgame altogether. Add to that the fact that you have over 16 million possible color combinations, and things can get confusing very quickly.

Tip

The figure of 16 million is arrived at by multiplying the maximum number of possible values for each primary color (256) by one another. Thus, you multiply 256 x 256 x 256, and the result is 16,777,216.

Easy Color Mixing

With a palette of nearly 17 million possible color combinations, how is it possible to simplify things? First, you must reduce your palette to a manageable size. No artist on the planet would ever use a palette of 16.7 million colors, and neither should you. Second, you should find a simple way to express the colors you are choosing. Third, you need to take advantage of available resources and color charts.

Reduce Palette Size

How do you reduce palette size? The easiest way is by making use of what was formerly known as the "browser-safe" palette. Joe Gillespie, on his *Web Page Design for Designers* Web site, provides a brief history of the "browser-safe" palette. He points out that in the early days of the PC and Mac, computer systems were less complex and had fewer capabilities, and color display was fairly simple. In fact, the 16 basic colors mentioned in the preceding section were about all you would have had to work with. As systems became more sophisticated, color palettes were expanded to display 256 colors, although the Macintosh and Windows systems went in somewhat different directions in the palettes they chose. When Web browsers were developed, in order to provide consistency of display across the different platforms, they incorporated a palette of 216 colors that the Mac and Windows systems had in common. This eventually became known as the browser-safe or Web-safe palette, because a designer could use these colors without worrying about *dithering*. The essence of mixing colors for the browser-safe palette is that you always mix in increments of 20%. For instance, 20% Red, 80% Green, and 60% Blue would be considered "browser-safe." On the other hand, 12% Red, 37% Green, and 92% Blue would not.

Hint

Dithering is the mottled or "speckled" effect you sometimes get when your system is trying to approximate a color that it doesn't support. The easiest way to see what dithering looks like is to set your system for a 16-color display, then view a photo or other image that has a smooth transition from one color to another. Under a 16-color display, the formerly smooth transition now looks mottled and choppy. That's an extreme example of dithering.

So, what happened with the browser-safe palette? With the advent of computer systems and video cards that can display millions of colors, the browser-safe palette is no longer considered "safe." Quite simply, there are too many possible combinations of systems and monitors and other variations in display to consider it absolutely safe. In addition, since most systems can handle a vastly expanded array of colors now, it really isn't necessary to adhere strictly to the browser-safe palette. However, there are good reasons that this palette still makes sense from a design standpoint. It is smaller, more manageable, and easier to mix, and there are numerous resources that support it.

If you keep in mind that you can mix any of the browser-safe colors by simply using amounts of Red, Green, and Blue, ranging from 0-20-40-60-80-100%, you will find that mixing colors for the Web is very easy. Plus, this smaller and more manageable palette provides you with a greater range of colors than you are ever likely to need.

4

Use Percentage Values

Although CSS gives you the option of using hexadecimal or decimal notation, unless you have some strong attachment to these methods, you're better off using percentage values. To specify a color value with percentages, you merely write the letters "RGB" followed by the amount of each color you want to include in the mixture. The colors should be in "RGB" order, that is red, green, and blue; and they should always have a percentage sign after each value. They must also be separated by commas. Thus, if you were going to set a page's background-color value to red, it would look like this:

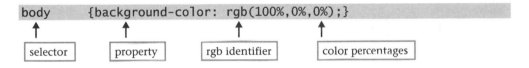

```
body      {background-color: rgb(100%,0%,0%);}
```
↑ selector   ↑ property   ↑ rgb identifier   ↑ color percentages

In the preceding listing, the color red is created by adding 100% of the color red, and 0% blue and green. You would produce green by using 100% green instead of red, and so on. The rest of the browser-safe colors are produced by using different combinations of red, green, and blue, in amounts of 0, 20, 40, 60, 80, and 100 percent. It's really quite simple.

Use Color Resources

Now that you understand how you can easily mix color for the Web using the browser-safe palette, you still face another problem. If the colors mix differently than they would with standard pigments, how can you know the mixtures you need to create the color you want? Visibone (**www.visibone.com**) offers a number of different free resources, such as downloadable color swatches that can be plugged into your image editing software. One of their most helpful resources is an online color "lab" that will enable you to select several different colors from a chart and see how those colors work together. Some other color resources are listed in Table 4-3.

Alternative Color Values

Although percentages are the easiest way to specify color in CSS, it's not a bad idea to be familiar with the other ways to accomplish the same goal. Keywords, hexadecimal, and decimal notation are not all that difficult to work with, once you know how they work.

Note

The style rule below each bullet produces the same result, blue text on a white background.

- **Keywords**   As mentioned earlier in the module, you can use keywords to set color values. CSS recognizes the 16 basic colors listed in Table 4-1 and, although there are other "named" colors (such as the Netscape named colors), it's not a good idea to use them with CSS. Because CSS does not

Resource	Site Title	URL
Color swatches and Online Lab	Visibone	www.visibone.com
Cat 'n Moose Web Safe Color Sampler	Cat 'n Moose	www.catnmoose.com
216 Web Safe Color Chart	Web Source	www.web-source.net/ 216_color_chart.htm
Web Safe Color Chooser	HSB Designs	www.hsbdesigns.com/clients/ colors.html
Web Templates Color Picker	Web Templates	www.webtemplates.com/ colors
"Is the Web Safe Palette Dead?"	Joe Gillespie, Web Page Design for Designers	www.wpdfd.com

Table 4-3   Web Color Resources

recognize these other named colors, your results will be unpredictable and will likely vary from browser to browser.

```
body      {color: blue; background-color: white;}
```

● **Hexadecimal**   Hexadecimal code is, in effect, the language of computers and, although it may seem confusing, it's not significantly different from percentages, aside from how it's written. When you use hexadecimal (or *hex*) to specify a color, you are still giving the rgb values. The only difference is that the amounts are given through hexadecimal's "base-16" numbering system. For example, the browser-safe percentages in hex are as follows: 0%=00, 20%=33, 40%=66, 60%=99, 80%=cc, and 100%=ff. Thus, if you want to specify red in hex code, you simply begin with a hash mark (to identify the value as hexadecimal), then you supply 100% red (ff) 0% green (00) and 0% blue (00). The complete value will look like this: #ff0000. An 80% red value would be written like this: #cc0000.

```
body      {color: #0000ff; background-color: #ffffff;}
```

● **Hex-3**   This is simply an abbreviated form of hexadecimal. Notice in the previous bullet that the hex code is in matched doublets (00, 33, 66, 99, cc, ff). It doesn't always occur this way, but with browser-safe colors it does. You can use a shortened version that supplies only one of each. For instance, the hex code for white (#ffffff) can be shortened to #fff.

```
body      {color: #00f; background-color: #fff}
```

● **Decimal**   You can also specify rgb values in decimal notation. Using decimal notation, you have a possible value range from 0-255 for each primary color. Thus, if you wanted to specify white in decimal, it would be written: rgb(255, 255, 255). The browser-safe amounts in decimal are: 0%=0, 20%=51, 40%=102, 60%=153, 80%=204, and 100%=255

```
body      {color: rgb(0,0,255); background-color:
rgb(255,255,255);}
```

Ask the Expert

Question: What is Hexadecimal?

Answer: Hexadecimal is simply a different way of numbering things. Having grown up with a base-10 numbering system, we often find it difficult to comprehend anything else. However, if you keep in mind that our base-10 system simply thinks of numbers in groups of 10 (0,1,2,3,4,5,6,7,8,9), you'll begin to understand how Hexadecimal works. Hexadecimal is base-16. That means that hex must find a way to represent some "numerals" that do not exist in the base 10 system. To represent the additional numerals, Hexadecimal uses letters: 0,1,2,3,4,5,6,7,8,9,a,b,c,d,e,f. A chart comparing our base ten values with hex values would look like this:

0=0	1=1	2=2	3=3	4=4	5=5	6=6	7=7
8=8	9=9	10=a	11=b	12=c	13=d	14=e	15=f

Simplifying Measurement Units

Measurement units can also be pretty confusing when you are trying to decide which is best to use. A simple rule of thumb for Web design in particular is that you should develop the habit of always using relative measurements, particularly *ems* and percentages. Although pixels are a relative measurement, they do not provide quite the flexibility that *ems* and percentages do. Also, pixel-per-inch counts will be affected by different monitor resolutions, and therefore they are not reliable measurement tools. Fixed measurements will be useful when you are designing for print media, but with all the possible variations in monitor displays, your pages will be most consistent if you use measurements that will be able to adjust to each display environment.

Project 4-1: Create a Color Table

One way to become acclimated to working with colors in CSS is by creating a table that forms an "online" chart of colors. While quite a few different programs will practically automate the color choice process for you, the more you work with color in CSS, the easier it will be for you to know which combinations of color will produce the results you want. In this project, you will begin creating an HTML page that will display colors for you and show you how they interact when mixed.

Step-by-Step

1. Create an HTML document and save it as colorchart.htm.

2. Insert a set of <style> tags in the <head> portion of the page.

3. Inside the style tags, add style rules that will set background and text colors for the following page elements: body, h1, h2, th (table header):

```
body    {background-color: rgb(60%,60%,60%);
         color: rgb(0%,0%,0%);}
h1, h2 {color: rgb(80%80%80%);}
th      {background-color: rgb(65%65%65%);}
```

4. Use the <div> element to align the page contents to the center:

```
<div align="center"> </div>
```

5. Add a heading and subhead using the <h1> and <h2> elements:

```
<h1>"Browser-Safe" Color Mixing Chart</h1>
<h2>Gray Scale</h2>
```

6. Add a set of table tags, inside the <div> element:

```
<div align="center">
<table> </table>
</div>
```

7. In between the table tags, add a header row with six cells, using the table header <th> element. Each header cell should list a percentage of red, green, or blue in amounts of 0-20-40-60-80-100%:

```
<tr>
<th>0% Red, Green, Blue</th>
<th>20% Red, Green, Blue</th>
```

4

```
<th>40% Red, Green, Blue</th>
<th>60% Red, Green, Blue</th>
<th>80% Red, Green, Blue</th>
<th>100% Red, Green, Blue</th>
</tr>
```

8. Add a data cell row with six cells, using the table data <td> element . With each cell, add an inline style that assigns a background color to the cell in equal amounts of red, green, and blue (in browser-safe amounts):

```
<tr><!-- Row 1 -->
<td style="background-color: rgb(0%0%0%)"> </td>
<!-- Col 1 -->
<td style="background-color: rgb(20%20%20%)"> </td>
<!-- Col 2 -->
<td style="background-color: rgb(40%40%40%)"> </td>
<!-- Col 3 -->
<td style="background-color: rgb(60%60%60%)"> </td>
<!-- Col 4 -->
<td style="background-color: rgb(80%80%80%)"> </td>
<!-- Col 5 -->
<td style="background-color: rgb(100%100%100%)"> </td>
<!-- Col 6 -->
</tr>
```

9. Create a second table that displays pure red, green, and blue colors in their browser-safe amounts:

```
<h2>Pure Colors</h2>
<table border="1" cellpadding="15" width="90%">
<tr>
<th>Color</th>
<th>20%</th>
<th>40%</th>
<th>60%</th>
<th>80%</th>
<th>100%</th>
</tr>
<tr><!-- Row 2 -->
<th>Pure Red</th>
<td style="background-color: rgb(20%0%0%)"> </td>
<!-- Col 2 -->
<td style="background-color: rgb(40%0%0%)"> </td>
```

4

```
<!-- Col 3 -->
<td style="background-color: rgb(60%0%0%)"> </td>
<!-- Col 4 -->
<td style="background-color: rgb(80%0%0%)"> </td>
<!-- Col 5 -->
<td style="background-color: rgb(100%0%0%)"> </td>
<!-- Col 6 -->
</tr>
<tr><!-- Row 3 -->
<th>Pure Green</th>
<td style="background-color: rgb(0%20%0%)"> </td>
<!-- Col 2 -->
<td style="background-color: rgb(0%40%0%)"> </td>
<!-- Col 3 -->
<td style="background-color: rgb(0%60%0%)"> </td>
<!-- Col 4 -->
<td style="background-color: rgb(0%80%0%)"> </td>
<!-- Col 5 -->
<td style="background-color: rgb(0%100%0%)"> </td>
<!-- Col 6 -->
</tr>

<tr><!- Row 4 ->
<th>Pure Blue</th>
<!- Col 1 ->
<td style="background-color: rgb(0%0%20%)"> </td>
<!- Col 2 ->
<td style="background-color: rgb(0%0%40%)"> </td>
<!- Col 3 ->
<td style="background-color: rgb(0%0%60%)"> </td>
<!- Col 4 ->
<td style="background-color: rgb(0%0%80%)"> </td>
<!- Col 5 ->
<td style="background-color: rgb(0%0%100%)"> </td>
<!- Col 6 ->
</tr>
</table>
```

10. Using the preceding tables as a model, create a table that displays the possible mixtures of red and green in browser-safe amounts. The first two rows are given in the following listing:

```
<h2>Mixture of Red and Green</h2><br />
<table border="3" cellpadding="15" width="90%">
```

```
<tr>
<th>Color Mixture</th>
<th>0% Red</th>
<th>20% Red</th>
<th>40% Red</th>
<th>60% Red</th>
<th>80% Red</th>
<th>100% Red</th></tr>
<tr>
<th>0% Green</th>
<td style="background-color: rgb(0%0%0%)"> </td>
<td style="background-color: rgb(20%0%0%)"> </td>
<td style="background-color: rgb(40%0%0%)"> </td>
<td style="background-color: rgb(60%0%0%)"> </td>
<td style="background-color: rgb(80%0%0%)"> </td>
<td style="background-color: rgb(100%0%0%)"> </td></tr>
<tr>
<th>20% Green</th>
<td style="background-color: rgb(0%20%0%)"> </td>
<td style="background-color: rgb(20%20%0%)"> </td>
<td style="background-color: rgb(40%20%0%)"> </td>
<td style="background-color: rgb(60%20%0%)"> </td>
<td style="background-color: rgb(80%20%0%)"> </td>
<td style="background-color: rgb(100%20%0%)"> </td>
</tr>
```

11. Notice how the red value progresses with each cell from 0 to 100%, while only one green value is used per row, the first being 0%, the second 20%, and so on. Now add another row with the green value set at 40%.

12. After that row, add a row with green set to 60%, following the same pattern.

13. After that row, add a row with green set to 80%.

14. Add a final row with green set to 100%. When you have finished, you will have a chart similar to the one in the illustration that follows:

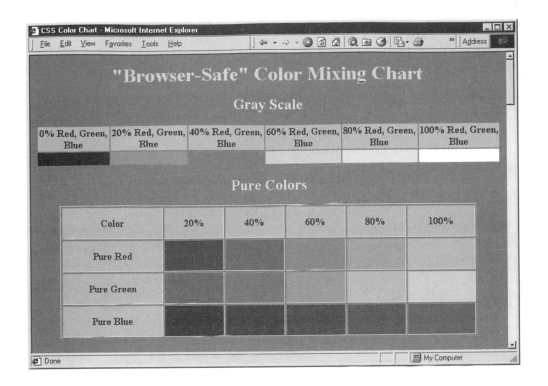

Note

The illustration shows only the beginning of the chart. If you use large table cells, as in the illustration, the chart will be quite long. However, the larger size makes it easier for you to perceive the subtle color differences between cells.

Project Summary

As you create a table that involves mixing various amounts of red, green, and blue, you begin to learn how these colors interact with one another. Keep developing your chart until you have constructed tables that mix colors in the following ways:

● Mixtures of red and green

● Mixtures of green and blue

● Mixtures of red and blue

● Mixtures of red, green, and blue

Mixing all three colors in a chart can be tricky, but try creating a chart that will have a row with 20% red and 20% green and then have each cell increase the blue amount from 0 to100%. The next row can be 20% red and 40% green, and each cell will increase the blue amount from 0 to 100%. Remember that there are 216 possible combinations with these browser-safe amounts, so you could end up with six color tables, not counting the gray scale and pure color tables done in this project. This is a lot of work, but by the time you're finished, you will be mixing colors of light just as easily as you did with those finger paints when you were a child.

☑ *Mastery Check*

1. Which of the following measurement units would be best to use if you were designing a page to be printed on paper rather than viewed on a monitor?

    A. Ems

    B. Percentages

    C. Inches

    D. Pixels

2. There is an error in the following url value. Correct it.

```
body   {background-image: (url)mypicture.gif; }
```

3. The color value #ff00cc corresponds to which of the following rgb values?

    A. rgb(0%, 100%, 50%)

    B. rgb(100%, 0%, 80%)

    C. rgb(100% 20%, 0%)

    D. rgb(0%, 100%, 60%)

4. If you want your pages to be scalable, you need to use _____ measurements.

5. True or false. An ex is the best choice for a measurement unit when you want to use relative measurements.

_____

6. True or false. Percentages are a form of absolute measurement.

_____

7. True or false. In additive color mixing, 100% of all the primary colors results in black.

_____

8. URI stands for _____ _____ _____

9. RGB stands for _____, _____, _____.

4

Module 5

Understanding Cascade and Inheritance

The Goals of this Module

- Understand How Inheritance Works
- Learn to Determine Specificity
- Understand the !important Declaration
- Learn How the Cascade is Applied

Are you familiar with the adage "Too many cooks spoil the soup"? It doesn't take a rocket scientist to figure out the meaning of that proverb. If anything, whether soup or a style sheet, receives too much conflicting input from multiple sources, the result is not likely to be good. As CSS was being developed, its creators had to balance the wishes of page designers against those of Web surfers. On top of this, all browsers have their own built-in style sheets. Add to that the possibility of imported, external, embedded, and inline style sheets all applying to the same document and you have a huge potential for confusion. Thus, the developers of CSS had to design mechanisms for setting style priorities. After all, if you have five different style sheets all trying to set the color and size of the <h1> element, which one does the browser choose? The answer to that question and other questions of conflicting style can be found in inheritance, specificity, and the cascade.

Understand Inheritance

In Module 2 an HTML document was compared to a "family tree." Actually, in HTML and CSS terminology, it's called a "document tree"; however, the concept is essentially the same. Just as with a family tree, a document tree has "parents" and "children." It even has grandparents and great-grandparents, although these are generally grouped under the collective name "ancestors." Likewise, grandchild and great-grandchild elements are called "descendents."

Another concept in CSS that parallels a family tree is that of *inheritance*. Inheritance is the mechanism by which the styles (properties) of a parent (ancestor) element are passed on to its children (descendents). The easiest way to learn how inheritance works is by simply assigning some styles to the <body> element of an HTML document.

How Inheritance Works

For instance, take the definition of inheritance from the previous paragraph and convert it into an HTML document. Use the <h1> element to create a heading that reads: **Inheritance:**, then place the definition in a paragraph, <p>, element. To get a few more levels of inheritance in there, use the <i> element to italicize the following terms: styles (properties), parent (ancestor), and children (descendents). Make it even more interesting by using the bold text, <b>, element to cause the following words to display in boldface: styles, parent, and children, as in the following code listing:

```html
<html>
<head><title>Inheritance</title></head>
<body>
<h1>Inheritance:</h1>
<p>Inheritance is the mechanism by which the <i><b>styles
</b>(properties)</i> of a <i><b>parent </b>(ancestor)</i>
element are passed on to its <i><b>children </b>
(descendents).</i></p>
</body>
</html>
```

Note

You could use CSS to create the italicized and bold text, but the <i> and <b> elements give you a simple way to observe inheritance at work.

Your finished page should look something like the following illustration:

Inheritance:

Inheritance is the mechanism by which the *styles (properties)* of a *parent (ancestor)* element are passed on to its *children (descendents)*.

This simple page has at least five "generations," and would look like this if drawn as a document tree:

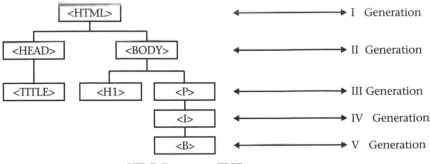

HTML Document TREE

As you can see, both the <h1> and <p> elements are children of the <body> element. The <i> element is a child of <p> and the <b> element is a child of <i>.

Inheritance:

Inheritance is the mechanism by which the *styles (properties)* of a *parent (ancestor)* element are passed on to its *children (descendents)*.

Hint

Just a reminder, an element is a "child" or "descendent" of another element only if it is contained (nested) completely within another element. Thus in the code <h1><b>Text</b></h1>, the <b> element is a child of the <h1> element. On the other hand, the elements in <h1>Text</h1> <p>More text</p> are siblings.

Now, to see inheritance at work, write some style rules for the <body> element only. Set the background color to dark gray, rgb(20%,20%,20%); the text to white, rgb(100%, 100%, 100%), the font family to Arial or sans-serif, and the font size to 1.2em. Embed the styles in the <head> portion of the page by using the <style> element. When your style sheet is applied, your page will look something like this:

Inheritance:

Inheritance is the mechanism by which the *styles (properties)* of a *parent (ancestor)* element are passed on to its *children (descendents)*.

```
<html>
<head>
<title>Inheritance</title>
<style type="text/css">
<!--
body    {background-color: rgb(20%,20%,20%);
         color: rgb(100%,100%,100%);
         font-family: Arial, sans-serif;
         font-size: 1.2em;}
-->
</style>
</head>
```

```
<body>
<h1>Inheritance:</h1>
<p>Inheritance is the mechanism by which the <i><b>styles
</b>(properties)</i> of a <i><b>parent </b>(ancestor)</i>
element are passed on to its<i><b>children </b>
(descendents).</i></p>
</body>
</html>
```

As you can see, all of the styles you specified for the <body> element have also been "inherited" by the <h1>, <p>, <i>, and <b> elements. You can probably also see what a time saver this is. If CSS properties did not inherit, then to accomplish the results in the preceding illustration, you would have had to write style rules for each of the elements in the document.

Non-Inherited Properties

Although most CSS properties inherit, some do not—and for a good reason. One example of a "non-inheriting" property is the "padding" property. If this property inherited, your design problems could approach "nightmare" status every time you used it. Suppose you added some padding to the <p> element in the preceding document. If the padding property inherited, its style rule would be applied to the <i> and <b> elements as well. This would create significant problems for your layouts. In general, the categories of properties that do not inherit are:

- Background properties
- Border properties
- Display properties
- Margin properties
- Padding properties

Hint

CSS's padding property functions something like HTML's "cellpadding" attribute. In HTML, cellpadding enables you to add space *inside* a table's data cell. CSS takes that much further by enabling you to add space "inside" any element. For more on the padding property, see Module 9.

Although there are other non-inherited properties that do not fit into the preceding categories, it is not necessary to learn each one. Just being familiar with the general categories will be enough. As you work through this book, the listing for each property will specify whether or not it is inherited.

Forcing Inheritance

Although the inheritance mechanism was put in place for a good reason, it is possible to override it and force a property to inherit, if you want to. You simply supply the keyword "inherit" in the child or descendent element in place of a value. For example, to cause the <i> and <b> elements to inherit the padding from the <p> element, the following style rules were added to the style sheet:

```
p       {padding: 1.3em;}
i       {padding: inherit;}
b       {padding: inherit;}
```

The primary problem with the "inherit" keyword is that at this writing it is supported only by Netscape 6. Thus, it is not a tool you will be able to use effectively any time soon. Also, as a rule it's not a good idea to override the inheritance mechanism. There may be times when it is to your advantage to "break" the rules, but for the most part the wisest course is to allow inheritance to perform its natural function, that of simplifying the overall process of writing style sheets by reducing the number of rules you must write.

1-Minute Drill

● What is inheritance?

● What general types of properties do *not* inherit?

● How does inheritance make writing style sheets easier?

● Inheritance is the mechanism by which the styles (properties) of a parent (ancestor) element are passed on to its children (descendents)
● Properties that do not inherit are: background, border, margin, display, and padding properties
● Inheritance makes it easier to write style sheets by reducing the number of rules you must write to apply the same style to multiple selectors

Determining Specificity

Although inheritance is an important part of style sheets and how individual styles are implied, it doesn't play much of a part if competing or conflicting style rules are involved. As a matter of fact, inheritance is one of the last things the browser checks when sorting out conflicting style rules. However, what *does* make a difference in which selector carries more weight is *specificity*.

How to Understand Specificity

Although the term "specificity" may sound confusing at first, it's really not that difficult to understand. The term simply refers to how "specific" a selector is. By way of comparison, suppose you visit your local used car dealer and tell the salesperson that you have decided to buy a car. When the salesperson asks you what kind of car you want, you reply, "A red car." Since there are probably 200 red cars on the lot, you are asked if you could be more specific. You then say, "A red sports car." The choices have now been drastically narrowed; however, there are still several models of sports cars on the lot. You then make your selection more "specific," by saying, "A red Grand Prix." Now the salesperson can take you to exactly the car you want. In becoming more "specific," you have not only chosen a car, but you have eliminated a large number of other choices. The analogy isn't perfect, but it might help you to understand the concept of specificity.

Specificity is a means of calculating the amount of "weight" a browser will give a particular style rule, on the basis of the selectors that are used in the rule, and is a key mechanism for choosing between conflicting style rules. Essentially, the more "specific" a selector is, the greater importance a browser assigns it. The selector with the highest specificity is the one that will be used (assuming there are no other determining factors involved). Although the actual calculation process can be a bit confusing, the rules for determining a selector's specificity are fairly simple. A numerical value is assigned to each selector based on:

- The number of id selectors in the style rule

- The number of other selectors and/or pseudo-class selectors in the rule

- The number of element names in the rule

Note

In determining specificity, pseudo-elements are ignored.

How to Calculate Specificity

How, then, do you use these rules to calculate a selector's specificity? Unfortunately, it's not as easy as just adding up the total of the three items listed in the preceding section. Instead, you must think of each of those items as separate categories, like columns in a table. The value of each of the indicators above is placed in a separate column with the id selectors first, the "other" and pseudo-class selectors second, and the element names third. Then, those values are "concatenated" or combined into one. Thus, the specificity of a simple <p> selector would be calculated this way: p = 0-0-1, giving that selector a specificity of 001.

Hint

The term *concatenate* when used in programming basically means to combine. It is to be distinguished from "adding," in that values (whether numbers, letters, or text strings) are combined in a linear fashion rather than totaled mathematically. For example if you add 1+1+1, you get three. If you *concatenate* 1+1+1 the result is 111.

Why did the selector in the previous paragraph receive such a low value? Because this selector had no id selectors, no "other" selectors or pseudo-classes, and only one element name. What if, on the other hand, the selector were written using a class selector like this: p.special? In this case, its specificity would be: p.special = 0-1-1. It gets a value in the second column for the class selector and one in the third column because the <p> element is named. If an id selector were added to this mix (p.special #412), you would add a value in the first column, thus calculating its specificity as: p.special #412 = 1-1-1.

If you're still having difficulty following how specificity is determined, it may be helpful to view it as a table, with columns identifying each of the value indicators:

Selector	ID Selectors	Other Selectors and Pseudo-Classes	Element Names	Specificity
h1 em l	0	0	3	003
#myid	1	0	0	100
table td.bold	0	1	2	012
div.blue #21s em i.reg	1	2	3	123

How to Use Specificity

How do you use specificity to your advantage? You can design your selectors to have a high specificity if you want to lessen the chances that they will be overridden by someone else's style sheet. For example, suppose that as you create a style sheet, you decide that you want all of the <h1> elements to be navy blue, set to 2.2em, and to use a fantasy font. You could write a style rule that looks like this:

```
h1      {color: navy;
          font-size: 2.2em;
          font-family: fantasy;}
```

Although this is undoubtedly the *easiest* selector to use, because it will not require you to make any special changes to your HTML code, it has a very low specificity of 0-0-1. Thus, it can be overridden by virtually anything. However, if this particular style is one that you do not want to be overridden, you can raise the specificity by using a class selector:

```
h1.navy      {color: navy;
              font-size: 2.2em;
              font-family: fantasy;}
```

Because this style rule has one class selector and one element name, it now has a specificity of 0-1-1. While that's still not very high, it improves the standing of this selector in the overall ranking. However, if you want to make this selector even stronger, you could add an id selector, as in the following style rule:

```
h1.navy #special{color: navy;
                  font-size: 2.2em;
                  font-family: fantasy;}
```

By adding the id selector, you have now raised the overall specificity to 1-1-1. However, even though you have significantly raised this selector's specificity, you might be wondering if there are any other ways to reduce the chances that a selector might be overridden by one with a higher specificity. The answer is yes. You can use the !important keyword.

The !important Declaration

There may be times when you want to do everything possible to ensure that a style rule or declaration is not overridden by another style sheet. CSS provides a simple means for indicating that a style is to be considered important, and (not unexpectedly) it is by using the !important declaration.

Understand the !important Declaration

Because the !important declaration is not a selector, it is not included in the overall specificity calculations; however, it is a very powerful tool for giving your styles the greatest possible weight. When you add !important to a style declaration, it is something like giving that declaration "VIP" status. It means that the browser will generally not allow it to be overridden by any other styles. For example, to ensure that the font color of the previous code listing is not changed, you would simply add the !important declaration, like this:

```
h1.navy #special{color: navy !important;
                 font-size: 2.2em;
                 font-family: fantasy;}
```

Note

The !important declaration will generally not allow your style to be overridden. However, there is one circumstance when even !important can be "bumped" by another style. That is if your visitors have created their own style sheets and used !important to define some of their styles. In CSS 2, a user's "!important" takes priority over an author's "!important." This is a reversal from CSS 1, where the author's use of !important had priority.

Ask the Expert

Question: Why did the W3C change the !important rule to give the user's styles precedence over the author's?

Answer: It has to do with accessibility. Some people who visit your Web site may be visually impaired and need pages to display in larger fonts or with particular color combinations. By giving the user control over presentation, the W3C hopes to improve accessibility to the Web.

Question: Does this mean that any user can override my styles, just by using !important?

Answer: In theory, yes; however, given the current status of browser support for CSS, all of this discussion is pretty much moot. Netscape and Internet Explorer do not allow users to create their own style sheets and attach them to the browsers. At best, a user can select font styles and background colors by using the browsers' "preferences" options. Opera, a Web browser that does allow you to create your own style sheets, provides a button on the toolbar that allows the user to toggle between the document style sheet and the user style sheet. Thus, users will have to wait a while before the !important property will really be a practical tool for them. However, as a style sheet author, you can still use !important to add extra weight to "important" declarations.

How to Use !important

The syntax for !important is not difficult, as long as you keep a few basic rules in mind. To apply the !important keyword within a style rule, you simply attach it to the end of whatever *declaration* you want it to be attached to. Also, keep in mind that !important must be placed *after* the value and *before* the semicolon, as in the following rule:

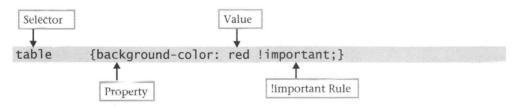

Another nice feature of !important is that you can choose to apply it to only *part* of a style rule, if you want. For instance, in the example on specificity, a rule was created that contained three declarations. What if you only want to apply !important to the font color? As the following rule demonstrates, you merely attach !important to that declaration and leave the others as they are.

```
h1              {color: navy !important;
                font-size: 2.2em;
                font-family: fantasy;}
```

On the other hand, if you want all of the declarations in that rule to be preserved, then you must add !important to all three declarations, as in the following rule:

```
h1              {color: navy !important;
                font-size: 2.2em !important;
                font-family: fantasy !important;}
```

One exception to this rule applies if you are using one of the "shorthand" properties. As you'll learn in Modules 6 through 10, shorthand properties enable you to combine several different values in a single declaration. For example, the "font" property would allow you to write a declaration like the one contained in the following rule:

```
h1      {font: bold 1.3em cursive !important;}
```

In the case of this rule, !important will be applied to all three of the values attached to the "font" property.

Tip

One interesting feature of the !important declaration is that it does *not* inherit. It functions only for the selector/declaration to which it is directly applied. So, if you want to use !important to preserve, say, a certain font style or color, you will need to reapply it at every level of your "document tree."

Thus, !important can enable you to "safeguard" your styles from other style sheets that could potentially override them. Could you attach !important to each of your style declarations, thus making your pages "tamper" proof? Yes, you could. Do you really need (or want) to? Probably not. For one thing, if you did this, you would in most cases need to add it to every single declaration you wrote. The result would be more work for you and an unnecessarily large style sheet file. Besides, since your visitors can conceivably override those !important rules anyway, all your hard work could be for naught. Use selectors with high specificity and save the !important declaration for when you really want to preserve something "important."

Thus far, this module has covered the basic pieces of the CSS puzzle: inheritance, specificity, and !important rules. You know that, generally speaking, child elements inherit their values from parent elements. Also, you are aware that selectors with a higher specificity will be chosen over those with a low specificity, unless the !important declaration is used to override that process. However, you may still be wondering how it all fits together. The mechanism that assembles a final product from whatever style sheets may be competing for attention is known as the *cascade*.

1-Minute Drill

● Specificity simply refers to how _____ a selector is.

● What selectors have the greatest specificity value: element, class, or id selectors?

● In CSS 2, whose !important rules have priority?

5

Understand the Cascade

Have you ever wondered why Cascading Style Sheets are called "cascading"? When most people hear the term "cascade," they tend to think of water cascading over a waterfall, or even someone's long hair cascading over her (or his) shoulders. If these illustrations don't help you understand the concept of "cascade," try thinking about how windows can be made to "cascade" on your computer. If you have several windows open at one time, and you choose the cascade option from a menu, then all of the windows overlap one another in sort of a "waterfall" arrangement. No matter how you picture it, the "cascade" basically refers to a set of rules for determining the order in which multiple style sheets and style rules are applied to an HTML document.

● Specific
● Id selectors
● The user's (or visitor's)

Competing Style Sheets

The need for the cascade becomes obvious when you consider the number of different possible style sheets that can be applied to any given HTML document. When a browser displays a Web page, it could conceivably have to choose its styles from among:

● **The Author's Style Sheet(s)**   It is possible for the author or page designer to specify multiple style sheets for a single document. Style sheets can be linked, imported, embedded, or inline. Using the @import rule, it is even possible to import a style sheet that imports other style sheets. Thus, in the author's arena alone, the potential for multiple, conflicting styles is great.

Note

The @import rule allows you to import a style sheet from virtually any other location. Its styles will then be treated as if they were part of your linked style sheets. To use the @import rule in an HTML document, you would write it this way:

```
<style>
@import  "http://www.anothersite.com/styles/newstyle.css";
</style>
```

● **The User's Style Sheet(s)**   Users (visitors, Web surfers) can create their own style sheets (see the preceding "Ask the Expert" box) and set their browsers so that their own preferences are applied to Web pages. These can conceivably conflict with the author's style sheets.

● **The User Agent's Default Style Sheet**   The user agent (Web browser) will have its own default style sheet, which can also be applied to a document that is being displayed. For instance, it is possible to "turn off" style sheets in your Web browser. If you do that, then the browser's default styles will be applied rather than any from an author or user.

Note

If you read information on CSS or HTML from the W3C and other technical sources, often you will see the term UA used. UA is simply an abbreviated form of "User Agent" and refers to Web browsers.

With all of these possible style sheets to apply, the cascade provides the rules needed to sort them all out.

Sort Out Style Sheets

So, how does a browser go about sorting all those styles and determining which ones to apply? The cascade provides a set of rules for browsers to follow that provide a means for prioritizing different styles. In performing the cascade, the browser must perform the following tasks in order:

1. Locate all declarations that apply.

2. Sort declarations by weight and origin.

3. Sort declarations by specificity.

4. Sort declarations by the order in which they occur.

   When a browser loads a page, it collects the information from all style sheets that apply to that page, then it uses a process called "pattern matching" to locate all of the declarations that apply to any given element on the page. Pattern matching simply means that the browser examines all of the selectors and targets the ones that "match" a construction in the HTML document. For instance, if you have a style sheet that specifies a style rule for underlined text <u> that occurs in an <h1> element, the selector would look like this: h1 u. Upon finding that selector in a style sheet, the browser would then look for a corresponding construction in the HTML document. If it finds a construction that matches the h1 u pattern— for instance: <h1>This is <u>important</u></h1>—then it applies the style. What if the browser finds multiple style sheets using an h1 u selector, all specifying different styles? Then it must choose from among the different styles using the rules of the cascade.

Sort by Weight and Origin

The browser first sorts the declarations by origin and weight. *Origin* refers to the source of the style sheet (author, user, or browser default). The author's style sheet is given priority over the user's style sheet; the user's style sheet takes precedence over the browser default style sheet. *Weight* refers to the relative importance of the style sheet. An inline style is given priority over embedded, linked, or imported styles. An embedded style has priority over linked and imported styles. Linked and imported styles carry the same weight.

Note

Over the years there has been some inconsistency of application where the cascade is concerned. For example, an earlier version of Netscape gave priority to linked style sheets over embedded. The process described here is according to the CSS 2 specification.

It is also in this sort order that the !important declaration is considered. An author's !important declarations take precedence over all others; however, a user's !important declarations are given priority over those of the author.

Sort by Specificity

The next sort is by *specificity*. The browser calculates the specificity of the individual declarations, giving priority to the ones with the highest specificity. Thus, if the browser found an h1 u selector (specificity=002), an h1 u.special selector (specificity=012), and an h1 u#xtraspecial selector (specificity=112), h1 u#xtraspecial would be applied because of its high specificity.

Sort by Order Specified

If, after all these "sorts," there are still conflicting styles, then the browser chooses based upon the order in which the styles occur. For example, suppose the browser found two "h1 u#xtraspecial" selectors: one in an imported style sheet and one in the linked style sheet. It would ignore the selector from the imported style sheet because imported styles are considered as coming "before" any styles found in the linked style sheet. A simpler illustration could be found in the following listing:

```
p       {color: blue;}
p       {color: red;}
p       {color: green;}
p       {color: magenta;}
```

Suppose a browser comes upon a single style sheet with the preceding rules listed one after another. Granted, this isn't likely to happen if the author knows anything about CSS, but for purposes of illustration let's assume it did. What color would the <p> selector be? They all have the same pattern, origin, weight, and specificity. Yet, the browser has to choose one of them. Actually, the browser's solution is simple: "last goes first." The paragraph text will be magenta, because it was specified last.

If you're not convinced, try it out. Create an HTML page and embed a style sheet by placing your selectors between <style> tags in the <head> portion of the page. Add the four style rules from the preceding example and then include a line of text in the <body> of the page. Make sure your text is enclosed in the <p> element. When you display it, the text will be colored magenta.

Project 5-1: Experiment with Conflicting Styles and !important

While it's interesting to talk about the theory behind the cascade, you might find it easier to grasp if you actually see it at work. For this project, you are going to create several conflicting style sheets and apply them to the CSS test page you developed in Module 1. As you see how the browser sorts out the different styles that you have created, you will hopefully gain an increased appreciation for what is meant by *Cascading* Style Sheets.

Step by Step

1. Open up the test page you created in Module 1 (csstestpage.htm). It will provide you with a representative, though not exhaustive, display of key HTML elements. It includes a set of three headline elements, horizontal rules, a sample table, an unordered list, two sample lines of text, and a sample link. You may choose to expand the scope of this project by adding some other elements. Your test page should look something like Figure 5-1.

2. Create a blank text page in Notepad or another text editor and save it as cascade.css. This will be your external style sheet. You will also be adding embedded and inline styles to csstestpage.htm. Thus, you will be applying three different style sheets to a single page.

3. Add some styles to cascade.css that a user with poor vision and/or difficulty viewing color might use. Use the font-size property to set the body font size to 1.3em and add the !important declaration to the rule.

4. Use the background-color property to set the default background color to white and the color property to set text color to black. Attach the !important declaration to both of those as well.

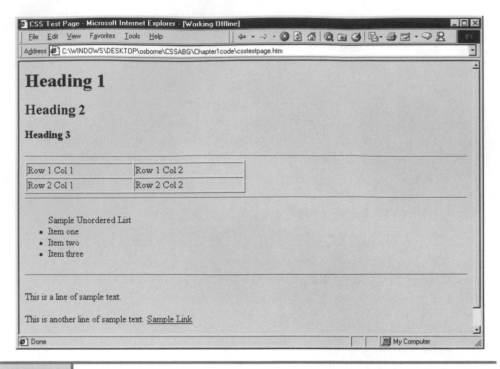

Figure 5-1 CSS test page with no styles attached

5. Just for fun, add a few styles that do not have !important attached. Set all three of the headline elements to use a sans-serif font with the font-family property and color them navy with the color property.

6. Set the background color for the table element to magenta.

7. Apply the text-decoration and font-style properties to the list-item element to cause it to display underlined and in italics.

8. Link the style sheet to csstestpage.htm by using the <link /> element in the <head> portion of the HTML page. Don't forget to include the attributes: rel="stylesheet", type="text/css", and href="cascade.css". Be sure you have saved cascade.css in the same directory as csstestpage.htm; otherwise, the browser may not be able to locate it. After you have saved csstestpage.htm, display it in your browser. It should look something like the following illustration:

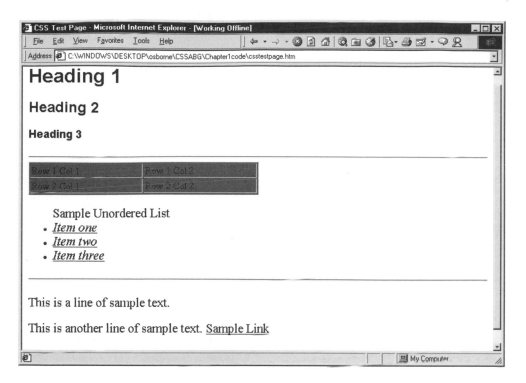

9. As you compare the preceding illustration with Figure 5-1, you will see that all of your styles have been applied. Of course, this is because there are currently no competing styles (except the browser defaults) and your styles take priority over the browser's styles. You may notice also that even though you set the body text to display at 1.3em, the text inside the <table> element is unchanged. However, based on the rules of inheritance you would have expected the table text to be in a larger font since font properties are inherited. Get used to little quirks like this. It's part of working with CSS.

10. Now that you have applied a linked style sheet, carry the experiment a little further by adding an embedded style sheet to the head portion of the page. However, instead of creating an entirely different style sheet, simply cut and paste the style rules from cascade.css into the <head> portion of csstestpage.htm. Don't forget to enclose the style rules inside the <style> element.

Hint

To get the table characters to display at 1.3em, apply the font-size property to the<td>selector.

11. Once you have pasted the styles into the page, change the values to match the following list:

● For the body element, change the font size to 1.1em, the color to navy, and the background color to yellow. *Delete the !important declarations from each of these.*

● For the h1, h2, and h3 elements, change the font family to fantasy, and the color to red.

● For the table, change the background color to yellow.

● For the list-item selector, remove the "font-style" declaration and replace it with a "font-variant" declaration with a value of "small-caps." Change the text-decoration value from "underline" to "none."

12. Save csstestpage.htm and reload it in your browser. All of your new styles should display, with the exception of the body text, color, and background styles. This is because in the cascade, an embedded style sheet will override a linked style sheet. However, because you used the !important declaration with the body text, color, and background-color properties in the linked sheet, its styles are given priority in those areas.

13. Add a third level of style to the csstestpage.htm document by inserting an inline style. Inside the <p> tag opening the line that reads "This is a line of sample text," add a style attribute that sets the color of that <p> element to red. When you save and display the page in your browser, you will notice that the text displays in red, even though the linked style sheet applied the !important property to all body text. Did the inline style override the !important declaration? Not exactly. Remember, the !important declaration does not inherit. Since <p> is a child of <body>, the !important declaration is not passed on.

14. To complete the exercise, remove the !important declarations from cascade.css and see how your test page displays. Now all the styles from the three pages will be weighed and applied based on their specificity and relative weight. If you wish to experiment further, create some class and id selectors and apply them to one or more of the style sheets. For example, create a class named p.maroon and set the color to maroon. Try applying it to the linked sheet first, then embed it or apply it as an inline style. No matter which sheet it is in, it *will* be applied, because it has a higher specificity.

External Style Sheet

```
cascade.css
body         {font-size: 1.3em !important;
              color: black !important;
              background-color: white !important;}
h1, h2, h3   {font-family: sans-serif;
              color:  navy;}
table        {background-color: magenta;}
li           {font-style: italic;
              text-decoration: underline;}
```

CSS Test Page

5

```
csstestpage.htm
<head>
<title>CSS Test Page</title>
<link rel="stylesheet" type="text/css" href="cascade.css" />
<style>
body         {font-size: 1.1em ;
              color: navy ;
              background-color: cyan ;}
h1, h2, h3   {font-family: fantasy;
              color:  red;}
table        {background-color: yellow;}
li           {font-variant: small-caps;
              text-decoration: none;}
</style>
</head>
<body>
<! - Heading samples -->
<h1>Heading 1</h1>
<h2>Heading 2</h2>
<h3>Heading 3</h3>
<!-- Horizontal Rule -->
<hr />
<!-- Sample Table -->
<table border="1"  width="50%">
```

```
<tr><!-- Row 1 -->
<td>Row 1 Col 1</td><!-- Col 1 -->
<td>Row 1 Col 2</td><!-- Col 2 -->
</tr>
<tr><!-- Row 2 -->
<td>Row 2 Col 1</td><!-- Col 1 -->
<td>Row 2 Col 2</td><!-- Col 2 -->
</tr>
</table>
<!-- Sample Unordered List -->
<ul>
<lh>Sample Unordered List</lh>
<li>Item one</li>
<li>Item two</li>
<li>Item three</li>
</ul>
<hr />
<p style="color: red;">This is a line of sample text.</p>
<p>This is another line of sample text.
<a href="http://www.nolink.com">Sample Link</a></p>
<hr />
</body>
</html>
```

Project Summary

In this exercise, you created three conflicting style sheets for one HTML document and observed how the cascade sorted them out. The inline and embedded styles took precedence over the linked styles, except when !important was attached to the declarations in the linked style sheet. You saw that certain properties do not always inherit (for example, the font properties in the table element), even though you might expect them to. You also learned that !important does not inherit. It applies only to the declaration it is directly attached to. In the modules that follow, you will have the chance to work with the cascade in more detail as you learn to use the various properties that comprise CSS.

☑ Mastery Check

1. Define inheritance.

   _____

   _____

2. What is specificity?

   _____

   _____

3. What is the cascade?

   _____

   _____

4. What happens when you add !important to a style declaration?

   _____

   _____

5. Calculate the specificity for the following selectors:

   A. ul li em.red #123

   B. table td i

   C. body h1 #9394h

6. According to the CSS 2 specification, whose !important declaration should take priority?

   _____

   _____

7. If several identical selectors remain after the cascade is complete, how does the browser choose which style to apply?

   _____

   _____

5

Part 2

Exploring the CSS Toolbox

Module 6

Working with Font Properties

The Goals of this Module

- Understand the Problem of Browser Support
- Become Familiar with the Font Properties
- Learn How to Use the Font Shorthand Property
- Know Which Font Properties and Values are Best Supported
- CSS and Weak Browser Support

CSS and Browser Compatibility

The first thing you have to understand about working with CSS is that you will have to take browser differences seriously if you plan on using style sheets very much. For example, if you display the Web page created in the previous module's project and display it in Internet Explorer 5.5, Netscape 6, and the W3C's "Amaya" browser, you will see some not so subtle differences between them all. For example, the illustration that follows shows how the page displayed in Internet Explorer:

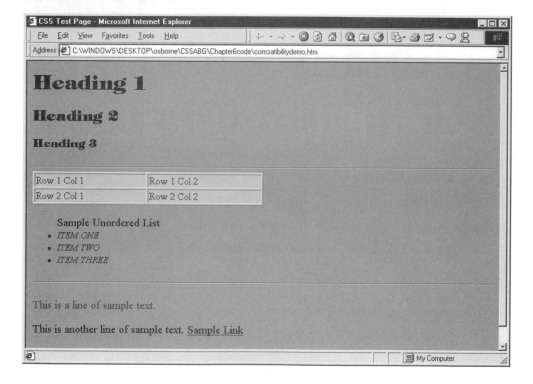

Suppose that you designed the preceding page and tested it only on your IE browser. You might be surprised when you see it in Netscape 6:

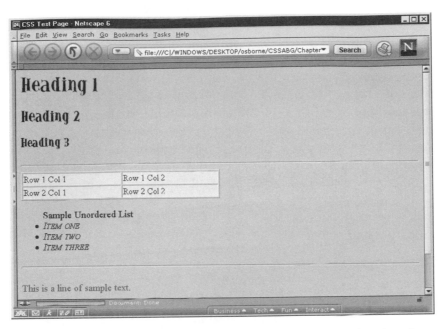

Notice that Netscape has chosen an entirely different font for the "fantasy" font that is specified in the style sheet. It also handles the table differently. Netscape applies the body background color to the table border; Internet Explorer uses the table background color. However, the surprises increase when you look at how the page displays in Amaya:

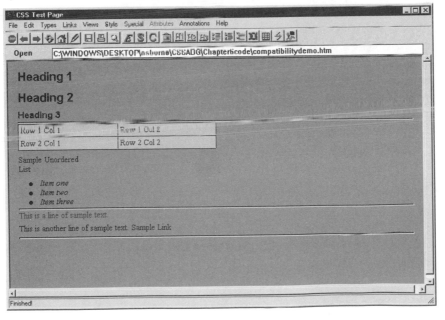

6

Amaya supplies a sans-serif font instead of a fantasy font, and it seems to have problems getting the headings to size properly. Also, it doesn't apply the "small caps" font variant to the unordered list and doesn't handle the list heading the same way as the other browsers do. Granted, these are minor differences, but when you consider that the properties used in the cascade.css style sheet are among the most common from CSS 1, you begin to appreciate how big the browser support problem can be. So, from the outset you need to understand that no matter how careful you are at designing pages with CSS, there *will* be differences from browser to browser. Sometimes they will be minor, sometimes major. How, then, do you design for maximum compatibility?

- Unless you know the browser your audience will be using, stick to "safe" properties and values.

- Test your pages in as many browsers as you can.

- Test your page *without* a style sheet.

- Restructure your page, if necessary.

- Create alternate style sheets if you need to.

Use "Safe" Properties and Values

Begin by sticking with "safe" properties and values. What are "safe" properties and values? Strictly speaking there probably aren't any if you consider the possibility that someone may visit your site using a browser that doesn't support CSS at all. However, since most browsers include at least *some* support for CSS nowadays, that's not likely to be a big problem. With that in mind, you can increase the compatibility of your pages by choosing the properties and values that enjoy the strongest cross-browser support. As you work through Modules 6 through 10, the properties and values will generally be presented by strength of support, from the strongest to the weakest. In the interest of keeping up to date, you may also wish to visit some of the Web sites listed in Table 6-1.

Tip

Another good resource on browser compatibility can be found in Osborne/ McGraw-Hill's *Cascading Style Sheets 2.0: A Programmer's Reference* by Eric A. Meyer. It's an excellent reference book overall and has an entire chapter devoted to browser compatibility.

Web site	URL	Resources available
RichinStyle.com	www.richinstyle.com	Browser support chart, plus browser specific "bug" pages
WebReview	www.webreview.com	Browser support chart by Eric A. Meyer, covering both Windows and Mac browsers
Index DOT CSS	www.blooberry.com/indexdot/css	Extensive browser support charts covering both CSS 1 and 2
CSS Pointers Group	http://css.nu/pointers.bugs.html	Charts that describe specific CSS bugs with Internet Explorer, Netscape, and Opera
The Web Standards Project	http://www.webstandards.org/css.html	Multiple resources, including a link to a support chart that focuses on CSS 2 support and rates the browsers accordingly

Table 6-1   CSS Browser Support Resources

6

Test Your Pages

Although browser support charts are invaluable tools for Web designers who are serious about using CSS, they should not substitute for actually testing your pages in as many browsers as you can. Obviously, it would be too time consuming to try to test your pages in every possible browser that they might be viewed on. However, if possible, you should at least test on Netscape 4 and 6, IE 4 and 5, and Opera 5. Testing gives you the advantage of actually seeing the bugs that might appear on your page rather than just knowing they are a theoretical possibility. As you see how your page displays in different browsers, you can make corrections that will minimize the "damage" to your design caused by browser incompatibility. And don't forget to test your page *without* a style sheet applied. If your page crashes or is incomprehensible, you probably need to redesign the HTML before worrying about the style.

Create Alternate Style Sheets

It may be a little more work for you, but once you have tested your pages on other browsers, one of the best solutions is to tailor some style sheets for those browsers. You needn't create ten or eleven different sheets to try and accommodate every possible browser that may be used to view your site. With two or maybe three style sheets (and generally minor variations between them), you should be able to cover most of the possibilities. Then, all you need to do is either include links for your visitors to use in accessing more compatible pages or automate the process with a JavaScript that detects the browser and redirects it toward the correct style sheet.

Note

Module 12 will cover how to create a JavaScript redirection script to use with your Web pages.

Once you have a strategy in hand for creating style sheets with maximum compatibility in mind, you're ready to begin exploring the world of CSS properties. Although, you could start anywhere, the font properties are the most logical place to begin. The Web, after all, began as a predominantly "text" medium. What better place to begin to work with styles than in learning how to apply them to make your text more interesting?

1-Minute Drill

● How should you test your pages for cross-browser compatibility?

● If you find compatibility problems, what is one way to get around them?

Typewriters to Desktop Publishing

How far things have come in a little over a century and a quarter! In 1874, E. Remington introduced the "Sholes and Glidden" typewriter. For the first time in history, the average person was able to do something that only printers had previously been capable of—writing with type. The "type" revolution continued when in 1935 IBM introduced the first electric typewriter. Twenty-six years later, IBM introduced the "Selectric," with interchangeable type "balls." Now, writers actually had more than one choice of typestyle. In the eighties, Macs and PCs paved the way for further change by bringing with them the word processing program. Computer users now saw their work on video screens before it was ever reproduced on paper. When desktop publishing came along shortly thereafter, interchangeable and scalable fonts were added to the mix, again enabling people to do something only printers could do previously—

● View your pages in as many browsers as possible
● Create alternate pages and/or style sheets and redirect your visitors to the appropriate pages

create professional-looking layouts with multiple fonts in different sizes and styles. In just over a century and a quarter, writing with "type" has moved from the primitive results of the simple typewriter to sophisticated, multi-font and multi-color design. Interestingly, when you examine the development of the World Wide Web, a similar pattern emerges.

The Web, <font>, and HTML

When the Internet first came on the scene in the late 1980s, fonts weren't really much of an issue. Since text-based browsers were all that were needed to access resources such as Gopher, HTML remained plain and unsophisticated. The advent of the Web and graphical browsers such as Mosaic paved the way for change by allowing the heading elements <h#> to display in a range of different sizes. You could also display bold, italic, and underlined text, but that was about all. However, it wasn't long before Web designers were crying out for more variety. In response, Netscape introduced a new proprietary element for its Navigator browser: the <font> element. This new element enabled Web authors to choose from seven different sizes of fonts and for the first time to specify their own fonts for Web pages. Now, authors were no longer limited to designing with a browser's default font in mind; they could choose whichever fonts they wanted to. On top of that, they could actually define colors for their fonts. The old "black and white" Web page quickly followed the black and white television into virtual disuse. A limitation still existed in that a user's browser couldn't display a font unless it was resident on the user's machine; however, that didn't slow down designers. Soon, <font> became a key part of virtually every Web author's toolkit, and it was eventually incorporated into the HTML specification. However, <font> eventually became perceived as a liability rather than an asset. When the W3C made Cascading Style Sheets an official recommendation in 1996, <font> was on its way out, displaced by a set of CSS font properties that give page authors a range of control similar to that of desktop publishers.

The Problem with HTML's <font> Element

The problem created by the <font> element's wild popularity was that the practical usage of HTML drifted further and further from the intent of its

Hint

To *deprecate* simply means to express disapproval. By deprecating elements and attributes, the W3C is merely discouraging you from using and browser companies from supporting them.

developers. HTML quickly became used to govern presentation rather than structure. When the W3C introduced Cascading Style Sheets, it was with the hope of returning HTML to its roots (governing structure). To encourage Web authors to jump on the bandwagon, the W3C *deprecated* <font> in the HTML 4 specification, along with a number of other presentational elements and attributes.

An element or attribute that has been deprecated is still supported by all the major browsers and can still be used. However, the W3C encourages browser developers to drop their support for the deprecated elements and attributes in future versions of their software. Thus, while you can still use elements such as <font> now, the time will come (theoretically) when you will not be able to. Even more problematic, if you continue to use <font> and make your pages dependent on it, the day could come when you will either have to rewrite your existing pages, start from scratch, or just resign yourself to allowing browsers to supply their default fonts in place of your design. However, the eventual demise of <font> is not the best reason for abandoning it in favor of CSS. The font properties built into CSS give you so much more control that, once you learn how to use them, you'll wonder why you clung to <font> for so long.

Note

The <font> element, though deprecated, will likely be around for a while. Even after the W3C recommended its disuse, both Internet Explorer 5.5 and Netscape Navigator 6.0 continued their support of <font>. Thus, while <font> may officially be "dead," it will probably be quite a few years before it stops "kicking."

The Advantages of CSS Font Properties

Although <font> represented a huge leap forward when it was introduced, it is quite limited when placed side by side with the CSS font properties. The <font> element enables you to choose your typeface, specify a limited number of sizes, and choose font color. That's it. In contrast, the CSS font properties enable you to do that much and more:

- **Font-family**   Specify generic or named fonts
- **Font-size**   Specify a virtually unlimited range of sizes
- **Font-style**   Choose between normal, italic, or oblique (slanted) styles
- **Font-variant**   Choose between normal and "small caps"
- **Font-weight**   Choose from as many as nine "boldness" settings

- **Font-size-adjust**   Make certain fonts more legible with aspect ratio adjustment.

- **Font-stretch**   Make characters wider or narrower without affecting the font's height.

- **Font**   Streamline your style sheet with a *shorthand* property that enables you to specify values without including properties.

Note

Font colors are set with the color property, rather than a font property.

CSS 1 Font Properties

"Font" is a printer's term that describes a collection of type in a particular face and size. Thus, Times New Roman and Times New Roman Bold are two different fonts. Likewise, Arial 12pt italic is a different font from Arial 14pt italic. While these technicalities are not essential for working with the font properties, they do help you maintain an important distinction. The term, "font," is basically concerned with the appearance and size of characters (typeface). Thus, the font properties also deal primarily with the appearance and size of characters. The reason this is important is that CSS also includes a set of properties called "text properties." Sometimes, newcomers to CSS can become confused as to the distinction between the font and text properties. Just remember that the font properties are concerned with the actual appearance of the characters. Text properties deal with line spacing, spaces between characters, underlining, alignment, and so on.

Note

The argument could be made that CSS 2 blurred that distinction between font and text properties when it added the text-shadow property. This property enables you to add a "drop shadow" to letters. However, no browsers support the text-shadow property at this writing.

The font-family Property

The font-family property enables you to specify a selection of fonts for your HTML document. In this respect, it performs the same basic function as the <font> element. However, one distinction that makes font-family stand apart from <font> is the ability it gives you in specifying generic fonts.

6

Values

You can specify virtually any font with the font-family property; you also can choose from five generic fonts. This is a change from HTML, where, if your visitor's system didn't have any of the fonts you specified, you had to be content with the browser's default font. The generic fonts are

- **Serif**   *Serif* fonts are distinguished by decorative strokes (called *ascenders* and *descenders*) at the ends of each character. These strokes are referred to (unsurprisingly) as "serifs." Times New Roman is a common serif font.

- **Sans-serif**   *Sans-serif* means "without serif." Thus, the characters of a sans-serif font are plain and unadorned. Arial is a common sans-serif font.

- **Monospace**   The characters of a *monospace* font all take up the same amount of space on a line. This font has what you might call a "typewriter" look.

- **Cursive**   A *Cursive* font uses a style resembling calligraphy. Normally, but not always, the individual characters will display separately, as opposed to a true cursive style where the letters are all connected. However, some cursive fonts connect the letters. Brush script is a well-known cursive font.

- **Fantasy**   *Fantasy* fonts are best described as those fonts that are styled to have a unique or different look. They may have characteristics of one or more of the above fonts, but they also have extra stylistic elements added to give them a "distinctive" look. Fantasy fonts can often be recognized by unique names such as Western, Chalk Dust, Alley Cat, and so on. Because the choice of which fantasy font to display is left up to the browser and dependent on which fonts your visitors have installed on their systems, selecting a "fantasy" font can yield wildly unpredictable results.

As the following illustration shows, these five fonts provide a somewhat larger range of possibilities than simply using the browser default:

This is a serif font.

This is a sans-serif font.

This is a monospace font.

This is a cursive font.

This is a fantasy font.

Note

Cursive and fantasy fonts tend to be displayed very inconsistently between browsers and different systems. While you may use these generic fonts, be forewarned that your results will be largely unpredictable.

Of course, you are not limited to using generic fonts with CSS any more than you would be with the <font> element. However, if your visitors do not have the font resident on their systems, then it will not be displayed. The solution is basically the same as that with HTML's <font> element: you specify a number of fonts in the order in which you want the browser to attempt to use them.

Syntax

Using the font-family property is straightforward and simple. You simply list the fonts in the order of your preference, separated by commas. The browser will try to load the first one in the list. If it isn't present, it will move on to the next, and so on. Some examples of the font-family property in action can be seen in the following listing:

```
body        {font-family: Arial, Verdana, sans-serif;}
p           {font-family: "Times New Roman", serif;}
.mono       {font-family: Courier, monospace;}
#29fs       {font-family: "Brush Script", cursive;}
```

The syntax for an inline style is the same, but remember that you'll be enclosing your declaration in quotation marks rather than curly braces.

```
<p style="font-family: 'Times New Roman', serif;">Text</p>
```

Tip

One important aspect of the font-family syntax is that if a font's name uses more than one word, you must enclose the entire name in quotation marks. If, as in the preceding example, you are using an inline style, you will need to use single quotation marks around the font name, so as not to conflict with the double quotes used around the style declaration.

A good rule of thumb is to specify several similar fonts, and always use a generic to finish the list. That way, you will significantly increase the odds that one of your fonts will be found on your visitor's system. Table 6-2 lists some other important things to know about the font-family property.

Does it inherit?	**Default value**	**Browser support**	**Works with**
Yes	Determined by the browser	Excellent	All elements

Table 6-2	Characteristics of the font-family Property

The font-size Property

With HTML's <font> element you had seven font sizes to work with. CSS gives you a virtually unlimited range of font sizes and multiple ways to express them. Your only real limits are set by the capabilities of the systems on which your pages are viewed. As for the different ways you can specify a font's size, you have plenty of choices.

Absolute and Relative Values

The easiest place to begin learning to work with the font-size property is with its *absolute values*. These are similar to HTML's seven font sizes, although the actual size that is to be applied is left up to the browser. The absolute values are:

xx-small   x-small   small   medium   large   x-large   xx-large

Strictly speaking, these values are not truly "absolute" in that they are referring to a specific size that is the same across all platforms. The definitions for these font sizes are left up to the "User Agent" (browser). Thus there can be variations in how different browsers define a "small" font and choose a default size. Why, then, are these values called "absolute?" Probably because they represent "fixed" sizes similar to the seven font sizes common to HTML. To use absolute values and class selectors together, you might write them like this:

```
p.xxsmall      {font-size: xx-small;}
p.xsmall       {font-size: x-small;}
p.small        {font-size: small;}
p.medium       {font-size: medium;}
p.large        {font-size: large;}
p.xlarge       {font-size: x-large;}
p.xxlarge      {font-size: xx-large;}
```

Displayed in Internet Explorer 5.5, the absolute values look like this:

This is font-size xx-small

This is font-size x-small

This is font-size small

This is font-size medium

This is font-size large

This is font-size x-large

This is font-size xx-large

6

Another easy way to manipulate font sizes is with *relative values*. In this case, you simply use the value keywords *larger* or *smaller*. The value of "larger" and "smaller" is always in relation to the parent element. For example, if you added the following style rules to the preceding style sheet, you would cause all <strong> elements to display one step larger than their parents and all <em> elements to display one step smaller.

```
strong      {font-size: larger;}
em          {font-size: smaller;}
```

The following illustration demonstrates how the "larger" and "smaller" values affect the display when applied. In this case, the "larger" value was applied with the <strong> element to the font-size text, while the "smaller" value was applied with the <em> (italics) element to the xx-large text.

```
<p style="font-size: xx-small;">This is
<strong>font-size</strong><em>xx-small</em></p>
<p style="font-size: x-small;">This is
<strong>font-size</strong><em>x-small</em></p>
<p style="font-size: small;">This is
<strong>font-size</strong><em>small</em></p>
```

```
<p style="font-size: medium;">This is
<strong>font-size</strong><em>medium</em></p>
<p style="font-size: large;">This is
<strong>font-size</strong><em>large</em></p>
<p style="font-size: x-large;">This is
<strong>font-size</strong><em>x-large</em></p>
<p style="font-size: xx-large;">This is
<strong>font-size</strong><em>xx-large</em></p>
```

This is **font-size**xx-small

This is **font-size**x-small

This is **font-size**small

This is **font-size**medium

This is **font-size**large

This is **font-size**x-large

This is **font-size**xx-large

Percentage Values

You can also specify font sizes by using percentages. The browser will regard 100% as the default value of any given font. Therefore, if you want to reduce the size of the font, use a value of less than 100%. On the other hand, to enlarge a font, use a figure higher than 100%. As an example, consider the following inline styles applied to a line of HTML code:

```
<p>Absolute and relative values are easy.</p>
<p style="font-size: 200%;">However, there's a lot
to be said for the convenience of percentages.</p>
```

As the following illustration demonstrates, increasing a font's size to 200% (twice normal size) makes a huge difference in the overall font size. If you plan on using percentages, you would be wise to experiment with them to get a feel for how to create the sizes you want:

Absolute and relative values are easy.

However, there's a lot to be said for the convenience of percentages.

Length Units

You can even use standard length units (inches, millimeters, centimeters, pixels, points, picas, ems, and exes) when specifying font size. Remember that inches, millimeters, and centimeters are absolute measurements and will not be able to scale or adjust to your visitors' settings. Likewise, although they are relative measurements, pixels and exes are less predictable in their results. If you decide to use a length unit for font size, your best choice is the em unit. (See Module 4 for more on em and ex units). However, as the following illustration shows, the different length units can give you a great variety of results.

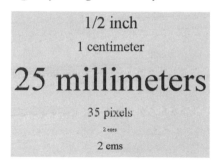

1/2 inch

1 centimeter

25 millimeters

35 pixels

2 exes

2 ems

If you plan on using length units, be sure to write the measurement identifier correctly. If it is incorrectly written, the browser will ignore the instruction. Table 6-3 lists the length units given in the preceding example.

Note

When specifying values with length units, do not put a space between the value and the unit. For example, font-size: 1.2 em is incorrect. You should write it, font-size: 1.2em.

6

Length unit	Should be written as	Example
Inches	in	font-size: .5in;
Centimeters	cm	font-size: 1cm;
Millimeters	mm	font-size: 25mm;
Pixels	px	font-size: 35px;
Points	pt	font-size: 14pt;
Picas	pc	font-size: 2pc;
Exes	ex	font-size: 2ex;
Ems	em	font-size: 2em;

Table 6-3   Length Unit Designations

Don't be intimidated by such a large array of value choices. Remember that you want to use relative values as much as possible, so try to stick with ems or percentages when specifying font sizes. Table 6-4 lists some other important characteristics of the font-size property.

1-Minute Drill

● List the absolute font size measurements.

● List the relative font size measurements.

● Font size is measured in relation to what element?

Does it Inherit?	Default value	Browser support	Works with
Yes	Medium (absolute value)	Excellent	All elements

Table 6-4   Characteristics of the font-size property

● Inches, centimeters, points, picas and millimeters
● Pixels, percentages, ems, and exes
● The parent element

The font-style Property

In HTML, if you wanted text to display in italics, you would use either the italics, <i>, element or the emphasized text, <em>, element. CSS allows you to specify italicized text using the font-style property, and oblique (slanted) text is thrown into the mix as well. With the font-style property, you can choose from normal, italic, or oblique fonts.

In contrast to the font-size property, font-style only has three possible values:

- **Normal**   {font-style: normal;}

- **Italic**   {font-style: italic;}

- **Oblique**   {font-style: oblique;}

Since the default value for font-style is "normal," you really only need to be concerned with the difference between the oblique and italic fonts. The characters of an oblique font are slanted to the right, with no other changes being made to the font face. A true italic font is not merely slanted. As the following illustration shows, the characters are actually drawn differently:

<div align="center">

Times New Roman (Normal)

AaBbCcDdEeFfGgHhIiJjKk

Times New Roman (Italic)

AaBbCcDdEeFfGgHhIiJjKk

</div>

6

Note ————————————————————————

Any given font family needs to have an oblique typeface designed by the typographer for this to work. Many font families only have italic, bold, and normal. Thus, if a particular font does not have an oblique typeface, the browser will either ignore the style or substitute an italic typeface.

However, there doesn't seem to be a great deal of consistency in how the browsers apply the different values for this property. For instance, as the following illustration shows, Internet Explorer 5 uses the same font face for oblique as for italics. Netscape 6 does the same thing.

"Normal" AaBbCcDdEeFfGgHhIiJjKk

"Italic" AaBbCcDdEeFfGgHhIiJjKk

"Oblique" AaBbCcDdEeFfGgHhIiJjKk

On the other hand, Netscape 4.7 ignores the oblique value altogether and displays the text as normal, as in the following screen shot:

"Normal" AaBbCcDdEeFfGgHhIiJjKk

"Italic" AaBbCcDdEeFfGgHhIiJjKk

"Oblique" AaBbCcDdEeFfGgHhIiJjKk

Thus, it appears that, for the present at least, you will find the greatest consistency in using the italic value rather than oblique. In future years, when the oblique value is better supported, it will be a more realistic option for you. Table 6-5 provides some other important characteristics of the font-style property.

The font-variant Property

Font-variant is perhaps the easiest of the font properties to summarize, as this property only gives you a choice between a normal font and small caps. Also, since normal is the default value, you can almost look at this property as a toggle switch for turning on the small caps option. However, the support issue causes some problems for those wanting to make use of this property.

To apply the font-variant property, include the small-caps value as in the following style rule:

```
p       {font-variant: small-caps;}
```

Does it Inherit?	Default value	Browser support	Works with
Yes	Normal	Inconsistent	All elements

Table 6-5   Characteristics of the font-style property

When your page displays on a browser that supports font-variant, the browser will display the lowercase letters as small caps. For this illustration, a style rule was written that instructed the browser to display each of the five "generic" fonts with the small-caps variant. The results in the following illustration demonstrate how the page displays in Internet Explorer 5.5.

> **Font variant is a nice, but weakly-supported property.**
>
> THIS IS A SERIF FONT, USING THE SMALL CAPS VALUE.
>
> THIS IS A SANS-SERIF FONT, USING THE SMALL CAPS VALUE.
>
> THIS IS A MONOSPACE FONT, USING THE SMALL CAPS VALUE.
>
> *THIS IS A CURSIVE FONT, USING THE SMALL CAPS VALUE.*
>
> THIS IS A FANTASY FONT, USING THE SMALL CAPS VALUE.

Unfortunately, only Internet Explorer 5.5 and Opera 5 displayed the small caps correctly. Even the state-of-the-art Netscape 6.0 had a glitch when it tried to display the generic "fantasy" font in small caps:

> **Font variant is a nice, but weakly-supported property.**
>
> THIS IS A SERIF FONT, USING THE SMALL CAPS VALUE.
>
> THIS IS A SANS-SERIF FONT, USING THE SMALL CAPS VALUE.
>
> THIS IS A MONOSPACE FONT, USING THE SMALL CAPS VALUE.
>
> THIS IS A CURSIVE FONT, USING THE SMALL CAPS VALUE.
>
> ?????????????????????? ???????????????????????

Thus, while you may find some uses for the font-variant property, be sure that you have tested your pages out in other browsers. You don't want your visitors to see a line of question marks instead of a line of text. Table 6-6 provides some other key information about the font-variant property.

Does it Inherit?	Default value	Browser support	Works with
Yes	Normal	Weak	All elements

Table 6-6   Characteristics of the font-variant Property

The font-weight Property

Just as the font-style property regulates whether a font displays in normal or italics, the font-weight property governs the boldness of a font. However, font-weight gives you a greater number of choices to work with. In HTML, all you could do was toggle boldness on or off. The font-weight property promises a broad range of boldness settings. Unfortunately, in actual practice you're not likely to get more than three or four different "weights."

Note

The biggest problem with the CSS boldness settings is that many fonts do not have such a wide variety available. Thus, depending on the font you are using, a browser often will have only two, three, or at the most four different "boldnesses" that it can display.

Values and Syntax

Font-weight allows for nine different boldness settings, plus "bold," and the relative settings "bolder" and "lighter." The values and syntax for font-weight are as follows:

- **100-900**   {font-weight: 400;} In theory, this causes the font to display in one of nine degrees of boldness, with 100 being the lightest and 900 the boldest. In practice, you will generally find that 100–500 are identical (normal), 600–800 are a medium bold, and 900 is *sometimes* a heavy bold.

- **Normal**   {font-weight: normal; This is the default value and need not be specified. It is equivalent to the 400 numerical setting.

- **Bold**   {font-weight: bold;} Toggles on bold text, equivalent to the 700 numerical setting.

- **Bolder**   {font-weight: bolder;} Causes the font to display one step bolder than the parent element

- **Lighter**   {font-weight: lighter;} Causes the font to display one step lighter than the parent element

Unfortunately, because many fonts are not available with nine different degrees of boldness, the browsers often are limited in what they can display. The CSS specification outlines how a browser should handle fonts where different boldness values are "unassigned." As the following illustration shows, in Internet Explorer 5.5 the values 100 through 500 are the same, while 600 is bolder, but slightly less bold than 700 and 800. The 900 value appears to be the heaviest.

6

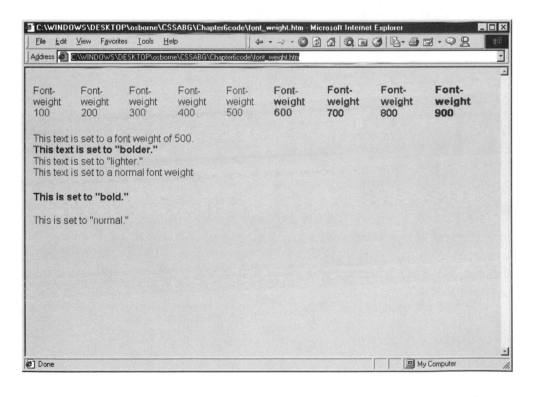

If you display the same page in Netscape 6, you'll see that Netscape follows IE's pattern of making 100-500 the same weight.

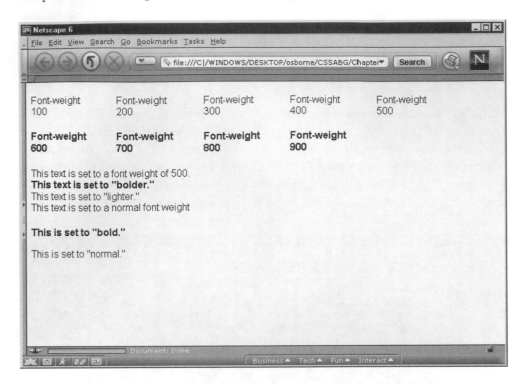

However, Netscape makes no distinction between 600-900 with this particular font. You'll get similar results with Opera 5 and Netscape 4.

How do you use the font-weight property? Don't expect to get a full range of nine different boldness weights for now. You will get the best results if you use the value 400 for normal, 700 for bold, and 900 for extra bold. However, remember that the 900 setting will not always produce an extra heavy font weight.

Ask the Expert

Question: Why don't the browsers support the nine different values for font-weight?

Answer: It's not as much a question of browser support as it is limited materials. Browsers are limited by what they have to work with. Remember, the browsers do not create the fonts that are displayed on your screen; they pull them from the user's computer system. That's why if you specify a certain font on a page and your visitors don't have it on their machines, then the browser can't display that font. Likewise, for a browser to display nine different varieties of boldness, it must have access to a font that *has* nine different varieties of boldness. The browsers are designed to handle the different values, but if a particular font does not support that large a variety, then the browsers substitute the nearest equivalent, based on the CSS specification.

Using "bolder" and "lighter"

The "bolder" and "lighter" values enable you to adjust a font's boldness based on the boldness of the parent element. This comes in handy, particularly if you are using a bold font and for some reason want to lighten it. Consider how these lines of HTML code display in the illustration that follows:

```
<p style="font-weight: 600;">
This paragraph will display bold,
<span style="font-weight: lighter;">
except for this phrase.</span></p>
```

This paragraph will display bold, except for this phrase.

The "lighter" property that was inserted with the <span> element causes the last phrase in the sentence to display at the lighter weight of 500. The calculation for boldness or lightness for this property is relative to the parent's value. Thus, since the parent has a value of 600, the value is reduced to 500. If you add a sentence to the paragraph, this time using the "bolder" value, you might reasonably expect it to display with a heavier weight than the first sentence. You may or may not be correct. As the following illustration shows, Internet Explorer 5.5 correctly displays the "bolder" value:

```
<p style="font-weight: 600;">
This paragraph will display bold,
<span style="font-weight: lighter;">
except for this phrase.</span><br />
<span style="font-weight: bolder;">This
phrase should be even bolder than the first.</p>
```

This paragraph will display bold, except for this phrase.
This sentence should be even bolder than the first.

On the other hand, the same code displayed in Netscape 6 shows no distinction between the last sentence and the first:

This paragraph will **display bold**, except for this phrase.
This sentence should be even bolder than the first.

Does this mean that Netscape 6 doesn't support the "bolder" value? Not at all. The problem goes back to the different numerical values and different browsers' abilities in displaying them. Internet Explorer displays an "extra bold" font at the 900 value; Netscape does not. Thus, when Netscape displays a 600 value for the first sentence, it can't make the font any bolder for the second. For Netscape, 600 *is* as bold as it can make the font. However, if you change the preceding code to have a value of 400, look at how Netscape's display changes:

This paragraph will display bold, except for this phrase.
This sentence should be even bolder than the first.

Now, Netscape is able to provide a bolder value for the second sentence. However, it is unable to display a "lighter" value, because it can't display anything lighter than 400.

In the final analysis, you probably will be able to produce all the results you want by using the 400, 600, and 900 values. Or, simply use the "bold" value to turn boldness on or off. As you work with the font-weight property, keep in mind some of its other characteristics, such as those shown in Table 6-7.

Does it Inherit?	Default value	Browser support	Works with
Yes	Normal	Excellent, but display usually limited to a fraction of possible values	All elements

Table 6-7   Characteristics of the font-weight Property

The font: Shorthand Property

If you want to keep your style sheets as simple as possible, you have another option when specifying font properties. CSS provides a *shorthand* property that enables the user to insert multiple declarations in a single rule by specifying only the values, not the properties' names. For instance, instead of writing a rule like this,

```
p       {font-weight: bold;
         font-variant: small-caps;
         font-style: italic;
         font-size: 18pt;
         font-family: "Times New Roman", serif;}
```

you can write it this way:

```
p       {font: bold small-caps italic 18pt "Times New Roman", serif}
```

The difference is that you omit each of the property names, listing only the values, and the values are not separated by any punctuation as in a normal declaration. Keep in mind also that you need to follow a certain order in listing the values; otherwise the browser will ignore them. The order is as follows, and the values are optional. You are not *required* to use a certain value for this shorthand to work; simply begin the declaration with the keyword "font:" and you're on your way.

- **Stylistic properties** (font-style, font-variant, font-weight) first, in any order.

- **Size** (font-size)

- **Line height** (if you want to adjust the line-height property, you may do it with this shortcut property, even though line height is a text property).

- **Font family**

Although this shortcut can save you time, its support tends to be inconsistent, particularly with Netscape 4. So, be sure to test your pages if you're using it.

6

Tip

You *do* need to separate the font-family choices by commas. However, no other commas or semicolons should be used in the line.

1-Minute Drill

● What are "bolder" and "lighter" measured in relation to?

● What is the default numeric value of "bold?"

● What is the order of values for the font: (shorthand) property?

● Do you have to include *all* possible values when using the font: (shorthand) property?

CSS 2 Font Properties

Two additional font properties were added to the CSS 2 specification: font-stretch and font-size-adjust. As of this writing, not even the most recent versions of Internet Explorer and Netscape support these properties. However, it's a good idea to at least be familiar with them for future reference.

The font-stretch Property

The font-stretch property's name summarizes its function well. It is designed to stretch or condense a font, while maintaining the font's height. The values of the font-stretch property are: normal, wider, narrower, condensed, semi-condensed, extra-condensed, ultra-condensed, semi-expanded, extra-expanded, ultra-expanded.

● "Bolder" and "lighter" are measured in relation to their parent element
● 700
● Style (style, variant, weight), Size, Line Height, Family
● No

The font-size-adjust Property

Because there can be significant differences in legibility between fonts of the same "point" size, the font-size-adjust property was added to CSS. The intent is to enable a page author to specify an adjustment value for a font that is listed as a backup font for a page, but that might be too small to read legibly if used at the size specified for the original font. The browser will then "adjust" the substitute font to a more legible size if it is used in displaying a page. This property would use a numeric value that expresses the ratio of the font's "x" height (the height of the lowercase letter x) to the overall height of the font. This value (called the *aspect value*) would then enable the browser to calculate an adjusted size for the font that would make its legibility comparable to that of the font it is replacing.

6

Project 6-1: Applying Font Properties

CSS font properties give you a degree of freedom in your page layouts that you never could have with plain HTML. In this project you will create a home page that steps "out of the box" in its use of fonts. By using fonts of multiple sizes and colors, placing them at different locations on the page, and using a few tricks with negative values, you can create a pleasing arrangement simply with fonts. To add a little visual interest in this page, you'll also need to apply some other CSS properties such as color, text-decoration, and text-align. As always, you'll want to check your results in more than one browser to be sure that your page displays well, no matter who is viewing it.

Step by Step

1. Begin by creating an HTML document. In the body of the document add some text that you might expect to see on a home page. For example, create a "Welcome to My Home Page!" heading with the <h1> element. Don't forget to put a title for your page inside the <title> element, as that's how some search engines will catalog your page.

2. Using <a href=" ">, add some navigational links such as: "About Me," "Family Album," "My Hobbies," "Favorite TV Shows," "Music I Like," "Sign my Guestbook," "Email Me." You don't have to link to actual documents unless you really want to, since this is just a sample page. Simply a URL such

as "nolink.htm" will be sufficient. Your results should look something like the following illustration:

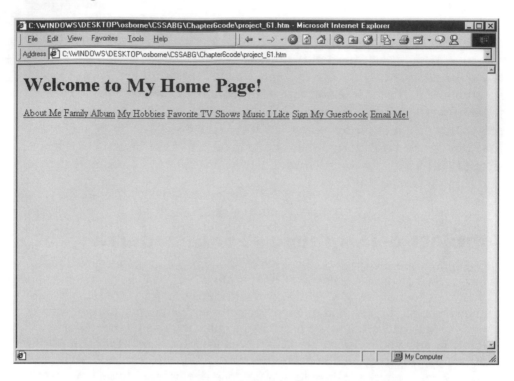

3. Embed a style sheet in the <head> portion of the document by adding a set of <style> tags.

4. Add a light blue background to the page by using the background-color property with the body selector. Try a color combination of rgb(0%,80%,80%). If you would prefer a different color or shade, adjust the color values until you find one you like.

5. Remove the underlines from the links, using the "text-decoration: none" declaration. Remember that you will have to use the pseudo-class a:link as your selector. Also, you will have to make the same declaration for a:active and a:visited. Otherwise, the underlines will reappear after a link has been visited.

Note

As a rule, it's not a good idea to alter the appearance of links this way, simply because people might tend not to recognize them as links. The blue color and underlining of links insures that your visitors will quickly recognize them as such. If you planned to use a page such as the one in this project, you would be well advised to at least add a set of plain, unstyled links at the bottom of the page.

6. Center the heading by applying the "text-align: center" declaration to the h1 selector. Use the color property to set the text color to silver. Use the font-size property to set the heading font size to 1.5em. Even though 1.5em is equivalent to 150%, this percentage setting will actually reduce the <h1> font size, because it is relative to the *parent* element (in this case "body"). Thus, 1.5 em is one and one half times the size of the default body text.

7. Now, you will begin creating some classes that you will apply to the different links. These classes will adjust the font properties as well as some margin and text properties. Name your first class ".arial1in", then add a declaration that sets the font family to Arial or sans-serif. Then set the font size to one inch and the font style to italic. Finally, add the margin-left property, and set the value to 35%. You will cover margin properties in Module 9, but for now just add in the declarations as described. Your class rule should look like the following listing:

```
.arial1in      {font-family: Arial, sans-serif;
               font-size: 1in;
               font-style: italic;
               margin-left: 35%;}
```

8. Create a class and name it "times30px." Use the text-align property to set the alignment to center and add declarations setting the font family to Times New Roman or serif and the font size to 30 pixels.

9. Create a class named "courier," and add the declaration "margin-right: 35%." Use font properties to set the family to Courier or monospace and the font size to 1.5 centimeters.

10. Create a class named "fantasy" and add declarations for "margin-top: -5%" and "margin-left: 15%." Apply font properties to set the family to Western or fantasy, and the font size to 5 ems.

6

11. Create a class named "cursive" and add a "margin-top: -10%" declaration plus a "text-align: right" declaration. Use font properties to set the font family to Script or cursive and the font size to 3 exes.

12. Create a class named "arial" and use the text-align property to center the text. Apply font properties to set the font size to .5 inches and the font family to Arial or sans-serif.

13. Create a class named "timessmall" and use the text-align property to align the text to the left. With the font properties, set the font family to "Times New Roman" or serif, and the size to 2 ems. Use font-variant to apply the small-caps value and set the font-weight property to a value of 900.

14. Once you have created your classes, all that remains is to apply them to the various links you created earlier. The easiest way to do this is to make use of the <div> element. Remember that <div> and <span> are generic elements that can be used to apply styles. Div is a block level element and thus will add line breaks before and after the element it contains. Span is inline and will not mark off new divisions on a page. To apply a class to one of the links, simply enclose the entire link inside <div> tags and use the class attribute inside the opening <div> tag to apply the class name. Add a little more visual interest by choosing different colors for your links. These may be applied with an inline style inside the <a> element, as is shown in the listing below:

```
<div class="arial1in">
<a href="nolink.htm" style="color:maroon;">About Me</a>
</div>
```

15. As in the preceding listing, apply the arial1in class to the About Me link and color it maroon.

16. Apply the times30px class to the Family Album link and color it teal.

17. Apply the courier class to the My Hobbies link and color it green.

18. For the Favorite TV Shows link, use the fantasy class, coloring it yellow.

19. The Music I Like link should be colored navy and attached to the arial class.

20. Use the cursive class with the Sign My Guestbook link and color it maroon.

21. Use the timessmall class with the Email Me! link, coloring it white.

22. Once you have applied all the classes to the links: save the page and display it in your browser. Displayed in Netscape 6.0, it looks like this:

Project Summary

Using little more than the font properties, you have been able to take a plain HTML page and customize it with different fonts, sizes, and styles. If you display the page in Internet Explorer 5+, Netscape 4 and 6, and Opera, you will get slightly different results, but all should be acceptable. As a rule you should be able to use most font properties with only minor worries about compatibility problems.

```
<html>
<head>
<title>My Homepage</title>
<style type="text/css">
body {background-color: rgb(0%,80%,80%);}
```

```
a:link {text-decoration: none;}
a:active {text-decoration: none;}
a:visited {text-decoration: none;}
h1        {text-align: center;
            font-family: Western, fantasy;
            color: silver;
            font-size: 1.5em;}
.arial1in {margin-left: 35%;
            font-family: Arial, sans-serif;
            font-size: 1in;
            font-style: italic;}
.times30px {text-align: center;
            font-family: "Times New Roman", serif;
            font-size: 30px;}
.courier  {margin-right: 35%;
            font-family: Courier, monospace;
            font-size: 1.5cm;}
.fantasy  {margin-top: -5%;
            margin-left: 15%;
            font-family: Western, fantasy;
            font-size: 5em;}
.cursive  {font-family: "Script", cursive;
            font-size: 3ex;
            text-align: right;
            margin-top: -10%}
.arial    {font-family: Arial, sans-serif;
            font-size: .5in;
            text-align: center;}
.timessmall {text-align: left;
            font-family: Times, serif;
            font-size: 2em;
            font-variant: small-caps;
            font-weight: 900;}
</style>
</head>
<body>
<h1>Welcome to My Home Page!</h1>
<div class="arial1in">
<a href="nolink.htm" style="color:maroon;">About Me</a>
</div>
<div class="times30px">
<a href="nolink.htm" style="color:teal;">Family Album</a>
</div>
<div class="courier">
<a href="nolink.htm" style="color:green;">My Hobbies</a>
</div>
```

```
<div class="fantasy">
<a href="nolink.htm" style="color:yellow;">
Favorite TV Shows</a></div>
<div class="arial">
<a href="nolink.htm" style="color:navy;">Music I Like</a>
</div>
<div class="cursive">
<a href="nolink.htm" style="color:maroon;">Sign My Guestbook</a>
</div>
<div class="timessmall">
<a href="nolink.htm" style="color:white;">Email Me!</a>
</div>
</body>
</html>
```

✓Mastery Check

1. Which of the following is *not* a value of the font-style property?

   A. normal

   B. small-caps

   C. italic

   D. oblique

2. On the font-weight scale of 100-900, which value is considered "normal"?

   A. 100

   B. 800

   C. 300

   D. 400

3. List the five "generic" font types that CSS recognizes.

   _____

   _____

4. List the different ways you can specify a value for font-size.

   _____

   _____

5. Of the previous different value types, which are recommended for use on Web pages?

   _____

   _____

Module 7

Work with Text Properties

The Goals of this Module

- Understand the Differences Between Font and Text Properties
- Adjust Word and Letter Spacing
- Learn How to Use the text-decoration Property
- Learn How to Align Text Horizontally and Vertically
- Use text-transform to Convert Text
- Create Indents with the text-indent Property
- Adjust Line Height

A frequent point of confusion when dealing with CSS is the distinction that is made between font-properties and text-properties. Often, beginning CSS users have trouble remembering what these properties control and why they are different. A possible reason for this is that many people tend to use the terms "font" and "text" interchangeably, as if the two words were synonymous. However, in CSS "font" and "text" refer to two very different aspects of an HTML document. You might try thinking of it this way: *font* refers to what a character or letter looks like; *text* refers to how it is positioned. As you'll see in this module, there are some exceptions to this, but as a rule of thumb, it's not bad. In this module, you will learn how to position text on your page with the text properties. However, before you begin learning the text properties, it might be helpful to take a few minutes to review the font properties and what they do.

What Font Properties Do

Font properties govern how letters, numbers, and other characters display on a Web page. With the font properties, you can control the size of your letters, what font they appear in, whether they display as normal, italic, bold, small caps, and so on. For example, in the following illustration, the first row of letters are set to a 24pt, normal Times New Roman font, while the second row is set to display a 32pt, italic, bold, Arial font.

AaBbCcDdEeFfGgHhIiJjKkLlMm
NnOoPpQqRrSsTtUuVvWwXxYyZz

What Text Properties Do

If font properties govern the overall appearance of letters, numbers, and other characters, where do the text properties come in? Essentially, they enable you to fine-tune the layout of characters on your page. You use the text properties to control things such as indent, alignment, character spacing, word spacing, and so on. For instance, you could take the preceding illustration and change it, simply by specifying the distance between the characters with the letter-spacing property. If you were to add a declaration that set the character spacing of line one to .5em (one half the size of the default font) and the line-height property to 2.5em (two and one half times the default font size), your results would be very different:

A a B b C c D d E e F f G g H h I i J j K k L l M m
NnOoPpQqRrSsTtUuVvWwXxYyZz

On the one hand, text properties duplicate many things you can do through the use of HTML elements. For instance, if you want to create a superscript in HTML, you can use the <sup> element; in CSS, the same effect can be created with the vertical-align property and the "super" value. Likewise, you can create subscripts, underlines, strikethroughs, and so on using either HTML elements or equivalent CSS style rules. Of course, you can also align text with either HTML or CSS, although the W3C has deprecated HTML's "align" attribute in favor of the CSS property.

In general, the CSS text properties enable you to easily perform simple tasks that present problems with HTML alone. For example, to indent text in HTML you must either resort to adding several "non-breaking space" entities ( ) at the beginning of a line or enclose the line in the *definition description*, <dd>, element. If you want some influence over letter or line spacing, you often have to use the preformatted text, <pre>, element. Unfortunately, this also results in a "monospace" text that doesn't usually look very good on a Web page. CSS text properties, on the other hand, give you greater control over letter, line, and even word spacing.

Note

The word "control" can be misleading. With CSS, your control is limited by a host of things, such as browser compatibility, user style preferences, and so on. When you think of CSS as giving you "control" over the appearance of your Web pages, keep in mind that it is in contrast to the lack of control you have with HTML alone.

The CSS Text Properties

The CSS text properties govern the positioning, alignment, spacing, and so on, of text in your HTML documents. Later in this module you will see each of the text properties in detail. However, as it is helpful to get a "bird's-eye" view of the properties, here is a list of each of the text properties with a brief description of its function:

- **word-spacing**   Allows you to increase (or decrease) space between words

- **letter-spacing**   Allows you to increase (or decrease) the amount of space between characters.

- **text-decoration**   enables you to add underlines, overlines, strikethroughs, or to cause text to "blink"

- **vertical-align** Alters the positioning of an inline element up or down

- **text-align** Aligns or justifies text inside a block-level element

- **text-transform** Enables you to change the case of characters or to make the initial letters of each word capital

- **text-indent** Adds indentation to the first line of a block level element

- **line-height** Increases the amount of space between lines

1-Minute Drill

- Generally speaking, font properties influence the _____ of text.
- Text properties influence the _____ of text.
- What text property is intended to replace HTML's "align" attribute?

Project 7-1: Experiment with Text Properties

The text-properties give you control over positioning, spacing, case, alignment, and decoration (underlining and so on). In this project, you will survey some (though not all) of the text properties and values by creating an HTML document that has a paragraph summarizing the text properties' capabilities. Then you will embed a style sheet in the <head> of the page and apply text properties to the document you created.

Step-by-Step

1. Create a blank HTML document and save it as text_properties.htm.

2. Create a level one (h1) heading that reads: **some things you can do with text properties**. Do *not* capitalize any of the letters.

3. Add the following text: Text properties enable you to align and indent text, position it vertically as in superscripts and subscripts, convert it to uppercase, lowercase, and title case, underline it, adjust letter spacing, adjust line

---

- Appearance
- Position
- text-align

spacing, and much more. Enclose the entire paragraph in a set of <p> tags and add <br /> tags wherever you want line breaks to occur. It should look something like the following illustration:

some things you can do with text properties

Text properties enable you to align and indent text,
position it vertically as in superscripts and subscripts,
convert it to uppercase, lowercase, and title case,
underline it, adjust letter spacing,
adjust line height,
and much more.

4. Add a set of <style> tags inside the <head> portion of the page.

5. Write a style rule using the body selector. Set the background color to white and the default font size to 1.2ems. This will set the font size to 120% of the browser's default font size.

6. Create a style rule using the h1 selector. Set the font size to 1.2 ems. (This will set the size to 120% of the body font size created in the preceding rule.) Use the text-transform property with the "capitalize" value to capitalize the first letter of every word.

Hint
Capitalize will render the first letter of every word as a capital letter. To change all of the letters in a block of text to capitals, you would use "uppercase" as your value.

7. Add a style rule using the "p" selector. Cause the paragraph to indent five percent of the screen width by using the text-indent property with a value of 5%.

8. Create a class selector named "sup." Add a declaration that sets the vertical alignment to superscript. You will need to use the vertical-align property with the "super" value. To apply the style to your text, enclose the word "superscript" within a set of <span> tags. Inside the first tag, add the attribute class="sup". It should look like this: **<span class="sup"> superscript</span>**

Tip
Remember that a class selector *must* be preceded by a period in the style sheet. Thus, your "sup" selector should be written **.sup {vertical-align: super;}**.

7

9. Create a class selector named "sub." Add a declaration that sets the vertical alignment to subscript. Use the vertical-align property with the "sub" value. Use <span> tags to enclose the word "subscript" in the text. Apply the style by adding the class="sub" attribute to the opening <span> tag.

10. Create a class selector named "upper" and use the text-transform property to set the value to "uppercase." Use span tags and the class attribute to apply the style to the word "uppercase" in your paragraph.

11. Create a class selector named "title." Write a declaration with the text-transform property, setting the value to "capitalize." Apply the style to the phrase "title case."

12. Create a class selector named "underline" and write a declaration with the text-decoration property and the "underline" value. Apply it to the word "underline" in your text.

13. Experiment with the letter-spacing property by creating a class selector named "letterspace." Use the letter-spacing property to set the spacing for the text that reads "adjust letter spacing." Set it to a value of .5ems.

14. Make one final change to your page by setting the line height for the phrase "adjust line height." Create a class selector named "lineheight" and use the line-height property. Set the value to 4 ems.

15. Save text_properties.htm and display it in your browser. The following illustration shows how it will display in Internet Explorer 5.5:

Some Things You Can Do With Text Properties

Text properties enable you to align and indent text, position it vertically as in superscripts and subscripts, convert it to UPPERCASE, lowercase, and Title Case, underline it, a d j u s t   l e t t e r   s p a c i n g ,

adjust line height,

and much more.

```
<html><head>
<title>Text Properties</title><style>
body    {font-size: 1.2em; background-color: white}
h1      {text-transform: capitalize; font-size: 1.2em;}
p       {text-indent: 5%;}
.sup    {vertical-align: super;}
```

```
.sub    {vertical-align: sub;}
.upper {text-transform: uppercase;}
.title {text-transform: capitalize;}
.underline {text-decoration: underline;}
.letterspace {letter-spacing: .5em;}
.lineheight  {line-height: 4em;}</style></head>
<body>
<h1>some things you can do with text properties</h1>
<p>Text properties enable you to align
and indent text,<br />
position it vertically as in
<span class="sup">superscripts</span>
and <span class="sub">subscripts,</span><br />
convert it to <span class="upper">uppercase</span>,
lowercase, and <span class="title">title case,</span><br />
<span class="underline">underline it</span>, <span
class="letterspace">adjust letter spacing,</span><br />
<span class="lineheight">adjust line height,</span><br />
and much more.
</body></html>
```

7

Project Summary

This project has given you a little taste of the capabilities of the text properties. Although not exhaustive, this demonstration is sufficient to show you how the text properties give you the same control you had with HTML...and much more. While you *can* create superscripts, subscripts, underlining, and text alignment with HTML elements, you have to resort to "workarounds" for things like indenting, adding extra spaces, or lines.. With CSS, these tasks are much simpler.

Working with Text Properties

Now that you have surveyed the text properties as a group and developed a basic understanding of what they are intended to do, it's time to examine each one more closely. As with Module 6, the section for each text property will cover the values it can take, its basic syntax, browser support, and any problems unique to it.

The Word-Spacing Property

For the most part, the function of a text-property can be inferred from its name. The *word-spacing* property, for example, allows you to add space between words.

You might want to use this property to balance a heading by increasing the space between the words. This property, along with the *letter-spacing* property can take negative values, thus you can use it to compress a portion of text as well as lengthen it. Word spacing can be used with all elements.

The word-spacing property will accept only length values (in, cm, mm, pt, pc, px, em, ex). You cannot use percentages with this property. As the default value of this property is "normal," you only need to use it if you want to adjust the spacing between words. The downside of this property is that it is currently supported only in Netscape 6.0 and Opera (all versions). Thus, it would be unwise to use it unless you knew that the overwhelming majority of your visitors would be using one of these browsers.

The syntax for word spacing is simple, as reflected in the following style rules:

```
h1      {word-spacing:  1.5em;}
h2      {word-spacing:  72px;}
h3      {word-spacing:  .75in;}
h4      {word-spacing:  12pt;}
```

Any of the above measurements will work with the word spacing property. As the following illustration demonstrates, the effect can be difficult to control and should be used with care:

This word spacing is unmodified.

This   word   spacing   was   increased   by 1.5   ems.

Thiswordspacingwasreducedby.25ems.

```
<h1>This word spacing is unmodified.</h1>
<h1 style="word-spacing: 1.5em;">This word spacing was
increased by 1.5 ems.</h1>
<h1 style="word-spacing: -.25em;">This word spacing was
 reduced by .25 ems.</h1>
```

As mentioned in the preceding paragraphs, support for this property is weak. However, should you plan on using it, Table 7-1 lists some important characteristics of the word-spacing property.

Does it inherit?	Default value	Browser support	Works with
Yes	Normal spacing for the default font	Poor	All elements

Table 7-1	Characteristics of the word-spacing Property

The Letter-Spacing Property

If you understand the concept behind the word-spacing property, then the letter-spacing property shouldn't pose much of a problem for you. Obviously, with this property you are adding or removing space between individual characters rather than between words. Like its "sibling," letter-spacing will accept only length values, and you can not use percentages. However, you can apply negative values. Also like the word-spacing property, letter-spacing with negative values can be tricky. As the following illustration shows, a small adjustment of one tenth of an em (one tenth the size of the default font) compresses the letters too much.

This letter spacing is normal.

This   letter   spacing   was   increased   by   .5   em.

Thisletterspacingwasdecreasedby.10ems.

```
<p>This letter spacing is normal.</p>
<p style="letter-spacing: .5em;">This letter spacing
was increased by .5 em.</p>
<p style="letter-spacing: -.10em">This letter spacing
was decreased by .10 ems.</p>
```

Browser support for this property is moderate. All browsers, except for the older versions of Netscape (Netscape 3 and 4) support it. Since these browsers are still commonly used, again you should use care with this property as well.

The syntax for letter-spacing is the same as for word-spacing, as the following code listing demonstrates.

```
p.wide    {letter-spacing: .45em;}
p.narrow  {letter-spacing: -5px;}
```

7

Ask the Expert

Question: Why do so many Web designers and Web authoring books speak negatively about the "blinking text" effect?

Answer: Although there are many effects that can make a Web page annoying (overuse of GIF animations, for instance), it seems that Netscape's <blink> element usually wins the award for the most annoying effect of all. When Netscape introduced <blink> it quickly became popular, most likely because it was the easiest possible way to create an "animated" effect on a Web page. Unfortunately, this effect tends to defeat the purpose of simple animation: to draw attention to a certain part of the page. The blinking text effect certainly does draw attention to itself, but since it cannot be stopped, it quickly moves into the realm of the obnoxious, much like a constantly dripping faucet or a flashing neon light. Have you ever watched a used car commercial on television that featured an "in your face" announcer that you just couldn't wait to turn off? That's the effect that "blink" tends to have on people. If you plan on designing Web pages, do yourself, your customers, and the online community a favor: don't use "blink."

Other characteristics of the letter-spacing property are listed in Table 7-2.

The Text-Decoration Property

HTML allowed you to create underlined and strikethrough text with the <u> and <strike> elements. The text-decoration property enables you to create these same effects and more. In fact one value, "blink," preserves for a future generation the effect created by Netscape's infamous <blink> element: text blinking on and off, ad infinitum, ad nauseum.

Does it inherit?	Default value	Browser support	Works with
Yes	Normal spacing for the default font	Inconsistent	All elements

Table 7-2 Characteristics of the Letter-Spacing Property

Values

The text-decoration property accepts only five specifically defined values.
These are

- **none**   Removes or prevents any text decoration

- **underline**   Adds an underscore to the text

- **overline**   Places a line over the text

- **line-through**   Creates strikethrough text

- **blink**   Causes the text to blink on and off (you cannot adjust the
  frequency or rate of the "blink")

Hint

Although it's generally considered poor design, if you wish to remove the
automatic underlines from hypertext links, you would use the following style rules:
a:link, a:visited, a:active   {text-decoration: none;}

7

As the following illustration demonstrates, the text-decoration property
doesn't allow for any adjustments. The effects are merely toggled "on" or "off."
You can see that, with the exception of "overline," which was not featured in
HTML, these text decorations are essentially the same as what you could create
with the <u>, <strike>, <del>, and <blink> elements. The code following the
illustration demonstrates the syntax for the text-decoration property.

Note

To view the "blinking text" effect, you will need to use either Netscape 4, 6,
or Opera 5.

Text with no decoration

Underlined text

Overlined text

~~Line-through~~

Blinking text

```
<p>Text with no decoration</p>
<p style="text-decoration: underline;">Underlined text</p>
<p style="text-decoration: overline;">Overlined text</p>
<p style="text-decoration: line-through;">Line-through</p>
<p style="text-decoration: blink;">Blinking text</p>
```

One "quirk" of the text-decoration property you should be aware of is that, although it is not inherited, all elements that descend from the "decorated" element will be affected by the decoration. To see how it works, try creating a paragraph with black text, using the <div> element, and set the text decoration to underline. Then, for added emphasis, enclose one of the sentences inside a set of <span> tags, setting its text color to white. When you display the page in a browser, the underline from the <div> element will be passed on to the text in the <span> element. However, as the following illustration shows, the line will still be black.

This text should be black with an underline.This text will be white but will still have a black underline.This text will be black again.

```
<div style="text-decoration: underline; font-size: 1.2em;">
This text should be black with an underline.
<span style="color: white">This text will be white
but will still have a black underline.</span>This text will
be black again.</div>
```

Hint

The only way around this problem is for you to add a declaration inside the <span> tags that specifies: "text-decoration: underline." Then, the underline will be white instead of black.

You are most likely to find the text-decoration property useful for creating underlines and strikethroughs or for removing underlines from links. You can't use this property to create a line without accompanying text (as in a horizontal rule), so its uses are fairly limited. Combine that with inconsistent browser support, and the conclusion is that this property should not be one you depend on much. Table 7-3 lists some of its important characteristics.

Does it inherit?	Default value	Browser support	Works with
No	None	Inconsistent	All elements

Table 7-3   Characteristics of the text-decoration Property

Tip

You can't use multiple values for this property. In other words, you can not combine underline and overline to create a partial "border" effect. In fact, when you try to use more than one value, the browser will either ignore them all or choose one (generally the "underline" value). Not surprisingly, in Netscape 6.0 the "blink" value is dominant when used in combination with other values.

1-Minute Drill

- Not including the default value of "normal," what are the specific values accepted by the text-decoration property?
- What would be a situation where you might want to use the value "text-decoration: none?"

The Vertical-Align Property

In HTML you can create superscripts and subscripts with the <sup> and <sub> elements. You can also control the vertical alignment of a table cell's contents with the "valign" attribute. CSS enables you to apply the same type of vertical alignment with the vertical-align property.

To understand how the vertical-align property works, you need to think "inside the box." That is, you need to understand the concept of *boxes* in CSS design. You'll cover this in greater detail in Module 8, but for now all you need to remember is that from a visual standpoint, CSS regards every HTML element as a *box*. If you find that difficult to visualize, you can make it concrete by simply using CSS to add a background color or border to any element of an HTML

- Underline, overline, line-through, and blink
- Removing underlines from links

document. The background/border will make the element's box visible, as in the following example:

Heading with invisible box

Heading box made visible

When you use the vertical-align property, you are aligning not only text or images, but also the boxes that enclose them. Because the vertical-align property only can be applied to inline-level or table cell elements, it is as if you are moving a box within a box. Again, this is difficult to follow without a visual reference. In Figure 7-1, all of the vertical-align values are displayed as boxes inside a larger box. Notice how the alignment of the entire box shifts when the value is changed.

Values

The vertical-align property gives you a much greater range of values to work with than HTML's valign property, which permitted you to specify only top, middle, or bottom. CSS on the other hand allows you to choose from three different value categories (keyword, percentage, or length). With eight different keywords to choose from, you'd think you'd have plenty of choices to work with. Unfortunately, the browser support for many of these values is weak. As you look through the following list of text-align values, refer to Figure 7-1 or to Figure 7-2 to see how the box for that value aligns inside its parent's box:

- **Baseline**   This is the default value, aligning the box with the baseline for the element's default font.

- **Super**   This creates a superscript, much like HTML's <sup> element.

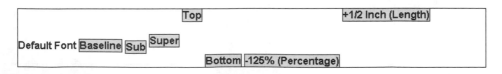

Figure 7-1   Text boxes aligned with the vertical-align property

- **Sub**   This creates a subscript, like HTML's <sub> element.

- **Top**   Top aligns the box with the tallest thing enclosed in the parent element.

- **Bottom**   This value aligns with the lowest thing enclosed in the parent element.

- **Text-top**   Aligns the top of the box with the top of the parent's font (See Figure 7-2).

- **Middle**   The official definition for this value as defined by the CSS2 specification is that it aligns the "vertical midpoint of the box with the baseline of the parent box plus half the x-height of the parent." However, for all intents and purposes, it aligns the boxes in the middle. (See Figure 7-2).

- **Text-Bottom**   Aligns the bottom of the box with the default font's baseline (See Figure 7-2).

- **Length**   This is a standard length value (in, cm, mm, pt, pc, em, ex, px).

- **Percentage**   This is a standard percentage value. The percentage is based on the size of the parent element's font. You can use either positive or negative values.

7

Syntax

The syntax for using the vertical-align property depends on whether you are using a keyword, length, or percentage. Any of the following style rules correctly apply a value to vertical-align:

```
em       {vertical-align: top;}
img      {vertical-align: -50%;}
.special {vertical-align: 3em;}
#si3e3   {vertical-align: middle;}
```

Note

At this writing, only Netscape 6.0 and Opera support all of the vertical-align values.

In view of the weak browser support for this property, you would be wise not to depend very heavily on it. You are generally safe using it for superscripts

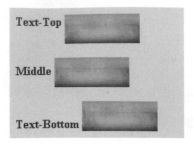

Figure 7-2   An image positioned with the text-top, middle, and text-bottom values

and subscripts and for minor element alignment on your page. However, the browser support is too inconsistent at this point to rely on it for much more. Table 7-4 provides some key characteristics of the vertical-align attribute.

The Text-Align Property

Just as the vertical-align property enables you to align page elements vertically, the text-align property allows you to align text horizontally. However, in contrast to the vertical-align property's weak browser support, the text-align property is strongly supported by all the major browsers. The text-align property is CSS's counterpart to HTML's deprecated "align" attribute. The values for this property are expressed in keywords only: left, right, center, and justify.

- **Left**   A value of left means that all of the text is aligned on the left side of the screen.

- **Right**   "Right" aligns text to the right side of the screen.

- **Center**   The middle of each line aligns with the center of the screen.

- **Justify**   The characters are aligned to both the left and right margins, rather than just one side of the page.

Does it inherit?	Default value	Browser support	Works with
No	Baseline	Inconsistent	Inline and Table Cell Elements

Table 7-4   Characteristics of the Vertical-Align Property

The following illustration shows how page elements are affected by the text-align property:

> This text is set to "text-align: left."
>
> This text is set to "text-align: right."
>
> This text is set to "text-align: center."
>
> This text is set to "text-align: justify." and so I've added extra text and indented the right margin 55% so that you can better see the justification effect.

An important characteristic of this property is that it can be applied only to block-level elements, such as <h#>,<p>, <div>, and so on. Thus, while you could align a heading by using this property, you could not align an image with it, because the <img /> element is not a block-level element. To align an image with the text-align property, you would need to enclose the image in a set of <div> tags, and then apply the alignment to the opening <div> tag. Your style rule and HTML construction might look something like the following:

```
<div style="text-align: center;"><img src="myimage.jpg" /></div>
```

Some other characteristics of the text-align property can be found in Table 7-5.

The Text-Transform Property

Another interesting CSS text property is *text-transform*. This property allows you to convert or "transform" text from lowercase to uppercase and vice versa. It also enables you to capitalize the first letter of every word in a sentence or paragraph, creating something similar to title case. However, you can not create a genuine title case with this property. Genuine title case will leave parts of speech such as articles, conjunctions, and prepositions uncapitalized; however,

Does it inherit?	Default value	Browser support	Works with
Yes	Left	Excellent	Block-level elements

Table 7-5 Characteristics of the Text-Align Property

the CSS text-transform property capitalizes every word to which it is applied. Nevertheless, it is a useful property to be familiar with. The text-transform property accepts only keywords as values. These are

- **None**   This is the default value and causes no change to any letters.

- **Uppercase**   All the letters will be converted to uppercase.

- **Capitalize**   Capitalizes the first letter of every word.

- **Lowercase**   Converts all characters to lowercase.

The effect of the text-transform property is easy to see by simply typing the following lines of code into an HTML document. The first line applies the "lowercase" value to a sentence typed only in capital letters. The second line does the opposite. The third line applies the "capitalize" value to a sentence typed in lowercase:

```
<div style="text-transform: lowercase;">
THIS WAS TYPED IN UPPER CASE!</div>
<div style="text-transform: uppercase;">
this was typed in lower case!</div>
<div style="text-transform: capitalize;">
this was also typed in lower case!</div>
```

When you view this portion of code in a browser, you should see something like the following illustration:

> this was typed in upper case!
> THIS WAS TYPED IN LOWER CASE!
> This Was Also Typed In Lower Case!

The text-transform property is strongly supported, and you can use it without much concern about compatibility. Table 7-6 lists some other characteristics of this property that you should be familiar with.

The Text-Indent Property

Of all the CSS text properties, text-indent is perhaps the most welcomed by Web designers. Ironically, although HTML was originally developed for presenting

Does it inherit?	Default value	Browser support	Works with
Yes	None	Excellent	All elements

Table 7-6	Characteristics of the text-transform Property

text-based documents, it has never had a good method for indenting text. The paragraph, <p>, element adds an extra line break to set off a new paragraph, but it doesn't indent text. Thus, Web designers tend to use the *non-breaking space* entity ( ) whenever they need to indent text. To indent a line five spaces, you would write your code this way:

```
     Text begins here . . .
```

While this method works, it is also rather tedious, particularly if you need to do a lot of indenting.

Another option is the use of the preformatted text, <pre>, element. Using this element, a designer can add spaces the conventional way, with the spacebar or by tabbing. The <pre> forces the browser to retain the designer's text formatting and, thus, the indents. Unfortunately, this involves a trade-off of sorts, because the browser displays the text in a typewriter-like monospace font.

If either of the two preceding options are not acceptable, a designer can always borrow the definition description, <dd>, element from the HTML code for definition lists. The definition description element is intended to be used in tandem with the definition term, <dt>, element. Definition description is intended to cause a "definition" to indent, thus highlighting the term being defined. However, in a pinch it also works pretty well for indenting text. Unfortunately, it also is one of those cases where a designer is using a structural element for presentational purposes—and that's exactly what the W3C is trying to get away from with CSS.

The text-indent property solves the problem neatly by enabling you to specify an indent for your text in a style sheet. For example, if you want every paragraph on your page to be indented by 1/2 inch, you can specify that with a single style rule. After that, the first line of every <p> element on your page will be indented by that amount. That sure beats having to add five non-breaking space entities for every paragraph. The text indent property enables you to specify your indents with either length or percentage measurements.

7

- **Length**   Text-indent will accept any standard length measurements (in, cm, mm, pt, pc, em, ex, px).

- **Percentage**   When using percentages with text-indent, the percentage is based on the width of the parent element. In most cases, this will probably be the <body> element. Thus, a value of 5% is, in effect, five percent of the width of the screen.

Keep in mind that if you choose a percentage value when you use the indent property, your indent will be able to "scale" or adjust with the browser display. For example, an indent of 5% adjusts up and down, depending on the size of the browser window. The following illustration shows the indent with the window at nearly full width:

> The text-indent property enables Web designers to indent their text using fixed values such as inches, centimeters, millimeters, points, and picas. It also makes it possible to use relative values such as pixels, exes, and ems. Perhaps the most versatile method for setting an indent is by using a percentage. For example, this paragraph was indented with a value of 5%. That means the indent will be five percent of the parent element. In this case, that's the browser window. If you display this paragraph in a browser, then adjust the size of the browser window, you will see that the indent adjusts as well.

Note

For this illustration and the one that follows, the entire paragraph was also indented. This was done by specifying right and left margins of 15%. If you want to learn how to set margins, check out Module 9.

When the window is reduced to about one fourth of the normal width, the indent shrinks to accommodate the smaller window size, as in the following illustration:

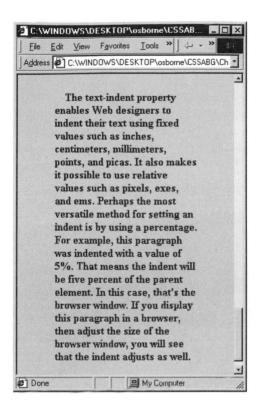

Another useful characteristic of the text-indent property is that it will accept
negative values, thus enabling you to create "hanging indents." Other important
characteristics of this property are listed in Table 7-7.

The Line-Height Property

There may be times when you want to either increase or decrease the amount of
space between lines on your pages. Perhaps you have a large portion of text and
you want to create a "double-spaced" effect. Or, you might want to move your

Does it inherit?	Default value	Browser support	Works with
Yes	None	Excellent	All elements

Table 7-7 Characteristics of the text-indent property

body text closer to your headings. This task, and many more, can be accomplished by using line-height. The line-height property enables you to specify the distance between baselines. In print terminology, this is controlling the "leading." That is, you are setting the space between the baselines, not the vertical dimensions of the letters.

Hint

The baseline is the line that the letter actually rests on. For example, if you are writing on lined notebook paper, the baseline would be the lines on the paper. Even though parts of some letters may extend beneath the baseline (these are called *descenders*), the line-height property adjusts only the space between the baselines.

The line-height property accepts length, percentage, or number values:

● **Length**   Line-height accepts standard length measurements. Keep in mind that when you specify a line height, you are specifying a minimum height.

● **Percentage**   Percentage measurements are figured relative to the font specified for the element to which the style is applied, not the parent element.

● **Number**   It is possible to specify a number value for the line height. The browser will multiply the number by the font size in calculating the line height. This is the generally recommended type of value to use when applying line-height to your pages.

Again, in this instance a visualization might help. The illustration that follows has four <h1> headings, each set with a different line height. The background for each heading reflects the difference in line height, based on the settings each heading describes

The line height is normal
The line height is set at 25%.
The line height is set at .50em.

The line height is set at 2.0

```
<h1 style="background-color: white;">The line
height is normal</h>
<h1 style="background-color: white; line-height: 25%;">
The line height is set at 25%.</h>
<h1 style="background-color: cyan; line-height: .50em">
The line height is set at .50em.</h>
<h1 style="background-color: yellow; line-height: 2.0;">
The line height is set at 2.0</h>
```

The line-height property does not accept negative values. Table 7-8 lists some other important characteristics of this property.

The Text-Shadow Property (CSS2)

The text-shadow property is one case where a text property's characteristics seem to overlap into the territory of the font properties. As was mentioned earlier in this module, text properties, as a rule, influence the *position* of text while font properties influence the *appearance* of text. However, the text-shadow property, introduced as part of the CSS2 specification, is intended to enable you to create a "drop-shadow" effect.

Unfortunately, since at this writing no browsers support this effect, you won't be able to practice it. However, if you could create a text shadow using CSS, you would only need to specify a vertical axis (x-axis), a horizontal axis (y-axis), a blur ratio, and a color. If you've ever worked with a graphics program such as Adobe Photoshop or Paint Shop Pro to create drop shadows, you're already familiar with this approach. You specify values using "lengths," such as pixels. The x-axis specifies how far below the text the shadow should drop, the y-axis specifies how far to the right of the text the shadow should display. The blur ratio will determine whether the shadow is sharp or "fuzzy." The higher the blur ratio number, the "fuzzier" the shadow. For example, the illustration that follows demonstrates what a drop shadow might look like if you used the following rule:

```
h1      {text-shadow: 4px, 4px, 0, black;}
```

This is text-shadow

The text-shadow property will accept negative values for the x and y axis values only. If you use negative values with these, it will cause the shadow to display

Does it inherit?	Default value	Browser support	Works with
Yes	Normal	Inconsistent	All elements

Table 7-8 Characteristics of the line-height Property

up and left, rather than down and right. Other characteristics of this property are given in Table 7-9.

1-Minute Drill

● What property/value combination would you use to convert a line of text to all capitals?

● In creating an indent with text-indent, what type of value will enable your indent to adjust when the size of the browser window is changed?

Project 7-2: Create a Font Sampler

As you learn how to work with CSS, you need to develop skills in using selectors, properties, and values. In this project, you will apply the text properties you are learning about in this module to create a "font sampler" page. You will also have the opportunity to practice working with class selectors and some of the font properties you learned about in Module 6.

Step-by-Step

1. Create a blank HTML document and save it as font_sampler.htm. Create a second blank text document and save it as font_sampler.css.

2. Add a link in the <head> portion of font_sampler.htm that will link the page to font_sampler.css. Remember that you will need to use the <link />

Does it inherit?	Default value	Browser support	Works with
No	None	Not Supported	All elements

Table 7-9 Characteristics of the text-shadow Property

● text-transform: uppercase;
● A percentage value

element, along with the rel, type, and href attributes. If you're not sure of the correct values, check the complete code listing at the end of this project.

3. In the <body> of font_sampler, add an <h1> heading that reads: **Font Sampler**.

4. Add an <h2> that reads: **Serif**.

5. Below your <h2> heading, type out the alphabet with both uppercase and lowercase letters, like this: **AaBbCc**, and so on. Use the <br /> tag to create a line break after "Mm."

6. Repeat that process four more times, changing only your <h2> headings. You should have headings that read: "Sans-Serif," "Monospace," "Cursive," and "Fantasy." All five of your alphabet lists should be enclosed in a set of <div> tags. This will cause them to function as block-level elements, adding some spacing between the different font groups. Your completed page should look something like the following illustration:

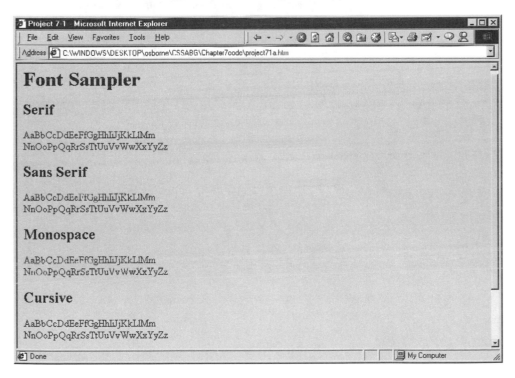

7. Set aside font_sampler.htm for a moment and work on font_sampler.css. Write a style rule for the h1 selector that will cause the text to align to the center of the page. You will need to use the text-align property for this.

8. Add an underline to all of your second-level headings by writing a style rule for the h2 selector. You will use the text-decoration property with "underline" as its value.

9. Create a class selector named ".serif" and write a declaration setting its font family as "serif." Align it to the right side of the page with the text-align property.

10. Create four more class selectors: .sans-serif, .monospace, .cursive, and .fantasy. Set the font family for each of your classes to be the same as the class name. Experiment with alignment by using the text-align property to align sans-serif to the right, set monospace to justify, align cursive to the left, and don't set any alignment for fantasy.

11. Save font_sampler.css and then open font_sampler.htm in your text editor.

12. Add the "class" attribute and the appropriate class name to each of the opening <div> tags in order to apply the style rules you just wrote. For example, to apply styles from the serif class selector, you would write <div class="serif">. Once you have added all of the class names to their respective <div> tags, save and reload font_sampler.htm in your browser. It should look something like the following illustration:

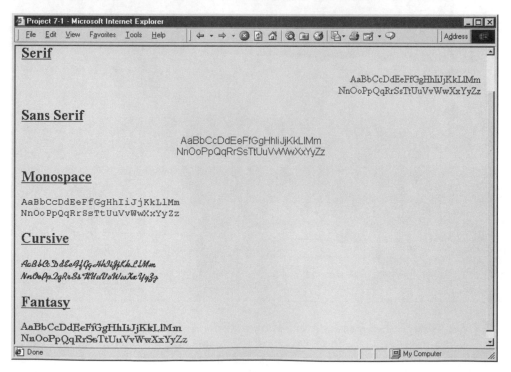

13. Once you've experimented with the text-align property, reset the alignment for all of your alphabet lines by removing the text-align declarations from the serif, sans-serif, monospace, and cursive rules. Because the default alignment is "left," all your alphabet lines will be aligned on the left side of the screen.

14. Transform all of your <h2> headings into capital letters by adding the text-transform property and the "uppercase" value to the h2 selector.

15. Bring your headings closer to the alphabet listings by using the line-height property with the h1 and h2 selectors. Set the line height to .5 ems.

16. Cause the alphabet lists to spread farther across the page by using the letter-spacing property with the div selector. Set the letter spacing to .5 ems.

17. Add a final touch of color by writing a style rule for the body selector. Set the background-color to a light beige by using a mixture of RGB 100%,100%,80%. Set the text color by using the color property. This time, use hexadecimal to choose a dark reddish brown color. The code you should use is #993300.

18. Save both font_sampler.css and font_sampler.htm and reload your sampler page in your browser. It should resemble the following illustration:

7

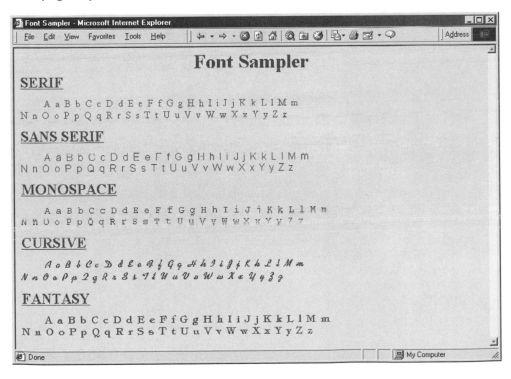

font_sampler.css

```
body                {background-color: rgb(100%,100%,80%);
                     color: #993300;}
h1                  {text-align: center; line-height: .5em;}
h2                  {text-decoration: underline;
                     text-transform: uppercase;
                     line-height: .5em;}
.serif              {font-family: serif;}
.sans-serif         {font-family: sans-serif;}
.monospace          {font-family: monospace;}
.cursive            {font-family: cursive;}
.fantasy            {font-family: fantasy;}
div                 {letter-spacing: .5em;}
```

font_sampler.htm

```
<html>
<head>
<title>Font Sampler</title>
<link rel="stylesheet" type="text/css"
href="font_sampler.css" />
</head>
<body>
<h1>Font Sampler</h2>
<h2>Serif</h2>
<div class="serif">AaBbCcDdEeFfGgHhIiJjKkLlMm<br />
NnOoPpQqRrSsTtUuVvWwXxYyZz</div>
<h2>Sans Serif</h2>
<div class="sans-serif">AaBbCcDdEeFfGgHhIiJjKkLlMm<br />
NnOoPpQqRrSsTtUuVvWwXxYyZz</div>
<h2>Monospace</h2>
<div class="monospace">AaBbCcDdEeFfGgHhIiJjKkLlMm<br />
NnOoPpQqRrSsTtUuVvWwXxYyZz</div>
<h2>Cursive</h2>
<div class="cursive">AaBbCcDdEeFfGgHhIiJjKkLlMm<br />
NnOoPpQqRrSsTtUuVvWwXxYyZz</div>
<h2>Fantasy</h2>
<div class="fantasy">AaBbCcDdEeFfGgHhIiJjKkLlMm<br />
NnOoPpQqRrSsTtUuVvWwXxYyZz</div>
</body>
</html>
```

Project Summary

By creating a font-sampler, you have been able to experiment with some of the basic text properties, including the text-align, text-decoration, text-transform, line-height, and letter-spacing properties. You have also been able to observe just how much control even a simple style sheet can give you over how a page displays. You have also had the chance to practice working with class selectors and to see how you can use them to apply style rules without being limited to using a type selector (an HTML element name).

7

Mastery Check

1. Which property would you use to create an "overline" effect?

    A. text-transform

    B. text-shadow

    C. text-top

    D. text-decoration

2. Which of these style rules is written incorrectly and why?

    A. h1 {word-spacing: 2em;}

    B. .extra {letter-spacing: -.25%;}

    C. #first   {line-height: -2.2em;}

3. The text-align property should be used in place of what HTML attribute?

    _____

    _____

4. A percentage value used with text-indent is measured relative to which of the following:

    A. The user's monitor screen

    B. The parent element

    C. The element in question

    D. The browser window

Module 8

Applying Color and Background Properties

The Goals of this Module

- Set Foreground and Background Colors
- Add a Background Image
- Learn How to Create Horizontal and Vertical "Tiles"
- Position Background Images
- Create a Fixed Background
- Learn How to Use the Background Shorthand Property

There's no doubt about it; color makes everything more interesting. If you don't believe it, try asking the average ten-year-old to watch an old movie with you. Very likely, the first question you'll get will be, "Is it in black and white?" The implication is that if the movie's not in color, it's not going to be fun to watch. The merits of the film notwithstanding, the point is well taken. People prefer color to black and white. Can you imagine how drab our world would be if there were no colors, if we lived in a grayscale universe? It wouldn't be a pretty picture. The same is true with Web pages.

The careful use of text colors, background colors, and background images can greatly enhance the appearance of a Web page. HTML provided means to add background and text colors and to add background images. CSS also enables you to accomplish these same goals with your pages—and more—with the color and background properties.

Add Color and Images

The best place to begin learning how to use the color and background properties is with those properties that correspond most closely to HTML. HTML provides an array of tools that enable you to easily add text and background colors as well as images to a Web page. For instance, to add a background color to a page you would use the "bgcolor" attribute inside the <body> tag, like this:

```
<body bgcolor="white">.
```

If you want to add an image you would use the "background" attribute, as in the following listing:

```
<body bgcolor="white" background="image.gif">
```

To set the default text color for a page, you would merely add the text attribute to the preceding tag, like this:

```
<body bgcolor="white" background="image.gif" text="navy">
```

To set colors for text other than the default, of course, you would use the now deprecated <font> element. Specifying red as a font color would involve writing a line of code similar to this:

```
<font color="red">This text is red</font>
```

You might be wondering how CSS improves on such a simple system and why you should bother learning to apply color and background images with CSS. The answers lie in the fact that CSS overcomes several limitations inherent in the way HTML allows you to work with color and image backgrounds. CSS opens up more design options by enabling you to add color and background images to *any element*; it also gives you greater control over the position of background images.

CSS Overcomes HTML's Limitations

If you are setting background colors and images with HTML, you are limited to applying them to entire pages or individual table cells, because only the <body>, <table>, <tr>, <td>, and <th> elements will accept the "bgcolor" attribute. Likewise, only the <body> element will allow you to add images with the "background" attribute. On the other hand, with CSS you can specify background colors and even background images for virtually any HTML. As you will see in this module and later ones, this ability provides an alternative to the use of tables for page layouts.

Note

In theory, you can add background images and colors to *any* element. However, certain HTML elements (<meta> for instance) do not display. Thus, there would be no real purpose in adding background styles to these.

CSS also demonstrates its superiority to HTML in the positioning of background images. If you use HTML to insert a background image on a page, you are limited to a single image, *and* that image will be "tiled" down the entire page. But what if you simply want to include a copy of your company logo at the top-right corner of every page. You can do this with HTML, but only by using the following code on every single page:

```
<img src="myimage.gif" align="right" />
```

Contrast this with CSS, where you can write a style rule *one time* that will add your logo to every page on your site, if you choose. This gives you many more design options than you have with HTML alone. Thus, as you begin to work

8

with the color and background properties, you will find that, although they can be a little more complicated than HTML, the benefits you reap will be worth the time you invest in learning how to use them.

The Color Property

If you have worked through Modules 6 and 7, you may have wondered why there were no font-color or text-color properties listed. It would, after all, seem logical that these properties would be used for controlling text color. In fact, as you begin working with CSS in your Web pages you might actually find yourself adding a declaration that reads "font-color: blue," then wondering why your text is still black. It just feels natural to specify your text colors that way. Unfortunately, if you plan on using CSS you'll have to get used to adjusting text with the "color" property.

The color property doesn't specifically set text color. Rather, you use it to set the *foreground* color of an HTML document. However, it is most commonly associated with text because an element's text content generally *is* considered to be its foreground. As the following illustration shows, adjusting the color property will affect the color of an element's text:

\<h1\> with color property set to rgb(0%,0%,0%)

\<h2\> with color property set to rgb(20%,20%,20%)

\<h3\> with color property set to rgb(40%,40%,40%)

\<h4\> with color property set to rgb(60%,60%,60%)

```html
<html>
<head>
<title>The Color Property</title>
<style> h1 {color: rgb(0%,0%,0%);}
        h2 {color: rgb(20%,20%,20%);}
        h3 {color: rgb(40%,40%,40%);}
        h4 {color: rgb(60%,60%,60%);}</style>
</head>
<body>
<h1>&lt;h1&gt; with color set to rgb(0%,0%,0%)</h1>
<h2>&lt;h2&gt; with color set to rgb(20%,20%,20%)</h2>
<h3>&lt;h3&gt; with color set to rgb(40%,40%,40%)</h3>
<h4>&lt;h4&gt; with color set to rgb(60%,60%,60%)</h4>
</body></html>
```

Ask the Expert

Question: In the preceding code, what does <h1> mean?

Answer: It may look like "gobbledygook," but it's the only way you can refer to an HTML tag in a portion of text. If the sentences were written "<h4> with color set to . . .", the browser would interpret the <h4> to be an HTML tag, rather than as part of the display. So, to display characters such as this, you have to use *entities*. Entities are simply code descriptions that tell the browser to insert special characters in the display. In this case you need the "less than" and "greater than" symbols to display an HTML tag. The entity for "less than" is <, and the entity for "greater than" is >. Thus, to display an HTML tag as part of a page, you would enclose the element name in the two entities mentioned in the preceding sentence. Your code will look like <h1>, but your display will look like <h1>.

The color property will accept any of the five standard methods for defining color. Since these were covered in detail in Module 4, only a brief summary will be included here. You can specify color by using

- **Keywords**   Any of the 16 Windows VGA color keywords will work. These are the following: black, white, silver, gray, red, blue, green, yellow, fuschia (magenta), lime, navy, maroon, olive, teal, purple, and aqua (cyan).

- **Hexadecimal**   You can specify values in hexadecimal code. For example, blue would be #0000ff.

- **Shortened Hex**   CSS will also accept a shortened version of the hexadecimal code. For instance, the code for blue in a shortened version would be #00f.

- **RGB Percentage Values**   You can also specify colors using percentage values that describe the amount of red, green, and blue contained in each color. In this case, blue would be described as rgb(0%,0%,100%)

- **RGB Numerical Values**   Numerical values for RGB are also acceptable for specifying color in CSS. Using numerical values, blue would be represented as rgb(0,0,255).

8

Does it inherit?	Default value	Browser support	Works with
Yes	Determined by the browser	Strong	All elements

Table 8-1   Characteristics of the color Property

Other important characteristics of the color property are listed above in Table 8-1.

The Background-Color Property

A close relative of the color property is the background-color property. This property is the CSS counterpart to HTML's "bgcolor" attribute. However, it has a great advantage over "bgcolor" in that it can be applied to any element. As you will learn in Modules 9 and 11, the ability to set backgrounds for any element combined with the ability to position those elements anywhere on the page will open up a host of design options for you.

Values

The background-color property accepts the same values as does the color property, plus one more. As with color, you can specify any color value through the five means listed in the preceding section. However, background-color also allows for a value of "transparent." In fact, this is the default value, and for good reason. To understand why, imagine that instead of transparent the default background-color for all selectors was white. This would work fine as long as you stuck with a white background overall. However, suppose you created a page and decided to set its background to aqua. When you displayed your page, you would get something like what you see in Figure 8-1.

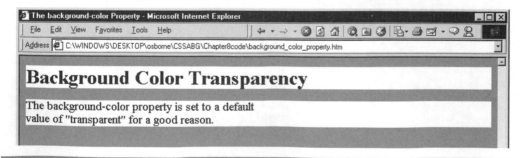

Figure 8-1   Page elements with non-transparent backgrounds

As you can see, if the background were not set to transparent, you would have a white background behind each of the page elements rather than the aqua background you wanted. There may be times when you want to create such an effect, but more often than not you will want the background color or image to "shine" through. That's why transparent is the default value.

Syntax

The basic syntax for assigning a background color is essentially the same as it is for the color property. To specify a background color for an entire page, you would apply the style declaration to the body selector. For example, to set a page's background color to yellow, you would write a style rule similar to the following one:

```
body        {background-color: yellow;}
```

You can also set background colors for individual selectors, just as you would assign any other styles. All of the following style rules are acceptable:

```
h1        {background-color: red;}
.olive    {background-color: olive;}
#1542     {background-color: rgb(122,232,85);}
ol li em  {background-color: #f0f;}
table     {background-color: #33cc00;}
p.spec    {background-color: rgb(35%,35%,85%);
```

─*Hint*─────────────────────────────────
Figure 8-1 was created by assigning a background-color of white to the "h1" and "p" selectors.
───

8

Characteristics

The background-color property is easy to use and apply. However, you should keep in mind some of its key characteristics when you work with it. An essential characteristic of background-color and all the rest of the background properties is that they are *not* inherited. The basic reasoning is simple. If background properties inherit, then you are going to wind up with a confusing jumble of backgrounds for your Web pages. Therefore, for the sake of consistency, the W3C has designed CSS to prevent background properties from being passed on from ancestor to descendent elements. As mentioned earlier in this section, this is also why the default value for background colors is set to "transparent." Table 8-2 lists some other important characteristics of the background-color property.

The Background-Image Property

As its name implies, the background-image property enables you to use an image for a background, rather than simply a color. Again, strictly speaking there is nothing new in the ability to add a background image. However, as you'll discover later in this module, CSS enables you to do quite a bit more with background images than you can with HTML alone.

Values

The background-image property takes as its value the URL of the image you want to use. As with HTML, you can use either *absolute* or *relative* URLs to point to the image. For instance, if the image and your stylesheet are in the same directory, you could write a background image declaration like this:

```
body      {background-image: url(mypics.jpg);}
```

However, suppose you have a large site, and your style sheets are stored in one directory while your images are in another. In this case, either you would need to list the specific directory in your declaration (absolute URL), as in the following listing,

```
body      {background-image:
url(http://www.mywebsite.com/images/mypics.jpg);}
```

or you would need to use a relative URL to tell the browser where to look for the file, as is illustrated in the code that follows. An easy way to do that is simply to add two dots and a slash in front of the directory name. This tells the browser to back up one directory (from the stylesheet directory to the root directory), then to go down to the images directory, as in the listing that follows.

```
#s120     {background-image:
url(../images/mypics.jpg);}
```

Does it inherit?	Default value	Browser support	Works with
No	Transparent	Strong	All elements

Table 8-2   Characteristics of the background-color Property

Tip

You have to use the ../ code once for every directory that the browser must "back up." Thus, if the browser needed to back up two directories before going down to the images directory, the listing would look like this: ../../images/mypics.jpg.

You can also direct the browser to pull an image from a different Web site:

```
p.special       {background-image:
url(http://www.anothersite.com/images/image.gif);}
```

If you don't use any of the other background properties to define how background-image displays, then your image will tile to fill the page (if used with the body selector), as in the following illustration:

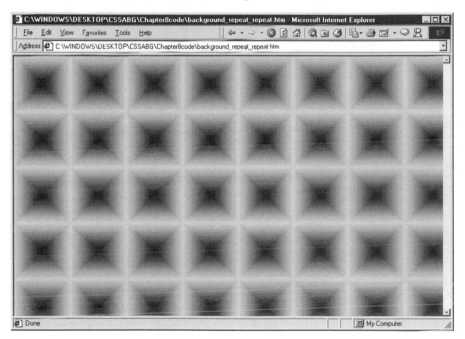

Syntax

The syntax for the background-image property is simple, but if you're not careful it can trip you up. If you're used to working with HTML, this is a case where it is easy to slip into HTML syntax without even realizing it. You might be working in a hurry, or maybe you're tired, and you dash off a line like this:

```
td      {background-image: newpicture.gif;}
```

It feels perfectly natural; unfortunately, it's also wrong. The worst part is that this is not the kind of syntax error that will jump out at you when you are trying to figure out why your background image isn't showing up. Therefore, make sure you are very familiar with the way you have to write a URL value with Cascading Style Sheets. It's not difficult, but it is different from the way you do it with HTML. For a URL value to work in CSS, it must be preceded by the letters "url," and the actual URL must be enclosed in parentheses. The listing below demonstrates the correct way to include a URL value for the background-image property.

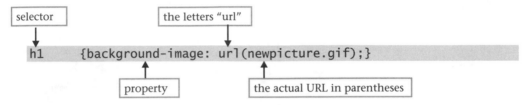

Characteristics

There are a few unique characteristics of the background-image property that should be noted. One of the most useful is that you are not limited to setting page or table backgrounds with this property. In fact, you can add a background image to virtually any element you wish. Headlines, paragraphs, tables, lists…you name it. The illustration that follows shows a level-one heading with a background image added.

Another important practice with the background-image property is to always use it in combination with the background-color property. Then, if for some reason your image does not load, you will still have the background color as a backup. Table 8-3 lists some other important characteristics of the background-image property.

Does it inherit?	Default value	Browser support	Works with
No	None	Strong	All elements

Table 8-3	Characteristics of the background-image Property

Tip

If you create your own images, you can achieve a nice effect by creating an image that has a transparent background, then using it with a background color. Your background color will show through those parts of the image that are transparent.

1-Minute Drill

● The "color" property sets the color for an element's _____.

● If you use the "background-image" property, what other property should you always use with it?

Project 8-1: Add Colors and a Background Image

One of the aspects of CSS that you will quickly come to appreciate is the ability it gives you to assign background colors and images to multiple pages from a single stylesheet. By taking advantage of this ability, you can create a distinctive "look" for your site without having to code each page separately. Another benefit of using stylesheets for background colors and images is that you can change the overall look of your site by merely modifying the stylesheet. In this project you will create several HTML documents and link them to the same stylesheet. In the stylesheet, you will add rules assigning foreground (text) and background colors as well as specifying an image that will "tile" across the page's background. If you get stuck and need help, the completed code is provided for you following the step-by-step instructions.

● Foreground
● Background-color

Step-by-Step

1. Create a directory on your hard drive and name it practice_site.

2. Create five blank HTML documents. Name and save them as page_1.htm, page_2.htm, and so on.

3. In the <title> element of each HTML document, give the pages a name. It can be simply "Page 1" (and so on), or you can name them as you might a regular Web site (home, faqs, links, and so forth).

4. Create a blank text document. Name it bgproperties.css and save it in the same directory as your HTML documents.

5. In the <head> element of each HTML document, add a <link /> tag that attaches the document to an external stylesheet. You will need to use the "rel," "type," and "href" attributes to properly link to the stylesheet.

6. Open bgproperties.css and add a style rule that sets the body text color to navy.

7. Write a style declaration setting the background color to a creamy off-white. The hex code would be #ffffcc. Try experimenting with other ways to write this color value.

8. Add a background image by writing a style rule that uses the background-image property. You can use an image (gif, jpg, png) from your system, or you can go to Osborne's Web site (**www.osborne.com**) and download the image used in the illustration for this project.

9. Use the background-repeat property (even though you haven't studied this property yet) to cause the background image to tile down the left side of the page. You do this by adding the following declaration: {background-repeat: repeat-y;}.

10. Add a rule that uses the text-align property to center the <h1> element.

11. Save and close bgproperties.css.

12. Go back to the five HTML documents you created earlier and add a line of text or two to each one, using the <h1> element. It doesn't particularly matter what you write; you just need to see how your text displays. After you've added text to your HTML files, save and close them.

13. Use your browser to display the HTML documents you created. Each one should have the same background image, background color, and text color, as in the following illustration:

bgproperties.css

```
body {color: navy;
      background-color: #ffffcc;
      background-image: url(ysample.gif);
      background-repeat: repeat-y;}

h1    {text-align: center;}
```

page_1.htm

```
<html><head>
<title>Index</title>
<link rel="stylesheet" type="text/css"
href="bgproperties.css" />
<style> </style></head>
<body>
<h1>CSS Background Properties</h1>
</body>
</html>
```

8

Project Summary

In this project, you learned how simple it is to add a professional touch to your site by setting the background properties for multiple pages with a linked stylesheet. If for some reason you want to modify an individual page without affecting the rest of the site, you could add different style rules in the <style> element of the page you want to change. Since the cascade favors an embedded stylesheet over a linked sheet, your changes would be applied. Later in this module, in Project 8-2, you will use this technique to modify the background properties of some of the pages you created in this exercise.

Control Image Placement and Attachment

The properties covered in the first section of this chapter all have their counterparts in HTML, and so they don't really add much that is new. However, major differences from HTML do come with the rest of the background properties. The background properties enable you to do much more with background colors and images than you could ever do with HTML alone. For instance, the *background-repeat* property makes it possible for you to control how (or if) your background image tiles. The *background-position* property gives you the ability to choose precisely where on the page an image should be placed or where the tiling should begin. The *background-attachment* property makes it possible for you to "fix" a background image's position so that it does not scroll along with the page contents.

The Backround-Repeat Property

With HTML's "background" attribute, you have virtually no control over how a background image displays. The image will repeat or tile until it fills the page. In contrast, background-repeat enables you to have an image tile vertically, horizontally, or until it fills the page. You can also specify that the image not repeat at all, but display only one time on the page. This capability is very useful if you want to display a logo or other single image on your pages.

Values

Background-repeat accepts only four specific values: repeat, repeat-x, repeat-y and no-repeat. *No-repeat* prevents the image from tiling and will display it only once. As you can see in the following screen shot, the image will display in the upper-left corner of the screen.

─┼─*Note*

The image in the following illustrations was used because it makes it easy to see how the tiling effect works. From a design standpoint, the background it creates is too "busy" and distracting.

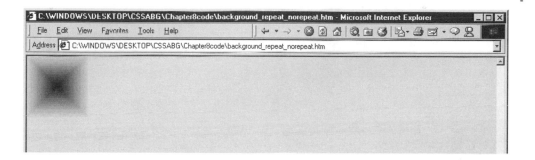

Repeat-x tells the browser to repeat the image along a single horizontal (x) axis. Unless its position has been specified with the background-position property, the image will tile across the top of the page. As the following illustration shows, this value can be used as an easy way to insert an image header in your pages:

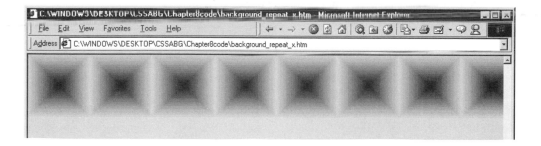

8

Repeat-y will repeat the image along a single vertical (y) axis. Its default position is on the left side of the page. Again, this value provides a nice quick way to add a sidebar effect to your pages, as the following illustration shows:

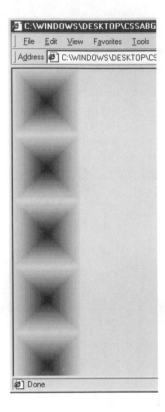

Repeat is the default value, and it will cause the image to tile until it fills the page or its containing "box." (For more on boxes and how they work in CSS, see Modules 9 and 11). If you specify a repeating background for the body selector, then the entire page will be filled with the image.

Tip

Since "repeat" is the default value, it is generally not necessary to actually use the "background-repeat: repeat" declaration. Anytime you add a background image, it will tile automatically.

Ask the Expert

Question: If a background image repeats automatically, what's the point of even having a "repeat" value?

Answer: There may be times when you want to override a style that has been set, but you don't want to do it "globally." Perhaps you have a background image set to "no-repeat" with a linked stylesheet, but there is a page where you would like it to repeat. You can use an embedded or inline style and set the value to "repeat" to force the image to tile.

Syntax

One thing to keep in mind about background-repeat syntax is that background-repeat must be used in conjunction with background-image. If no background image is specified, then background-repeat has nothing to work with. This is true of all the background properties. Remember also that you should always use the background color property as well. Thus, the following style rules would all be valid applications of the background-repeat property:

```
body      {background-color: white;
           background-image: url(image.jpg);
           background-repeat: repeat-y;}

p.bg      {background-color: white;
           background-image: url(pix.gif);
           background-repeat: repeat-x;}

p.logo    {background-color: white;
           background-image: url(logo.jpg);
           background-repeat: no-repeat;}

h1        {background-color: white;
           background-image: url(image.jpg);
           background-repeat: repeat;}
```

Characteristics

As you work with background-repeat, keep in mind two important characteristics of this property. First, if you do not specify a position for the image, the browser

8

will always default to the top and/or left of the screen or containing "box." Also, if you use any of the "tiling" values, part of the image may be cut off at the edges of the page. For a seamless tile image, that won't be a problem; however, for a company logo, it may be. Table 8-4 lists some other key characteristics of the background-repeat property.

The Background-Attachment Property

The background-attachment property is possibly the simplest of the background properties to explain. It simply gives you the option of allowing a background image to "scroll" along with the page or element content or of "fixing" it in place. If you choose the "fixed" value, then the image will remain stationary, but the foreground contents (text, images, and so on) will scroll when the user operates the scroll bar. Among other things, this property is useful for creating a "watermark" effect with a faint background image. It also is an easy way to add a header image at the top of your page that stays in place while the page's content scrolls over it. The values for this property are either "scroll" or "fixed," with scroll being the default value. The following style rule shows how the background-attachment property might be used to create a fixed background that fills the entire page.

```
body      {background-color: aqua;
           background-image: url(imagetile.png);
           background-attachment: fixed;}
```

As with the background-repeat property, it is generally not necessary to use background-attachment if you want the image to scroll along with the page contents. Other characteristics of the background-attachment property are listed in Table 8-5.

Does it inherit?	Default value	Browser support	Works with
No	Repeat	Strong	All elements

Table 8-4   Characteristics of the background-repeat Property

Does it inherit?	Default value	Browser support	Works with
No	Scroll	Strong	All elements

Table 8-5   Characteristics of the background-attachment Property

The Background-Position Property

The background-position property is perhaps the most versatile of the background properties; it can also be the most confusing to learn how to use. The potential for confusion is primarily due to the numerous ways you can specify a value for a background image's position. As you will see, the array of choices can become a bit overwhelming. However, once you learn how to use background-position, you'll be a long way down the road to understanding a key concept in CSS—the positioning of elements.

The background-position property tells the browser where to place the *initial* occurrence of your background image. In other words, since your background image can be displayed once, tiled horizontally or vertically, or repeated until the element's box is filled, there obviously must be a place where the *first* image goes. With the background-position property, you tell the browser where to place that image. For example, as the following illustration shows, if you create a page with a horizontal row of background tiles, and the background position is set to "left," the tile on the left side of the screen is complete, but the one on the right is partially cut off.

This is because the first image placed was on the left side. However, if you set the background position to center, as in the following illustration, you'll notice that the images on both ends are cut short. That's because the first

8

image was placed in the center of the page, and the rest of the images tiled out from there.

However, if you set the background position to right, then the complete image will be on the right side of the page, while the image on the left is cut off, as in the following illustration:

Simply put, the background-position property just tells the browser where to put the first "tile." If you've ever tiled a floor in your house, you'll know how important it is to place the first tile correctly. At least for your HTML documents, CSS does it for you with the background-position property.

Values

When applying a value to the background position property you need to keep in mind that the starting point is always the upper-left corner of the element's box. If you think in terms of coordinates, the upper-left corner would be (0%, 0%), with the first zero representing the horizontal axis and the second representing the vertical axis. Logically, then, the bottom-right corner will be (100%, 100%). If you understand that, you're ready to learn how to supply values for the background-position property. This property will accept percentages, length units, or keywords.

● **Percentages**   Percentage values may be supplied in any amount and even in negative values. However, keep in mind that a negative value or a value over 100% will move all or part of the image off the edge of its element's box, rendering that portion of the image invisible. Percentage values are the most versatile measurements, as they can "scale" along with the size of the browser window.

● **Length Units**   You can use length units (in, cm, mm, pt, pc, px) to set a position for an image. However, length units are absolute units of measure and will not scale or adjust to fit their environment. You can mix different length units, and you can even combine length units and percentages. However, length units cannot be combined with keywords.

Note

If you specify only one length value, it will be used for both axes.

● **Keywords**   A set of keywords [(top, center, bottom) (left, center, right)] can be used to place a background image; the words represent the percentage values of 0%, 50%, and 100% respectively. Keywords can be given in a combination of two words (not separated by commas), or the single words *top, left, center, right, bottom*. Single keywords will always result in the image being placed in the center of either the horizontal or vertical axis. For example, the keyword "top" will place the image at the top (0%) of the vertical axis, but since the horizontal axis isn't mentioned, it defaults to the center (50%) of the horizontal axis. Table 8-6 lists the positioning keywords and their corresponding percentage values.

8

top left	top	top right
left top	top center	right top
0% 0%	center top	100% 0%
	50% 0%	
left	center	right
center left	center center	center right
left center	50% 50%	right center
0% 50%		100% 50%
bottom left	bottom center	bottom right
left bottom	center bottom	right bottom
0% 100%	bottom	100% 100%
	50% 100%	

Table 8-6   Keyword and Percentage Values for background-position

Tip

If you don't specify anything, the default is top left, but if you specify one keyword coordinate, the default of the other will be center. Also, it doesn't matter what order keywords are in: "top center" *usually* lands you in the same place as "center top". (Explorer 3.0 does something different.) Also "top" and "bottom" apply only to vertical offsets, and "left" and "right" to horizontal.

Syntax

The syntax for the background-position property is easy to master, even if the actual positioning itself can be tricky. The style declaration should include two values, representing the x (horizontal) and y (vertical) coordinates where you want your image positioned. The only exception to this is if you are using the standalone keywords or a single length measurement, as mentioned in the preceding section. A comma should not separate the coordinates, and they do not need to be enclosed in parentheses. You can mix and match length units and percentages, but you cannot mix keywords with any other type of value. The following style rules demonstrate how background positioning can be applied:

```
body    {background-color: white;
         background-image: url(image.jpg);
         background-repeat: repeat-y;
         background-position: center center;}

div     {background-color: white;
         background-image: url(pix.gif);
         background-repeat: repeat-x;
         background-position: 37px 68%}

h1      {background-color: white;
         background-image: url(logo.jpg);
         background-repeat: no-repeat;
         background-position: top}

h2      {background-color: white;
         background-image: url(image.jpg);
         background-repeat: repeat;
         background-position: -15% 50%}
```

Characteristics

The background-position property works only with block-level or "replaced" elements. Thus, you would not be able to use the background-position property with inline elements, such as <b>, <span>, and so on. Other characteristics of the background-image property are listed in Table 8-7.

Ask the Expert

Question: What is a "replaced" element?

Answer: According to the CSS2 specification, a replaced element is "an element for which the CSS formatter knows only the intrinsic dimensions. In HTML, *IMG*, *INPUT*, *TEXTAREA*, *SELECT*, and *OBJECT* (italics mine) elements can be examples of replaced elements." Perhaps a simpler definition can be drawn from the term "replaced." Think of the <img /> element. The image element is an empty element that encloses no content of its own. Instead, it imports an image using the "src" attribute. Thus, the element itself is "replaced" by the image and it takes on that image's "dimensions."

The background: (shorthand) Property

In Module 6 you learned about the font: property. This is a "shorthand" property that allows you to make multiple declarations in a single style rule. With the background property, you can create a style rule that will set the values for the background-color, background-image, background-repeat, background-attachment, and background-position properties.

To use the background property, simply list the values for the background properties you want to adjust. It is not necessary to specify values for all of these properties, as CSS will automatically assign the default values for any that you do not include. There is no particular order in which the values must be listed. The only restriction is that if you set a value for the background-position property, the coordinates must be listed together (horizontal axis first). For example, the following style rule,

```
body      {background-color: yellow;
          background-image: url(bg.gif);
          background-repeat: no-repeat;
          background-attachment: fixed;
          background-position: center;}
```

Does it inherit?	Default value	Browser support	Works with
No	0,0	Strong	Block level and replaced elements

Table 8-7   Characteristics of the background-position Property

when used with the background property will look like this:

```
body
{background: yellow url(bg.gif) no-repeat fixed center}
```

Also, the following style rule is an acceptable application of the background property:

```
body {background: red url(bg.gif) 50% 100%}
```

Some other key characteristics of the background property are listed in Table 8-8.

1-Minute Drill

● Which values can not be mixed and matched when using the background-position property?

● What is the default value of the background-attachment property?

● In the background-repeat property, what do the letters *x* and *y* represent?

Project 8-2: Apply Background Properties

In Project 8-1 you created a mini Web site with five pages, linking all five pages to a stylesheet named "bgproperties.css." That linked stylesheet sets the overall style for your miniature site. However, you may wish to change some of the individual pages. In this project, you will get some practice using the background properties by embedding style rules in the individual pages you created. Should you need help, check out the code at the end of the Step-by-Step section. Since

Does it inherit?	Default value	Browser support	Works with
No	Not applicable with shorthand properties	Inconsistent	All elements

Table 8-8 Characteristics of the background Property

● Keyword values
● Scroll
● The horizontal and vertical axis, respectively.

the pages are otherwise identical, and the HTML code for them was provided in Project 8-1, only the style rules will be displayed.

Step-by-Step

1. Leave page_1.htm unchanged, but make changes to the background properties of the rest of the pages. As you make adjustments to each of the pages, use the shorthand "background:" property rather than the individual background properties. It is always advisable to set all five background properties at the same time, and the "background:" property is the easiest way to do that.

2. Open page_2.htm in a text editor and add a style rule that will change the background-repeat property to a horizontal axis instead of vertical. Change the text color to white. Change the background color to "rgb(0%,100%,100%)." Because the background: property resets the property values to their defaults, you will need to include a value for the background image, even though it is specified in the linked stylesheet. Your results should resemble the following illustration:

8

3. Open page_3.htm and change the background image to a logo image or a small photograph. Set the position of the image to center, the attachment to fixed, the background-repeat to no-repeat, and the background-color to white. This will create a "watermark" effect with the image fixed in the background. However, in order to see the effect, you will need to add enough text to make it scroll. You can do this by copying and pasting text from any file into the document. The following illustration shows how your document should look.

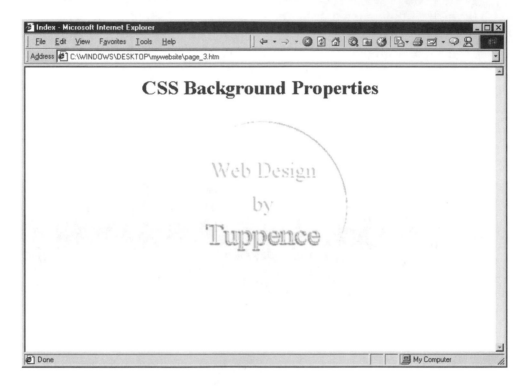

4. Open page_4.htm and change the text color to white, the background to maroon, and use a photograph for the background tile. If you don't have one of your own to work with, you can download the photo used in the following illustration from Osborne's Web site, along with all the other files created for this project.

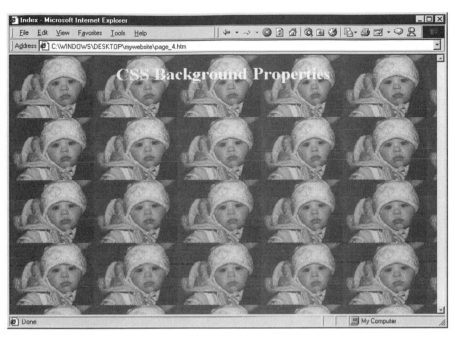

5. Open page_5.htm and set the background color to silver, then specify a background image with a horizontal repeat. Position the image so that it repeats across the bottom of the screen. Your results should resemble the following illustration:

8

page_2.htm

```
{color: white; background: repeat-x
rgb(0%,100%,100%) url(repeatsample.gif);}
```

page_3.htm

```
{background: white url(logo_sample.gif)
center fixed no-repeat;}
```

page_4.htm

```
{color: white; background: maroon url(cm2_150x112.jpg);}
```

page_5.htm

```
{background: #99ffff url(xsample.gif) bottom left repeat-x;}
```

Project Summary

In this project, you modified several HTML pages by adding embedded styles and using the "background:" property. You learned that since this property resets all five background property values to their defaults, when embedded on a page it will override all of the background styles and images specified in a linked stylesheet. Chances are that with an actual site you won't want to make so many drastic changes to your pages. Instead, you will be more likely to use the background properties to create a consistent "style" for all the pages on your site. With the background properties, this is easier than ever to accomplish.

☑ *Mastery Check*

1. Which of the following background-image declarations is *correctly* written?

    A. {background-image: (url)myimage.gif;}

    B. {background-image: newpix.gif;}

    C. {background-image: url goodpix.gif;}

    D. {background-image: url(oldpix.jpg);}

    E. {background-image: url="bgpx.png";}

2. To set the color for text, you use the _____ property.

    A. foreground-color

    B. color

    C. text-color

    D. font-color

3. Write a style rule for the <h1> element that will result in red text on a navy background.

    _____

4. Which of the following style rules will cause an image to tile vertically, down the right side of the page?

    A. body {background: white url(myimage.jpg) repeat-y right top;}

    B. h1   {background: white url(myimage.jpg) repeat-y right top;}

    C. body {background: white url(myimage.jpg) right top;}

    D. html {background: white url(myimage.jpg) repeat-x right top;}

5. Using the background: property, write a style rule for the <body> element that will set a white background and place a single logo image that is fixed in the upper-right corner of the page. Use percentage values for the positioning.

    _____

8

Module 9

Using Box Properties

The Goals of this Module

- Understand the Basics of the Box Model
- Set Margins with Margin Properties
- Add Padding with Padding Properties
- Create Borders with Border Properties

Creativity is sometimes described as "out of the box" thinking. This generally refers to thinking that is not bound by rigid constraints, but is free to try new approaches. Ironically, if you want to be set free from the "constraints" of HTML layout, you need to learn how to think "inside the box." In fact, you'll need to think inside, outside, and all around the box, because doing visual layout with CSS involves working with the "box" model. Among the essential aspects of the box model are the box properties. Although Module 11 devotes much greater detail to the box model and how it works, it's important to understand the basics if you want to learn how the box properties work.

Understand the Box Model

In previous modules you've read about how in CSS all elements are contained in invisible boxes. Although the concept of boxes for page layout might seem foreign to you, you've probably encountered it many times. If you've ever used a desktop publisher, image editor, or even one of the popular greeting card programs, you have probably worked with boxes. For example, if you enter text, often the text will appear outlined by a rectangular box that allows you to position it wherever you want on the page. Thus, when you move the box around, you also move its contents. That's also true of the content boxes on a Web page designed with CSS. When you work through Module 11 and learn how to position boxes, you will discover just how important the box model is to CSS layout.

HTML Tables and the Box Model

HTML tables are another area where you have possibly encountered concepts similar to the CSS box model. In fact, tables are a great place to start learning about the box properties, because most people who work with HTML have inevitably turned to tables as a means of doing page layout. Also, the areas of similarity between tables and boxes provide some common ground to help you make the transition from tables to CSS for your layout needs. For example, suppose you create a simple table in HTML that has three columns and three rows, as in the following illustration:

Content Content Content
Content Content Content
Content Content Content

```
<html><head><title>Table Demo 1</title>
<style>table  {background-color: white; font-size:1.5em;}
</style></head>
<body>
<table align="center" border="0">
<tr><td>Content</td><td>Content</td><td>Content</td></tr>
<tr><td>Content</td><td>Content</td><td>Content</td></tr>
<tr><td>Content</td><td>Content</td><td>Content</td></tr>
</table>
</body></html>
```

At first glance, it's difficult to tell whether the illustration is a one-celled table with the word "Content" written nine times, or whether it is a nine-celled table. However, as the following illustration demonstrates, if you add a border to the table the actual number of cells instantly becomes clear.

Content	Content	Content
Content	Content	Content
Content	Content	Content

```
<table align="center" border="1" bordercolor="black">
```

Now you know that you have nine cells, each containing "Content." However, as a designer you may feel that the layout is too cramped. So, you decide to add some "padding" inside each of the cells using HTML's "cellpadding" attribute. By modifying the opening <table> tag to add the attribute cellpadding="15", you add fifteen pixels of padding around the content of each table cell. As the next illustration demonstrates, this adds room inside each of the cells:

Content	Content	Content
Content	Content	Content
Content	Content	Content

```
<table align="center" border="1" bordercolor="black"
cellpadding="15">
```

Next, you can also add the "cellspacing" attribute. This will add space *between* the individual table cells. By giving a cellspacing value of 15 pixels, you will add 15 pixels of space around and between all of the cells, as is shown by the following screen shot:

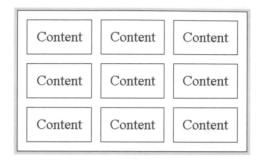

```
<table align="center" border="1" bordercolor="black"
cellpadding="15" cellspacing="15">
```

Thus, if you examine the preceding illustration closely, you'll notice that the table has four important characteristics:

● **Cell contents** Whatever is put inside the <td> element

● **Border** A line drawn around the outside of each cell

● **Cell Padding** Extra space inside the cell, surrounding its contents

● **Cell Spacing** Extra space around the outside of cells

If you're thinking that this doesn't sound all that difficult, congratulations. You've just grasped the essence of the box model.

Box Model Basics

The CSS box model closely parallels HTML tables in that you have the same four key characteristics coming into play: content, border (around the box), padding (inside the box), and margin (outside the box). However, in the case of CSS you are not limited to the restrictive "row and column" structure of a table. As you'll learn in Module 11, you can position elements anywhere on the page, even overlapping and stacking them. Another advantage you have with CSS is that you can apply borders, padding, and margins *selectively*. If you choose, you can add a border to the top of an element, some padding on the left side, adjust the margin on the right side, and leave the bottom untouched. It's all up to you.

Content

The basic idea behind HTML elements is that (with the exception of empty elements) they function much like *containers*. Thus, the first consideration when dealing with the box properties is the element's *content*. Consider the following illustration in which you have two lines of text, each contained in a separate <p> element. The background of each has been set to white so that you can see each element's containing box. This illustration represents the elements' content:

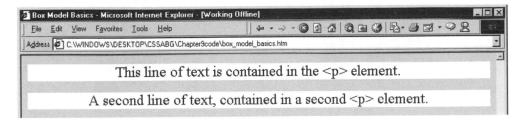

+Tip ───

Notice how the *baseline* of the text is not at the very bottom of the containing box. Instead, the box surrounds the element's contents completely, just as it does in a table.

9

```
<style>
body      {font-size: 1.5em;}
p         {background-color: white;
           text-align: center;}
</style>
```

Border

In addition to a containing box, each element can have a *border*. With tables, you are pretty limited in this area. A border must be drawn around all of the table cells or none of them; you can't "pick and choose." However, with CSS, you can add borders to certain elements while leaving others without borders. Also, with tables you have very limited control over the border style. You can control the pixel width of a table border and (with IE's bordercolor, bordercolorlight, and bordercolordark attributes) you can use color to alter the appearance of the table's border. As you'll see later in this module, CSS goes much further in providing ten different styles that you can assign to a border, not to mention providing the ability to adjust its width and color. By applying the border property to the preceding example, the appearance of the <p> element is changed to look like this:

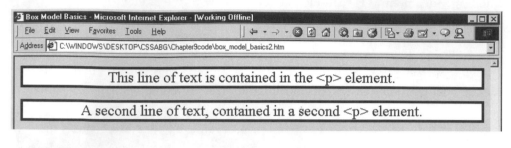

```
<style>
body      {font-size: 1.5em;}
p         {background-color: white;
           text-align: center;
           border-color: black;
           border-style: solid;}
</style>
```

Padding

With HTML tables you can add "cellpadding" inside individual table cells; with CSS you can add "padding" inside the containing box of any element. Padding essentially increases the size of the containing box, much like blowing up a balloon increases the size of the balloon by adding space inside it. For example if you add 15 pixels of padding to the "p" selector from the preceding illustration, your display will look like this:

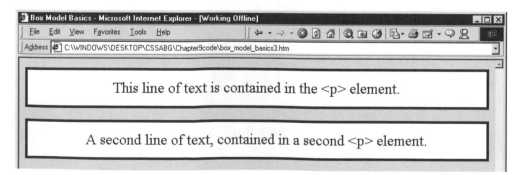

```
<style>
body       {font-size: 1.5em;}
p          {background-color: white;
            text-align: center;
            border-color: black;
            border-style: solid;
            padding: 15px;}
</style>
```

Margins

The fourth component of a "containing box" is actually the space *around* the box. With HTML tables, this is called "cellspacing"; with CSS, it is referred to as "margin." Among other things, by adding margin space you can increase the space around the outside of an element's containing box. For example, if you add a margin value of 25% to the "p" selector from the preceding illustration, the containing boxes look much different. The illustration that follows demonstrates the change in appearance created by adding margin space:

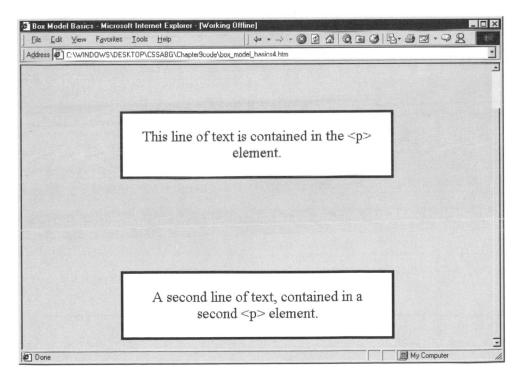

9

```
body       {font-size: 1.5em;}
p          {background-color: white;
            text-align: center;
            border-color: black;
            border-style: solid;
            padding: 15px;
            margin: 25%;}
</style>
```

There is much more to the box model than has been covered thus far. However, understanding these basics will enable you to grasp how the box properties work. As you work with CSS in general and the box properties in particular, keep in mind that by manipulating the four key components of the box model—content, padding, border, and margin—you can control the position of elements and the overall appearance of your page. Figure 9-1 illustrates the box model and its four components.

1-Minute Drill

● List the four components of the box model.

● What is the box model's closest counterpart in HTML?

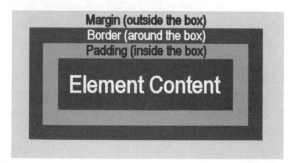

Figure 9-1   The four components of the box model

● Content, padding, border, and margin
● Tables

Project 9-1: Work with the Box Model

Although you'll learn about the box properties in detail in the next section of this module, you will benefit from doing a simple project that applies the box shorthand properties. Just as with the background and font properties, the box properties have shorthand versions that simplify their use. This is helpful because, as you will see later, if you are setting specific properties (for example, border-bottom-width, padding-left, margin-top), things can get complicated. However, if you want to set the same value uniformly all around, you can use the shorthand properties: border, padding, and margin. In this project, you will experiment with the shorthand properties by creating a welcome mat for your Web site's front door.

Step-by-Step

1. Create an HTML document and save it as "welcome.htm."

2. In the <body> of the document, use the <h1> element to create a heading that reads "Welcome to my Web site!"

3. Add a set of <style> tags in the <head> portion of the document.

4. Set the page background color to a dark green, rgb(20%, 40%, 0%), and the text color to gold, rgb(100%, 80%, 20%). Use the background-color and color properties, respectively.

5. Use the text-align property to center the <h1> element.

6. Resize the text for the h1 selector to 4 ems.

7. Set the text color for the h1 selector to the same gold mixture that you used in step number four. The h1 background-color should be set to a slightly lighter green than that of the page background. You can do this by simply increasing the "G" value from the value used in step four from 40% to 50%.

8. Use the padding property to add 10% of padding inside the h1 box. You can do this by writing a declaration for the h1 rule that reads "padding: 10%."

9. Set the margins for the h1 box by adding a declaration that reads "margin: 15%."

10. Add a medium border that uses the "outset" border style. Make it the same color as the text. Your declaration should read "border: medium outset rgb(100%, 80%, 20%)."

9

11. Save your page and view it in your browser. Although IE 5.5, Netscape 4.7 and 6.0, and Opera 5 all display the page with slight variations, the basic presentation is the same. Your results should resemble the following illustration:

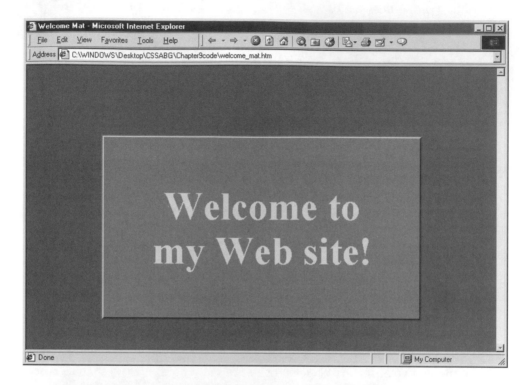

```
<html>
<head>
<title>Welcome Mat</title>
<style>
body     {background-color: rgb(20%,40%,0%);
          color: rgb(100%,80%,20%);}

h1    {background-color: rgb(20%,50%,0%);
       color: rgb(100%,80%,20%);
       text-align: center;
       font-size: 4em;
       padding: 10%;
       margin: 15%;
       border: medium outset rgb(100%,80%,20%);}
```

```
</style></head>
<body>
<h1>Welcome to my Web site!</h1>
</body></html>
```

Project Summary

If you observe the code from the preceding project, you may notice that none of the style came from HTML presentational elements. It was created entirely with CSS. You can see that the box properties allow you to create attractive layouts and styles, totally apart from HTML code. In fact, if you allow your creativity to run free, you can actually develop some very sophisticated designs with style sheets. The downside of this approach to page design is, again, the support issue. If you create beautiful page layouts that crash because of poor browser support, then you are defeating your purpose. However, if you test your pages and take care to stick with the better-supported CSS properties, you will find CSS to be a useful tool for your Web design work.

The Box Properties

As you have already learned, the box properties enable you to set margins, padding, and borders for virtually all HTML elements—at least in theory. In actual practice you will discover that there are some support problems that limit the applicability of these properties. For example, while the box properties seem to work well with block-level elements, browser support for inline elements is virtually nonexistent. Thus, even though you should be able to apply these properties to all elements, you will be safest using them only on block-level elements. As you will see in this section, support for some of the properties, even for block-level elements, can be inconsistent. However, that does not alter the fact that the box properties are a key tool of CSS design. If you plan to use CSS much, you had better become very acquainted with margin properties, padding properties, and border properties.

The Margin Properties

The margin properties can be applied to all or part of the outside of an element. In CSS, a *margin* is understood as the space between the outside edge of an element's box and the inside edge of that element's containing box. If that

9

seems confusing, consider how it works on the scale of a full page. If you create a simple HTML document and enclose a sentence or two inside the <p> element (making sure to set the "p" selector's background color to something different than the page's background color), you'll notice that the browser adds a small margin by default. As the following illustration shows, the element's containing box extends nearly to the edges of the browser window.

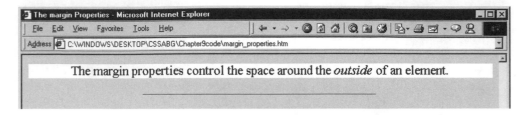

You can use margin properties to increase or even decrease the amount of space around any or all the sides of an element's containing box. The margin properties are

- **margin**   Enables you to set all four margins at once (a shorthand property)

- **margin-top**   Enables you to set a separate value for the top margin

- **margin-right**   Allows you to set a value for the right-hand margin

- **margin-bottom**   Sets the margin value for the bottom of the element box

- **margin-left**   Enables you to set the left-hand margin

Values

Margin values may be set using length measurements (in, cm, mm, pt, pc, px, em, ex), percentages, or a value known as "auto." One advantage of length measurements is that it's often easier to estimate the overall impact of your value choices when you're working with familiar measurements. However, if you use length measurements, remember that you are using a fixed measurement that will not scale or adjust to different screen displays. You may find that in the long run you are better off working with percentages.

Percentage measurements are generally based on the parent element. In other words, if you set a value of 25% for a left margin, the browser will calculate 25% of the distance from one of the parent element's inside edges to

the other. If, as in the following example, the parent element happens to be
<body>, then the calculation is essentially based on the overall screen width.
Figure 9-2 demonstrates how the margin properties affect the overall display
of the elements to which they are applied.

Note

The "auto" value is based on the idea that the browser will automatically adjust
the value so that the width of the element in question is the same as its containing
block. This value will be explored in more detail in Module 11.

It is also possible to use negative values with margins. As you'll notice
in Figure 9-2, the top margin of the fourth sentence has been set to -.75em,
effectively reducing the space between the two elements. Negative values can
even be used to cause elements to overlap. As the following illustration shows,

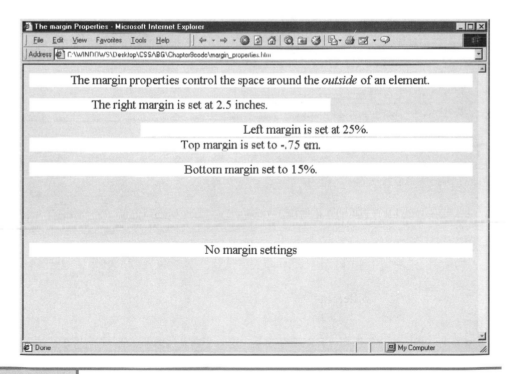

Figure 9-2   Margin properties applied to the <p> element

9

the "Heading Two" element has been made to overlap the "Heading One" element, simply by the use of a negative value for the top margin.

```
<h1 style="background-color: black;
           color: white;
           font-size: 1.5em;">Heading One</h1>
<h2 style="background-color: yellow;
           font-size: 1.5em;
           margin-top: -1.0em;">Heading Two</h2>
```

Syntax

One of the key syntax issues with all of the box properties is the order in which values should be listed when using the shorthand property. For example, suppose you want to use the margin property to specify your margins, but you want to supply two, three, or even four different values? In what order should the values be listed? The rules of value application are

- One value specified: applies to all four sides.

- Two values specified: first value applies to top and bottom; second value applies to right and left.

Tip

Don't put any punctuation (such as commas) between multiple values. They should be separated only by a space.

- Three values specified: first value applies to the top; second applies to left and right; third applies to bottom.

- Four values specified: the values are applied to the top, right, bottom, and left sides (in that order).

Tip

If you will think in terms of a clock, you'll find it easier to remember the order in which four separate values will be applied. The order begins at the top (12 o'clock) and moves clockwise around the clock face (12, 3, 6, and 9 o'clock).

Another syntax issue with the margin properties is that of mixing different types of measurements. It is possible to mix different length measurements and percentage measurements when specifying values for margin properties. For example, all of the following style rules would be acceptable

```
h1              {margin: 1in 7% 3em 15%;}

p               {margin-top: 2.5em;
                 margin-right: 13px;
                 margin-bottom: 22%;
                 margin-left: 10mm;}

.special        {10% -.50em;}

.offset         {2em 1.5pc 25%;}

.uniform        {10px;}
```

Although the margin properties are generally supported, the support is weak in older browsers (such as Netscape 4 and IE 4). When using these properties, be sure to test your pages in these browsers to make sure your layout has not "crashed."

Collapsing Margins

A unique characteristic of the margin properties is the ability of CSS to "collapse" margins. For example, suppose you have used a style sheet to set the top margin for all your <p> elements to 1/2 inch, and the bottom margin has been set to 3/4 inch. If both of these margins are applied, they would cause the margins between your paragraphs to be 1 and 1/4 inches. To avoid creating the extra space, CSS "collapses" the margins between the paragraphs by applying only the larger of the two. Thus, the margin between your paragraphs would be 3/4ths of an inch. Table 9-1 lists some other important characteristics of the margin properties.

9

Note

Only top and bottom margins collapse.

Do they inherit?	Default value	Browser support	Works with
No	Not defined for the "margin:" shorthand property; 0 for all others	Inconsistent	All elements

Table 9-1 Characteristics of the margin Properties

1-Minute Drill

● With collapsing margins, the _____ of the two values is used.

● Which margins do *not* collapse?

● Why are collapsing margins helpful?

The Padding Properties

As mentioned earlier in this module, the padding properties add space *inside* the containing box. Beyond that, there is not a great deal of difference in how you would apply the padding properties to an element on your page. As with the margin properties, you can use the shorthand "padding:" property to set all the values at once, or you can apply the values individually. The padding properties are:

● **padding**   Enables you to add padding to all four sides at once (a shorthand property)

● **padding-top**   Enables you to set a separate value for top padding

● **padding-right**   Allows you to add padding to the right-hand side of the element's contents

● **padding-bottom**   Sets the padding value for the bottom of the element box

● **padding-left**   Adds padding to the left side of the element's contents

---

● Larger
● Left and right
● Without collapsing margins, the top and bottom margin values of adjoining elements would be combined, increasing the space between them

Values

The padding properties are similar to margin properties in that they accept both length and percentage measurements as values, and the measurement types can be mixed. However, there is a key difference in that negative values are *not* permitted for padding properties. Thus, a declaration of "padding-right: -.50in" would be ignored by the browser.

The order in which values must be specified for the "padding:" shorthand property is the same as that of the "margin:" property: one value=all sides; two values=top-bottom and left-right; three values=top, left-right, bottom; four values=top, right, bottom, left. If you are using the non-shorthand padding properties (padding-top, padding-right, padding-bottom, padding-left), you can specify them in any order you wish. Figure 9-3 demonstrates the effect of the padding properties on several instances of the <p> element.

```
<html><head>
<title>The Padding Properties</title>
<style>
body             {background-color: silver;
                  font-size: 1.5em;}
p                {background-color: white;}
.padtop          {padding-top: 20px;}
.padright        {text-align: right;
                  padding-right: .50in;}
.padbot          {padding-bottom: 1em;}
.padleft         {padding-left: 25%}
.pad             {padding: 10%}
</style></head>
<body>
<p class="padtop">Top padding of 20 pixels</p>
<p class="padright">Right padding of .50 inches</p>
<p class="padbot">Bottom padding of 1 em</p>
<p class="padleft">Left padding of 25%</p>
<p class="pad">Padding of 10% all around</p>
</body></html>
```

Note

Because padding is "transparent," it's often difficult to notice its effects. In Figure 9-3, all the text has been aligned to the left *except* for the second line. Since this line demonstrates the padding-right property, the text has been aligned to the right. You can see in the second, fourth, and fifth lines how the padding actually moves the text. In the first and third lines, the padding is reflected by the extra space above and below the text.

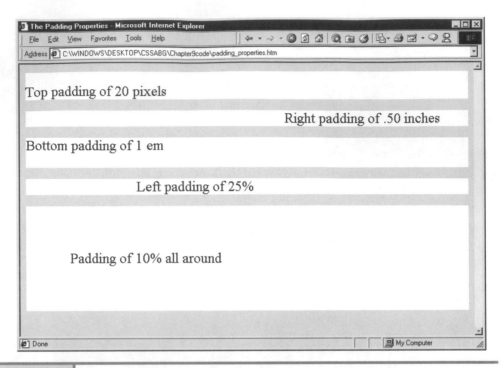

Figure 9-3 Padding properties applied to the <p> element

If you compare the padding properties to a table's "cellpadding," you can see an important advantage you have with padding. The padding properties enable you to do more than merely "inflate" an element's containing box by adding extra space inside. By applying padding selectively, you can control the placement of an element's contents. In Module 11, you will learn to use padding in creating page layouts. Table 9-2 lists some other important characteristics of the padding properties.

Do they inherit?	Default value	Browser support	Work with
No	Not defined for the "padding:" shorthand property; 0 for all others	Inconsistent	All elements

Table 9-2 Characteristics of the padding Properties

The Border Properties

The border properties are, perhaps, more fun to use than the other box properties because the results are more concrete. When dealing with margins and padding, you are primarily dealing with *space;* when using the border properties, you are drawing lines around the space. Also, although with HTML you can create borders for certain elements (such as tables), the border properties enable you to do more than simply draw lines around the exterior of an element. Eight different styles, combined with colors and the ability to specify borders for individual sides of a containing box, open many new creative possibilities to you as a Web designer. In contrast to the margin and padding properties, there are four different sets of border properties that you need to learn how to work with:

- **border**   Enables you to apply color, width, and style at one time (shorthand property)

- **border-color**   Enables you to set a color for your borders

- **border-width**   Allows you to specify the "thickness" of your borders

- **border-style**   Gives you a choice of eight different styles for your borders

The Border-Color Properties

This is the easiest of the border properties to work with, since all you need to do is specify a color value. As with the other box properties, you can do this for all four sides of a box, or for one to three sides. Also, the order of value specification is the same when using the shorthand property: one value=all sides; two values=top-bottom and left-right; three values=top, left-right, bottom; four values=top, right, bottom, left.

The syntax for applying colors with the border-color properties is

- **border-top-color**   Applies color to top border

- **border-right-color**   Applies color to right border

- **border-bottom-color**   Applies color to bottom border

- **border-left-color**   Applies color to left border

- **border-color**   Applies color to multiple borders

9

Internet Explorer added extensions to HTML a few years back, enabling Web authors to specify for tables a bordercolor, bordercolorlight, and bordercolordark. This gave designers the ability to create attractive borders for certain page elements visible in Internet Explorer. CSS takes this a step further by enabling you to use color creatively with your borders, applying different colors to different sides of an element's box. As you become skilled at using the border color properties, you can create some very nice effects. Other important characteristics of the border-color properties are listed in Table 9-3.

The Border-Width Properties

You can set the width or "thickness" of a border either by using the keywords *thin*, *medium*, *thick* or by specifying a length measurement. If you use a keyword, be prepared for the possibility that different browsers will render the border width differently. The actual definitions for the "thin," "medium," and "thick" keywords is left up to the user agent (browser), and each one tends to display these values differently. Also, you can't use percentage measurements for setting border widths—only length measurements (in, cm, mm, px, pt, pc, em, ex) are acceptable. For the shorthand property, the values should be specified in the same order as all of the other shorthand properties. The border-width properties are

- **border-top-width** Sets the top border width

- **border-right-width** Sets the right border width

- **border-bottom-width** Sets the bottom border width

- **border-left-width** Sets the left border width

- **border-width** Sets multiple border widths at one time

Do they inherit?	Default value	Browser support	Works with
No	Not defined for the "border-color:" shorthand property; Same as the "color" property for all others	Inconsistent	All elements

Table 9-3 Characteristics of the border-color Properties

The border-width property allows you to govern the size of your borders with a great deal of precision. As the following illustration demonstrates, by setting different values for each side of an element's box, you can create almost a "3-D" feel using nothing more than border-width.

This paragraph features a solid border style with the top set to "thin," the right set to "medium," the bottom set to "thick," and the left set to 3 pixels.

```
<html><head><title>Border Width Properties</title>
<style>
body      {font-size: 1.3em;}
p         {background-color: white;
            border-style: solid;
            border-top-width: thin;
            border-right-width: medium;
            border-bottom-width: thick;
            border-left-width: 3px;}
</style></head>
<body>
<p>This paragraph features a solid border style with
the top set to "thin," the right set to "medium,"
the bottom set to "thick,"
and the left set to 3 pixels.</p>
</body>
</html>
```

Other important characteristics of the border-width properties are listed in Table 9-4.

The Border-Style Properties

The border-style properties are arguably the most important of the border properties, because if a border style is not specified, then no border will be displayed at all. This is because the default value for border-style is "none." On the other hand, you can leave the border-color and border-width properties

Do they inherit?	Default value	Browser support	Works with
No	Medium	Inconsistent	All elements

Table 9-4   Characteristics of the border-width Properties

unspecified, and a border will still display. The color will be taken from the foreground color value, and the default width is "medium." So, keep in mind that if you plan to use borders, *always* specify a border style.

In contrast to HTML, which allows for only one style of border, CSS lets you choose from eight different styles. If you include the values "none" and "hidden" (which renders an invisible border), then CSS allows for ten border styles.

Note

Although CSS provides a large number of border styles, not all browsers support them. As a matter of fact, the only style they are required to support in order to be CSS 1-compliant, is the "solid" style. Be sure to check your pages out in several different browsers to make certain they are displaying the way you want them to.

These styles are the following: dotted, dashed, solid, double, groove, ridge, inset, and outset. As with the border-width keywords, the border styles can vary from browser to browser in how they actually display. As the following illustration and code demonstrate, the variety of border styles enables you to create a broader range of effects than you can with HTML alone:

```
<html><head><title>Border Styles</title>
<style>
body    {background-color: rgb(50%,50%,50%);
          font-size: 1.1em;
          color: yellow;}

.dotted {border-color: yellow;
          border-width: medium;
          border-style: dotted;
          margin-right: 75%;
          text-align: center;
          margin-left: 10%;}

.dashed {border-color: yellow;
          border-width: medium;
          border-style: dashed;
          margin-right: 75%;
          text-align: center;
          margin-left: 10%;}

.solid {border-color: yellow;
          border-width: medium;
          border-style: solid;
          margin-right: 75%;
          text-align: center;
          margin-left: 10%;}

.doubl {border-color: yellow;
          border-width: medium;
          border-style: double;
          margin-right: 75%;
          text-align: center;
          margin-left: 10%;}
.groov {border-color: yellow;
          border-width: medium;
          border-style: groove;
          margin-right: 75%;
          text-align: center;
          margin-left: 10%;}

.ridge {border-color: yellow;
          border-width: medium;
          border-style: ridge;
          margin-right: 75%;
          text-align: center;
          margin-left: 10%;}
```

9

```
.inset {border-color: yellow;
        border-width: medium;
        border-style: inset
        margin-right: 75%;
        text-align: center;
        margin-left: 10%;}

.outset {border-color: yellow;
         border-width: medium;
         border-style: outset;
         margin-right: 75%;
         text-align: center;
         margin-left: 10%;}</style></head>
<body>
<p class="dotted">Dotted</p>
<p class="dashed">Dashed</p>
<p class="solid">Solid</p>
<p class="doubl">Double</p>
<p class="groov">Groove</p>
<p class="ridge">Ridge</p>
<p class="inset">Inset</p>
<p class="outset">Outset</p>
<hr />
</body></html>
```

The border-style properties are

- **border-top-style** Specifies a style for the top of a containing box
- **border-right-style** Specifies a style for the right side of a box
- **border-bottom-style** Specifies a style for the bottom of a box
- **border-left-style** Specifies a style for the left side of a box
- **border-style** Specifies multiple border styles

Other important characteristics of the border-style properties are listed in Table 9-5.

Do they inherit?	Default value	Browser support	Work with
No	None	Inconsistent	All elements

Table 9-5 Characteristics of the border-style Properties

1-Minute Drill

- If three values are specified for a shorthand property, how does the browser apply them?

- What is the only border style that CSS 1-compliant browsers are required to support?

The Border Shorthand Properties

One final set of properties must be considered before you try working with the border properties. As you may have noticed, with three different border properties and four potential targets for these properties, you could easily have a stack of 12 declarations, just governing borders—and that's just for one style of border. What if you want to have several styles and colors of borders? If you want to streamline your stylesheets *and* take advantage of borders at the same time, you can use the "border:" properties. These shorthand properties combine the border-color, border-width, and border-style properties, enabling you to reduce the complexity of your style sheets somewhat. The border properties are

- **border-top**   Sets the border style, color, and width for the top of an element's box

- **border-right**   Sets border style, color, and width for the right side of an element's box

- **border-bottom**   Defines a border's style, color, and width for the bottom of an element's box

- **border-left**   Defines style, color, and width for a left-side border

- **border**   Defines style, color, and width for multiple borders

The syntax for the "border:" properties is essentially the same as for the other shorthand properties. For example, the shorthand property border-top can be used to add a solid, thick, red border to the top of an element. The rule to add such a border would look like this:

```
p       {border-top: solid thick red;}
```

The style, color, and width values may be presented in any order. This is because these shorthand properties accept only one value for each of the

---

- Top, left-right, bottom
- Solid

options. Even with the "border:" property, you may only supply single values that will be applied to all four sides of the element's box. As the following illustration and code demonstrate, this can make adding borders a much simpler process:

The Border Properties

A solid, thick, red border with border-top

A double, medium, blue border with border-right

A dotted, thin, green border with border-bottom

A dashed, thin, navy border with border-left

An inset, 3 pixel, yellow border with border

```
<html><head><title>Border Properties</title>
<style>
body      {font-size: 1.3em;}
p         {background-color: white;}
</style></head>
<body>
<h1><i>The Border Properties</i></h1>
<p style="border-top: solid thick red;">
A solid, thick, red border with border-top</p>

<p style="border-right: double medium blue;
text-align: right;">A double, medium, blue border
with border-right</p>

<p style="border-bottom: dotted thin green;">
A dotted, thin, green border with border-bottom</p>

<p style="border-left: dashed thin navy;">
A dashed, thin, navy border with border-left</p>

<p style="border: inset 3px yellow;">
An inset, 3 pixel, yellow border with border</p>
</body></html>
```

The downside of the "border:" properties is that support for them is weaker than for most of the other border properties. Thus, if you use these shorthand properties, you should be careful to test your pages in multiple browsers and make sure that your borders are displaying the way you want them to. Other important characteristics of the shorthand border properties are given in Table 9-6.

Do they inherit?	Default value	Browser support	Work with
No	Same as the individual properties	Inconsistent	All elements

Table 9-6	Characteristics of the Shorthand Border Properties

Project 9-2: Playing with the Box Properties

The purpose of this module was to introduce you to the box properties. In Module 11, you will learn how to combine these properties with some you haven't worked with yet in creating page layouts. However, to give you a sample of what is to come, try creating a "photo album" page using the box properties you have worked with thus far. You will need to have some digital photos to work with. If you have a scanner, you can personalize the project by scanning in some of your own photos. You can also capture some off of the Internet by simply right-clicking on any image. Your browser will then prompt you to save the images on your own machine. If you want to try reproducing the exercise exactly, then you can download the images used for this project from Osborne's Web site: **www.osborne.com**. All of the files for this project and all the others in this book (as well as the other examples and illustrations) can be found as a zipped file by clicking on the "free code" link and then on the title of this book.

Step-by-Step

1. Create an HTML document and save it as family_album.htm.

2. In the <body>of the document, add a headline that reads: **The "Family" Album**.

3. Add a set of <div> tags and put an <img /> element in between them. Using the "src" property, supply the url of the first picture you want to have on your page. For this project it is "boo250x203.jpg."

4. Add a second set of <div> tags and repeat the process, adding a second image. The image used in Figure 9-4 is "dandy221x182.jpg."

Hint

Your HTML code for this image and the others should include "width," "height," and "alt" attributes. This helps your page to load faster and provides your visitors with a text description of your image if it does not load properly.

5. Add a third set of <div> tags and use the <img /> element to add the image "bunbun250x230.jpg."

6. Add a set of <style> tags in the <head> of the document.

7. Write a style rule that sets the body background color to white and the text color to navy.

8. Write a rule that will set the alignment for the <h1> element to center.

9. For the div selector, write a style rule that will set the background color to navy, add 20 pixels of padding all around, adjust the right margin to 60%, and set a double, yellow, medium border.

10. Create a class named ".dandy," and specify a left margin of 15% and a top margin of -15%. Be sure to add the *class="dandy"* attribute to the opening <div> tag for that image.

11. Create a class named ".bunbun" and specify a left margin of 30% and a top margin of -12%. Add the *class="bunbun"* attribute to the opening <div> tag for that image.

12. Save your page and view it in a Web browser. It should look something like Figure 9-4.

```
<html><head><title>Photo Album</title>
<style>
body    {background-color: white; color: navy;}
h1      {text-align: center;}
div     {background-color: navy;
          padding: 20px;
          margin-right: 60%;
          border: double yellow medium;}
.dandy {margin-left: 15%;
         margin-top: -15%;}
.bunbun {margin-left: 30%;
          margin-top: -12%;}
</style></head>
<body>
<h1>The &quot;Family&quot; Album</h1>
<div><img src="boo250x203.jpg"
width="250" height="203"alt="My cat, Boo." /></div>
<div class="dandy"><img src="dandy221x182.jpg"
width="221" height="182" alt="My other cat, Dandy" /></div>
<div class="bunbun"><img src="bunbun250x230.jpg"
width="250" height="230" alt="A rescued bunny" /></div>
</body></html>
```

Figure 9-4   Pictures "framed" and positioned with CSS box properties

9

Project Summary

In this exercise, you took some simple images and used the box properties to "matte" and "frame" them. Then you used margin properties to position them on the page. Although this is a simple example, it will hopefully give you an idea of the potential of CSS for layout work. In Module 11, you will learn some additional properties that you can use for positioning elements on a page. These will give you an even greater ability to control how your pages look.

✓ Mastery Check

1. If four values are supplied for padding, margin, or border properties, in what order will browsers apply them?

_____

_____

2. Using shorthand properties, write a style rule for the <h3> element that will create a thick, red, grooved border on the top and bottom and a thin, solid, blue border on the right and left.

_____

_____

3. Write the same style rule for a <p> element, using the individual (top, right, bottom, left) properties.

_____

_____

4. Using shorthand properties, write a style rule that adds 15 pixels of padding, 15 pixels of margin, and a thin, yellow outset border to the <div> element.

_____

_____

5. Using individual (top, right, bottom, left) properties, write a style rule for an <h2> element that applies 15% of padding to the top, 20 pixel margins on the right and left, and a thick. green, double border on the left and top sides.

_____

_____

Module 10

Applying the Descriptive Properties

The Goals of this Module

- **Understand the Descriptive Properties**
- **Use Display to Change Element Performance**
- **Use White-Space to Control Text Display**
- **Work with List Style Properties**
- **Become Acquainted with Table Properties**

The descriptive properties are among the most powerful in CSS, because they enable you to literally alter the very structure of HTML. With descriptive properties you can change the behavior of elements from block-level to inline, and vice-versa. You can also change how list items display or convert other elements into list items. With CSS 2 you can even create your own table elements. In other words, you can essentially mold HTML and make it work the way *you* want it to work. You might be wondering why you would even want to do this—or if you even *should*. To learn the answer to that question, you must understand the purpose of the descriptive properties.

Understand the Descriptive Properties

The first step in understanding the descriptive properties is to find some analogy that describes what it is they do. Although all analogies tend to break down, try imagining that you are building a house. Suddenly you realize that you have run out of two-by-fours. You're at a critical point in your work, and you don't want to take the time to go buy more. However, you're in luck because you have a large pile of bricks nearby. You also have a handy new invention called the "building supply classification machine." All you have to do is put in your pile of bricks, change the classification setting to two-by-four, and *presto*…you now have a pile of lumber to work with. Then you happily go on with your construction—until you run out of nails. Then, it's back to the machine to convert some dry-wall screws into nails.

Granted, this analogy is a bit of a stretch, but at least it captures the essence of what the descriptive properties can do. Essentially the descriptive properties function like the "building supply classification machine" by enabling you to redefine how an element should function. With these properties you can virtually restructure HTML, making it work entirely differently than its designers intended.

Descriptive Properties and HTML

The *descriptive* properties (also known as *classification* or *display* properties) allow you to customize HTML elements so that they will behave the way you want them to. For example, a block-level element such as <p> or <h1> always includes a blank line before and after the element. Perhaps for some reason you want to prevent those extra lines from being added. You could change the display property for <p> or <h1> from "block" to "inline." Instantly, your entire page layout changes as those extra lines are no longer inserted.

Hint

There are actually much better alternatives for removing unwanted lines, as you'll learn in Modules 11-13, but it *could* be done this way.

Of course, doing this will also cause the element to behave exactly as an inline element. In other words, not only would you omit the extra line, but no line break at all would be added after the element's closing tag. Or perhaps you have an existing page that has a list, and you would rather have it display as inline. You can change the display property for the list with a simple style rule, altering its appearance entirely. The descriptive properties also enable you to substitute your own images for list item bullets, control how a browser handles white space, and more. However, the true power of the descriptive properties is not revealed until you see them at work *outside* of HTML altogether.

Caution

Although it's a good idea to know the descriptive properties and how to work with them, if you care about accessibility you should be very cautious about using them. Since non-visual browsers (such as aural and Braille) depend on HTML's structure to help them interpret your pages, if you alter the structure of your HTML too much, it might make it impossible for these browsers to decipher your pages.

Descriptive Properties and XML

The descriptive properties come into their own when used with a language like XML. XML (Extensible Markup Language) is sort of a "sibling" of HTML because they were both developed from the same "mother" language, SGML (Standard Generalized Markup Language). However, although XML and HTML look a lot alike, there is a huge difference between them. When you work with HTML, you use a set of elements, tags, attributes, and values that have already been created for you. When you use XML, you create *your own* elements, tags, attributes, and values. The descriptive properties are what you use to tell browsers how those elements should behave.

?→Ask the Expert

Question: Why does XML *require* a style sheet while HTML does not?

Answer: Actually, HTML *does* require a style sheet. However, since all of the elements, attributes, and values of HTML are predefined, all browsers have a style sheet built in. In the absence of any other style sheet, the browser supplies its own styles. Since the elements, attributes, and values of XML documents are all defined by the author, it is impossible for browsers to supply style sheets. There are simply too many different possibilities. Thus, the author of an XML document must also create a style sheet that tells a browser how to display the document.

Question: What other languages can be used to write style sheets for XML pages?

Answer: XSL (Extensible Stylesheet Language) is being developed by the W3C as the "official" language for XML style sheets. However, it is considerably more difficult to learn and work with than is CSS. If you plan on using XML for some of your Web pages down the line, you can do just fine with CSS.

If you use CSS to create a style sheet for an XML document, you will have to set the descriptive property for each of your elements. If you want to have lists, you will need to use the list-style properties and, if you want tables, the table-layout properties. In one sense, the descriptive or classification properties enable you to be a "do-it-yourselfer." You create your own markup language with XML, and then define how it should function with CSS.)

Descriptive Properties and Browser Compatibility

Another important factor to consider when learning the descriptive properties is that of browser compatibility. A few of the descriptive properties are part of the CSS 1 specification and enjoy fairly strong browser support. However, some of the properties and values are new additions with CSS 2, and the support for many of these is often weak at best. Thus, it's a good idea, in becoming familiar with these particular properties and values, to give higher priority to those with greater browser support. This module covers the properties and values with the strongest support first, then those that are weaker.

The descriptive properties are

- **display**   The display property enables you to make an element display as block, inline, list-item, or "none." A large number of new values have been added with CSS 2. Some of these (run-in, compact, marker) will be treated with the display property. The rest deal with causing elements to display as tables and will be dealt with in a special section at the end of this module.

- **list-style-type**   This property allows you to select the bullet that appears for an unordered list or the numbers/characters that display with an ordered list.

- **list-style-position**   With the list-style-position property, you can position the bullet on the outside (as it is in this list) or on the inside (lined up with the text's left margin).

- **list-style-image**   With this property, you can substitute your own images as bullets for list items.

- **list-style**   This is a shorthand property that enables you to set the list style type, position, and image with a single declaration.

- **white-space**   With the white-space property you can control how a browser handles "white space," that is, the extra spaces in code that are normally ignored by browsers. The white space also allows you to regulate things such as line breaks and text formatting.

10

Note

The circles, discs, squares, and so on that appear at the head of each list item are commonly called "bullets." However, in CSS they are referred to as "markers" and/or "marker-boxes."

The Display Property

In learning about the descriptive properties, it is best to start with the display property. Gaining an understanding of the display property functions will help you understand the basic idea behind the other descriptive properties. Also, the display property has undergone the most significant changes between the CSS 1 and CSS 2 specifications. Thus, it will be helpful for you to be aware of what those changes are and what they mean for CSS design. To begin with, let's examine the CSS1 version of the display property.

The display Property in CSS 1: Element Behavior Control

The display property enables you to change the fundamental behavior of an element. For example, you can change a block-level element to inline, list-item, or even "none." What this means is that the element will take on the behavior you have specified for it, rather than behaving as it normally would. The following illustration shows a level two heading, <h2>, which is a block-level element, and a <p> element.

Display can change elements from <u>inline</u> to block level.

Notice that the word "inline" is underlined. Since the underlined text, <u>, element is an inline element, no line breaks or extra lines are added. The element's contents (underlined text) remain "in-line" with the rest of the <h2> element. However, if you write a style rule that changes the display property for the <u> element from inline to block, the results are much different, as the following illustration demonstrates:

**Display can change elements from
<u>inline</u>
to block-level.**

```
<html>
<head>
<title>Display</title>
<style> u {display: block;} </style>
</head>
<body>
```

```
<h2>Display can change elements from <u>inline</u>
    to block-level.</h2>
</body>
</html>
```

With its display property changed to "block," the <u> element now appears on its own line, just as a block-level element would. By changing the value of an element's display property, you can make a list item behave like an inline, a block-level element display like a list, and so on.

Values

In CSS 2, as you'll learn later in this module, a large number of new values have been added to the display property. The values represented here are the original values this property had in CSS 1. For the most part, they are well supported by the major browsers with one exception: the list-item value. This value is currently supported only by the Opera 5 browser. The basic values for display are

- **block**   Causes an element to display as a block-level element. In other words, a line is inserted before and after the element's contents.

- **inline**   Makes an element display as an inline element. No extra lines or line breaks are added between the element's contents and that of the elements that surround it.

- **list-item**   Causes the element to behave as a list item: indented and with a space before and after each item. The element will also display a marker (or bullet), but this must be specified with the list-style-type, list-style-image, or list-style properties.

- **none**   Prevents the element from displaying at all. This property does not just hide the property (that is, make it invisible), but actually prevents it from having any presence on the page at all. The browser treats it as if it were not there and draws the page without reserving any space for it.

10

Tip

Another property that you will learn about in Module 12 is the "visibility" property. This property has a value named "hidden" that causes an element to be invisible; however, the browser still allots space for it, just as if it were visible. This is in contrast to the "none" value of the display property, which completely removes the element's presence from the layout.

Syntax

Since this property will accept only keywords, the syntax is simple. Simply use the keyword that describes the value you wish to apply. The following style rules are all acceptable:

```
h1 {display: inline;}
h2, h3, h4, h5, h6 {display: none;}
p {display: list-item;}
li {display: none;}
.blk {display: block;}
img {display: block;}
#83e {display: list-item;}
em, strong, i, u, span {display: block;}
div {display: inline;}
```

The display Property in CSS 2: Heading-Related Values

In CSS 2, the display property retains all of the values that were covered in the preceding section, with quite a few more added in. These essentially fall into two subcategories: those related to markers or headings and those related to tables. The heading-related values enable you to create more sophisticated headings; the table-related values enable you to specify any element as a table element.

The heading-related values are *compact*, *run-in*, and *marker*. These display values enable you to manipulate block-level elements in such a way as to create alternative heading and bullet styles for your documents. The functions of each of these values are described next.

Does it inherit?	Default value	Browser support	Works with
No	Inline; however in HTML when this property is not specified, the element's natural display property is the default	Strong, except for the list-item property, which is not supported by any browsers except Opera 5	All elements

Table 10-1   Characteristics of the CSS 1 display Property

display: compact

As mentioned in previous Modules, block-level elements are characterized by a line added before and after the element's content. This value, in effect, enables you to place two block elements side by side, omitting the line in between them. The key to making it work is that the content of the "compact" element must be small enough to fit in the margin of the next block-level element. If you think in terms of the "box" model, this display puts the two elements' boxes side-by-side. The following illustration demonstrates what happens when <h3> is set to display:compact and alternated with three <p> elements.

Title:	CSS: A Beginner's Guide
Author:	James H. Pence
Publisher:	Osborne/McGraw-Hill

```
<html>
<head><title>Compact</title>
<style>
body        {background-color: white;}
h3          {display: compact; background-color: silver;}
p           {margin-left: 15%; background-color: cyan;}
</style></head>
<body>
<h3>Title:</h3>
<p>CSS: A Beginner's Guide</p>
<h3>Author:</h3>
<p>James H. Pence</p>
<h3>Publisher:</h3>
<p>Osborne/McGraw-Hill</p>
</body></html>
```

10

Note

To view the illustrations in this section on your own browser, you will need to use Opera 5 or higher.

display: run-in

The run-in value causes the content of a block-level element to "share" the first line of the next element. In terms of the box model, the two elements virtually share the same box. As the following illustration shows, you might use this value to cause your headings to display as "run-in" headings that share the same margin and line spacing with the paragraph they introduce.

> **A run-in header** This is the paragraph content that follows the run-in header. You can see how this value for the display property can be a useful tool for page layout.

```
<html><head><title>Run-in</title>
<style>
h3    {display: run-in;}
p     {background-color: cyan;
      margin-right: 25%;}</style></head>
<body>
<h3>A run-in header </h3>
<p> This is the paragraph content that follows
the run-in header. You can see how this value for the
display property can be a useful tool for page layout.</p>
</body></html>
```

● **display: marker** The "marker" value will cause the browser to generate a bullet in front of an element, as if it were a list item. This value is a bit more complicated to use than the CSS 1 display values, because it also requires the use of the *:before* or *:after* pseudo-elements and the content property. (These will be covered in Module 14.) As the following illustration shows, you might use this property to add graphical bullets before or after an element.

★A black star should appear before and after this heading. ★

```
<html><head><title>Marker</title>
<style>
h3:before    {display: marker;
              content: url(blackstar.gif);}
h3:after   {display: marker;
            content: url(blackstar.gif);}
</style></head>
<body>
<h3>A black star should appear before
and after this heading.</h3></body></html>
```

Hint

The ":before" pseudo-element instructs the browser to generate content before an element, and ":after" tells the browser to generate content after an element. The content property specifies what kind of content should be generated.

Table-Related Values

In anticipation of the probability that XML will one day become the dominant language in Web design, a set of table display values has also been added to CSS 2. This is because XML does not come with predefined table elements. Thus, if you want to display tabular data with XML, you will need to define your own table elements and set their behavior with the display property. When you use the values in the following list with the display property, you can cause an element to behave as if it were a table, table cell, table heading, and so on. The table-related values that go with the display property are

- **display: table**   Corresponds to HTML's <table> element.
- **display: table-row**   Corresponds to the <tr> element
- **display: table-cell**   Corresponds to the <td> element
- **display: table-caption**   Corresponds to the <caption> element
- **display: table-row-group**   Corresponds to the <rowgroup> element
- **display: table-column-group**   Corresponds to the <colgroup> element
- **display: table-header-group**   Corresponds to the <thead> element
- **display: table-footer-group**   Corresponds to the <tfoot> element
- **display: inline-table**   Creates a table "inline" rather than as a block-level element

If you are working with HTML, it is unlikely that you will need to use these values, since HTML already provides table elements. Still, it is interesting to see how you can create a table using ordinary elements. The following illustration shows a simple, six-celled table created with nothing more than class selectors, the <div> and <span> elements, and the display property. Borders have been set

10

for each cell and for the table, and background colors have been added so you can better view its structure.

```
<html><head><title>Table</title>
<style>
.table      {font-size: 1.2em;
             display: table;
             background-color: cyan;
             border: solid thin;}

.row        {display: table-row;}

.cell       {font-size: 1.2em;
              display: table-cell;
              background-color: yellow;
              border: solid thin; }
</style></head>
<body>
<div class="table">
    <div class="row">
        <span class="cell">This</span>
        <span class="cell">table</span>
    </div>
    <div class="row">
        <span class="cell">was</span>
        <span class="cell">created</span>
    </div>
    <div class="row">
        <span class="cell">with</span>
        <span class="cell">CSS!</span>
    </div>
</div></body></html>
```

As you can see, it is possible to create a table with nothing more than the <div> and <span> elements. You could just as easily use all <div> or all <span> elements, or even <p> or <h1> elements, because you were using the display property to alter the fundamental display characteristics of those elements.

Using <div> and <span> merely helps to distinguish between the "row" and "cell" elements. One cautionary note, though. Since browser support for these values is weak, it's best to create tables for your Web pages with the HTML table elements. Otherwise, your table might wind up looking like the following illustration:

Project 10-1: Experiment with Display

In CSS 1, the basic function of the "display" property is to govern whether an element should display as block-level, inline, list-item, or not at all. The best way to understand how this powerful property works is by seeing it in action. In this project you will create a simple HTML document and then change the display properties of the major elements. When you see how the page changes, you will understand why you need to be careful when using the display property.

Step-by-Step

1. Create an HTML document and save it as display_property.htm.

2. In the <body> of the document, add a heading with the <h1> element. You can make the text say whatever you wish.

3. Add several sentences of text, enclosed in the <p> element.

4. Somewhere in the paragraph you just created, enclose a few words inside an inline element such as <i> (italicized text), <b> (bold text), or <u> (underlined text).

5. Write a single sentence, but enclose every two or three words in a set of <p> tags. In the opening tag for each of these, also add the following attribute: class="list".

6. Add a second level heading, <h2> at the bottom of the page. Make the heading say whatever you want it to say. When you are finished, save your page and display it. It should resemble Figure 10-1.

7. Add a set of style tags inside the <head> portion of the page.

8. For the h1 selector, set the display property to inline.

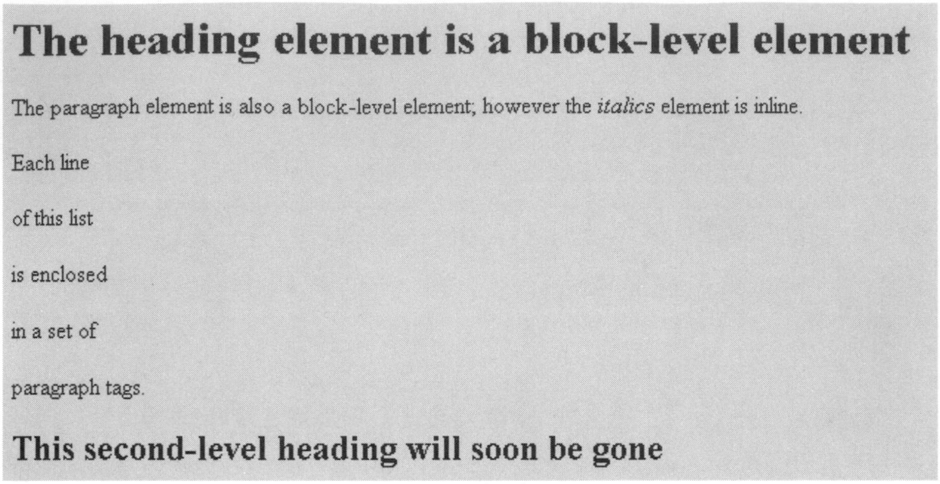

The heading element is a block-level element

The paragraph element is also a block-level element; however the *italics* element is inline.

Each line

of this list

is enclosed

in a set of

paragraph tags.

This second-level heading will soon be gone

Figure 10-1 HTML document with display properties unmodified

9. Set the display property for "p" to inline.

10. Create a class selector and name it "list." Set the display property for this selector to list-item. Also add the list-style-type property and set its value to "disc."

11. For the "i" selector, set the display property to "block."

12. Save the page again and display it in your browser. Your results should resemble Figure 10-2.

Note

To properly display the list items, you will need to use the Opera 5 browser. As of this writing, it is the only browser that supports the list-item value for the display property.

```
<html><head>
<title>Display</title>
<style>
h1      {display: inline;}
h2      {display: none;}
p       {display: inline;}
.list   {display: list-item;
         list-style-type: disc;}
i       {display: block;}
</style></head>
<body>
<h1>The heading element is a block-level element</h1>
<p>The paragraph element is also a block-level
element; however the <i>italics</i> element is
inline.</p>
<p class="list">Each line</p>
<p class="list">of this list</p>
<p class="list">is enclosed</p>
<p class="list">in a set of</p>
<p class="list">paragraph tags.</p>
<h2>This second-level heading will soon be gone</h2>
</body>
</html>
```

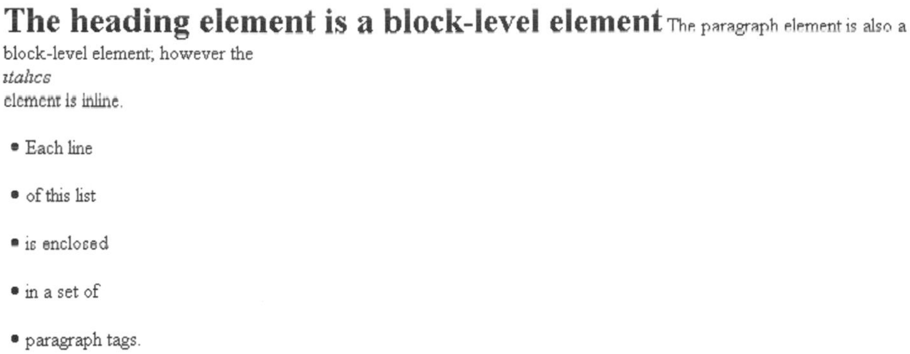

The heading element is a block-level element The paragraph element is also a
block-level element; however the
italics
element is inline.

- Each line

- of this list

- is enclosed

- in a set of

- paragraph tags.

10

| **Figure 10-2** | HTML document with display properties altered |

Project Summary

This project clearly demonstrates the impact that the display property can have on an HTML document. Because the display property for "h1" and "p" has been changed to "inline," these elements no longer appear on separate lines, but are all jumbled together. On the other hand, the italicized text now functions as a block-level element and is set apart on a line of its own. Most interesting are the individual paragraphs that follow. Now that their display property has been set to "list-item," they all function as a bulleted list rather than separate paragraphs. Interestingly, you didn't even have to use the unordered list, <ul>, element to create this bulleted list. However, you did have to add a marker (bullet) with the list-style-type property. Finally, the h2 element disappeared completely, because you set its display to "none."

While these aspects of the display property can be useful, be cautious. Using them is something like getting "under the hood" of your car and working on it yourself. If you know what you're doing, no problem; if you don't—watch out. The display property can literally overturn the entire structure of your document. While there may be times when you want to adjust an element's display property, you may find that it creates more problems for you than it solves. However, later in this module and in Module 16, you will see that the display property has some other very valuable uses.

1-Minute Drill

● What are two other names for the "descriptive" properties?

● What is the general function of the descriptive properties?

● Which property/value combination could you use to place two elements side-by-side?

● Display or Classification Properties
● To govern how elements behave in a document.
● You could do this with display: compact.

The Other Descriptive Properties

The display property is undoubtedly the most versatile of the descriptive properties. However, unless you work with XML, you probably will not find yourself using it all that often. There are several other descriptive properties, though, that you may find more useful: white-space and the list-style properties.

The white-space Property

If you've worked with HTML much, you already know that, as a rule, it ignores extra white space. In other words, if you type a line of code and add extra spaces between the characters or words, the browser will "collapse" them down to a single space. Thus, the code

```
<p>HTML      collapses      extra      white      space.</p>
```

is transformed into the following display:

HTML collapses extra white space.

If you want to use HTML to preserve your formatting, you must either add the nonbreaking space entity (one for each space you want to add) or use the preformatted text element, <pre>, as in the following lines of code:

```
<p>HTML     
collapses     
extra     
white     
space.     </p>

<pre>HTML      collapses      extra      white      space.</pre>
```

This code would produce the results you find in the following illustration:

HTML   collapses   extra   white   space.

HTML   collapses   extra   white   space.

10

HTML also will automatically add line breaks whenever the text would otherwise "spill" off the edge of the screen or window. This is called *text-wrapping*. If you want to override HTML's text-wrapping, you can do it by using the <pre> element or by adding your own line breaks with the line break, <br />, element. The CSS white-space property is designed to give you the same ability to control line breaks, text wrapping, and white-space with style sheets rather than HTML elements or character entities.

Values

The values for the white-space property are similar to their HTML counterparts, and they're easy to apply.

- **normal**   This is the default value. Extra white space is collapsed and text is wrapped.

- **pre**   This corresponds to the <pre> element in HTML. When you choose this value, the browser should preserve your spacing and line breaks.

- **nowrap**   This value will prevent the browser from inserting line breaks, thus allowing the text to flow off the edge of the screen.

Note

Most browsers support the "nowrap" value, but support for the "pre" value is weak. Even those browsers that do support "pre" are inconsistent in how it's applied. Although they preserve the essence of your text formatting, they do not reproduce it precisely.

Syntax

The white-space property accepts only the keyword values mentioned in the preceding section. Thus, the syntax for this property is basic and simple. Also, since "normal" is the default value, it is not necessary to use this property if you want a browser to handle formatting the way it normally would. One way you could apply this property would be by creating class selectors that apply the various values, then using the class attribute in any HTML element you want to modify. For example, the class selectors in the following code listing will produce the results found in Figure 10-3.

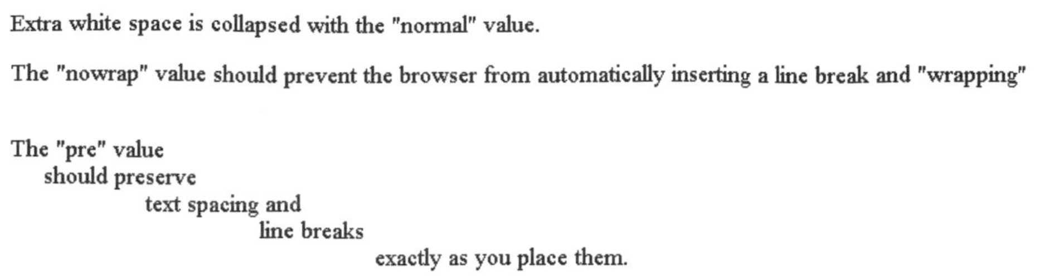

Extra white space is collapsed with the "normal" value.

The "nowrap" value should prevent the browser from automatically inserting a line break and "wrapping"

The "pre" value
    should preserve
        text spacing and
            line breaks
                exactly as you place them.

Figure 10-3 | Examples of the white-space property

```
<style>
.normal      {white-space: normal;}
.nowrap      {white-space: nowrap;}
.pre         {white-space: pre;}
 </style>
```

```
<html><head><title>White-space</title>
<style>
.normal {white-space: normal;font-size: 1.1em;}
.nowrap {white-space: nowrap; font-size: 1.1em;}
.pre    {white-space: pre; font-size: 1.1em;}</style>
</head>
<body>
<p class="normal">Extra      white      space      is      collapsed
    with     the      "normal"     value.</p>
<p class="nowrap">The "nowrap" value should prevent the browser from
automatically inserting a line break and "wrapping" the text to the next
line. This is the best-supported value, next to normal.</p>
<p class="pre">
The "pre" value
     should preserve
               text spacing and
                    line breaks
                         exactly as you place them.</p>
</body></html>
```

Characteristics

The white-space property doesn't have any unusual characteristics, except for the fact that it is not strongly supported by the major browsers. At this writing, the "pre" value remained unsupported in any version of Internet

Explorer—including the Version 6 beta. Therefore, if you are trying to preserve extra white space, you are better off using HTML's <pre> element instead. However, if you want to override line breaks and text-wrapping, you should have no trouble using the "nowrap" value. Table 10-2 lists some other important characteristics of the white-space property:

1-Minute Drill

- What is "white space" when used in the context of CSS?
- What do browsers normally do with white space?
- What values does the white-space property accept?
- Which value would you use to prevent the collapsing of white space?

The list-style-type Property

One of the first things you learn when you begin to work with HTML is how to create lists. Unordered (bulleted) lists, ordered (numbered) lists, and definition (glossary) lists are easy to work with, but they do have their limitations. For instance, with unordered lists you are limited to only three kinds of bullets: circle, square, or disc. With ordered lists, you have a greater range choices to work with, including uppercase and lowercase letters, uppercase and lowercase Roman numerals, and Arabic numerals. When you work with HTML, you set your preferences as to which type of bullet or number you want by using the "type" attribute. For example, if you want to create an unordered list with square bullets, you would write the list's opening tag this way: <ul type="square">. If you want to have a numbered list with Arabic numerals, the tag would look like this: <ol type="1">. A numbered list with lower case Roman numerals would begin with this tag: <ol type="i">.

Does it inherit?	Default value	Browser support	Works with
Yes	Normal	Weak	All elements

Table 10-2   Characteristics of the white-space Property

- Extra spaces in the code with no content.
- Browsers normally "collapse" all extra white space down to a single space.

With the list-style-type property you can use CSS to set the bullet or numbering type for list items. This can be particularly helpful on a large site where you are going to use a lot of lists. With this property you can set the style for all of your lists at one time, rather than needing to repeat the specification with each new list you start.

Values

The list-style-type property accepts keywords indicating both bullets and numbering systems. You can also specify a value of "none," which can suppress the bullet or number for an entire list or for a single list item.

Tip

Suppressing the display of an item number does not change the actual count. In other words, even if you suppress the number for a list item, the browser will still keep count, thus giving the next item the number it would have had anyway.

The CSS 1 values for the list-style-type property are essentially the same as those for the HTML "type" attribute. CSS 2 has added values for multiple language scripts, including Japanese, Greek, Chinese, Armenian, and Georgian. The values for the list-style-type property are

- **decimal**   Traditional Arabic numerals (1, 2, 3, and so on)

- **decimal-leading-zero**   CSS 2. This places a zero before the first number (01, 02, 03). The leading zero is only applied for the first nine numbers, as is illustrated in Figure 10-4.

- **lower-roman**   Lowercase Roman numerals (i, ii, iii)

- **upper-roman**   Uppercase Roman numerals (I, II, III)

- **lower-alpha**   Lowercase alphabet (a, b, c)

- **lower-latin**   CSS 2. Lower case Latin letters (same as lower alpha)

- **upper-alpha**   Upper case alphabet (A, B, C)

- **upper-latin**   CSS 2. Upper case Latin letters (same as upper alpha)

- **lower-greek**   CSS 2. Greek characters (α, β, γ)

- **hebrew**   CSS 2. Hebrew characters

10

- **armenian**   CSS 2. Armenian script

- **georgian**   CSS 2. Georgian script

- **cjk-ideographic**   CSS 2. Chinese ideographic characters

- **hiragana**   CSS 2. Japanese numbering system

- **katakana**   CSS 2. Japanese numbering system

- **hiragana-iroha**   CSS 2. Japanese numbering system

- **katakane-iroha**   CSS 2. Japanese numbering system

- **none**   Suppresses bullets or numbering

As of this writing, the CSS 2 values are not well supported by the major browsers. However, Netscape 6 does support the decimal-leading-zero, lower-greek, and hebrew values. Figure 10-4 demonstrates how these numbering systems look when applied to a list:

Syntax

The list-style-type property can be applied to any element with a display property of list-item. A numbering system or bullet may be specified for an entire list by using the "ol" or "ul" selector. You can also use the "li" selector to target all list items, or a class or id selector to focus on specific list items. For

Decimal Leading Zero	Greek	Hebrew
01. This is item one.	α. This is item one.	א. This is item one.
02. This is item two.	β. This is item two.	ב. This is item two.
03. This is item three.	γ. This is item three.	ג. This is item three.
04. This is item four.	δ. This is item four.	ד. This is item four.
05. This is item five.	ε. This is item five.	ה. This is item five.
06. This is item six.	ζ. This is item six.	ו. This is item six.
07. This is item seven.	η. This is item seven.	ז. This is item seven.
08. This is item eight.	θ. This is item eight.	ח. This is item eight.
09. This is item nine.	ι. This is item nine.	ט. This is item nine.
10. This is item ten.	κ. This is item ten.	י. This is item ten.

Figure 10-4   List style type values for decimal-leading-zero, lower-greek, and hebrew

example, if for some reason you wanted to suppress the numbering on a single item, you might create a class that was named "nonumber," then apply that class to the list item you wished to suppress, as in the following code:

```
<html><head><title>List Style Type</title>
<style>
ol    {list-style-type: decimal-leading-zero;}
.nonumber {list-style-type: none;}
<body>
<ol>
<li>This is item one.</li>
<li>This is item two.</li>
<li>This is item three.</li>
<li>This is item four.</li>
<li class="nonumber">This is item five.</li>
<li>This is item six.</li>
<li>This is item seven.</li>
<li>This is item eight.</li>
<li>This is item nine.</li>
<li>This is item ten.</li></ol>
</body></html>
```

The preceding list has a value of "decimal-leading-zero" specified for the entire list, but item number five is assigned the "nonumber" class. Notice in the following illustration that all of the items except for number five have item numbers. You might also take note that the count does not change, even though number five has been given a value of "none." The item is included in the browser's count, even though it is not given a number in the list.

10

Decimal Leading Zero
01. This is item one.
02. This is item two.
03. This is item three.
04. This is item four.
This is item five.
06. This is item six.
07. This is item seven.
08. This is item eight.
09. This is item nine.
10. This is item ten.

Characteristics

The CSS 1 values for the list-style-type property are well supported in the browsers. These are essentially the same values that you can create with HTML. Table 10-3 lists other important characteristics of the list-style-type property:

The list-style-image Property

One very nice feature of the CSS list-style properties is that it gives you the option of adding your own graphical bullets to lists. These can be any images that will display on a Web page, including photos, logo images, or simple graphics you design yourself. This can be a nice way of adding a personal touch to your Web pages, and it is simple to do.

The list-style-image property accepts either a URL value or a value of "none." Obviously, the URL value is the one you need to add your own image to a list. The syntax is the same as it would be for other URL values: the letters "url" precede the actual url, which should be enclosed in parentheses: url(myimage.gif). The following illustration and code demonstrate how a list might look if you used graphical bullets rather than those supplied by your browser:

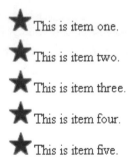

This is item one.

This is item two.

This is item three.

This is item four.

This is item five.

Does it inherit?	Default value	Browser support	Works with
Yes	disc	Inconsistent Strong support for CSS 1 Values. Others vary from browser to browser, with Netscape 6 being the strongest.	Elements whose display property is set to "list-item"

Table 10-3   Characteristics of the list-style-type Property

```
<html>
<head>
<title>List Style Image</title>
<style>
ul {list-style-image: url(blackstar.gif);}</style></head>
<body>
<ul>
<li>This is item one.</li>
<li>This is item two.</li>
<li>This is item three.</li>
<li>This is item four.</li>
<li>This is item five.</li>
</ul></body></html>
```

If you plan to use your own graphics for bullets, remember to keep them small (about 20 x 20 pixels or smaller). If the images are too large, then the entire layout of your list, not to mention your page, will be thrown off. Table 10-4 lists some other important characteristics of the list-style-image property.

The list-style-position Property

Another option that the CSS list-style properties give you is the ability to choose whether a number or bullet appears outside or inside the item. The list-style-position property allows you to specify a value of "outside," which places the bullet outside the list item box, or "inside," which places the bullet inside the list item box, as in the following illustration:

1. A value of **outside** will cause the number or bullet to be set apart to the left side of the list item. This is the default setting.

2. A value of **inside** will cause the first line of the list item to indent. The number or bullet will then be set inside the left margin of the list item, as it is in this item.

10

Does it inherit?	Default value	Browser support	Works with
Yes	None	Strong	Elements whose display property is set to "list-item"

Table 10-4   Characteristics of the list-style-image property

```
<html><head><title>List Style Position</title>
<style>
.outside   {list-style-position: outside;}
.inside    {list-style-position: inside;}</style></head>
<body>
<ol>
<li class="outside">A value of <b>outside</b> will
cause<br />the number or bullet to be set apart<br />
to the left side of the list item.<br />
This is the default setting.</li><br />

<li class="inside">A value of <b>inside</b> will
cause<br />the first line of the list item to indent.<br />
The number or bullet will then be set inside<br />
the left margin of the list item,<br />
as it is in this item.</li></ol>
</body></html>
```

Your decision as to which of these values to use will be based on aesthetics and your own personal preferences. If you are looking for a more compact layout, with the bullets or numbers being less obtrusive, then you will probably want to use the "inside" value. Table 10-5 lists some other key characteristics of the list-style-position property:

The list-style Property

In previous modules you were introduced to the shorthand properties. These properties enable you to set values for several properties at once, with a single style rule. The shorthand properties are helpful for keeping your style sheets brief and uncomplicated. Unfortunately, they are generally not supported as well as the individual properties. Thus, you need to use them with care.

Does it inherit?	Default value	Browser support	Works with
Yes	outside	Strong	Elements whose display property is set to "list-item"

Table 10-5 Characteristics of the list-style-position Property

The list-style property enables you to set styles for your lists with a single style rule. With this property you will need to supply only two values: one for the number, bullet, or image, and the other for the position.

Tip

If you decide to supply a graphical bullet, be sure to specify a keyword bullet (disc, circle, square) as a backup, in case your image fails to load.

The following style rules would all be acceptable applications of the list-style property:

```
ol     {list-style: upper-roman inside;}
ul ul  {list-style: url(myimage.gif) circle outside;}
.special {list-style: circle outside;}
ol ol ol {list-style: lower-alpha outside;}
#ls324  {list-style: lower-greek inside;}
```

Hint

Remember that when you see two or more selectors side-by-side and *not* separated by commas, they are *descendent* selectors. A descendent selector focuses on an element, class, or ID that is a child, grandchild, great-grandchild, and so on, of another selector. For example, in the preceding listing, the selector "ol ol ol" would set a style for an ordered list that is nested inside two other ordered lists.

Support tends to be a problem with all of the shorthand properties; however it is fairly strong for the list-style property. Netscape 4 does not support the URL value for graphical images. Aside from that, you are reasonably safe using this shorthand property. Table 10-6 supplies some other important things to remember about the list-style property:

10

Does it inherit?	Default value	Browser support	Works with
Yes	Not defined for shorthand properties	Good	Elements whose display property is set to "list-item"

Table 10-6   Characteristics of the list-style Property

Project 10-2: Create a Nested List

If you want to create an outline with HTML list item elements, you need to learn how to *nest* lists; if you want to use CSS to specify the outline's numbering scheme, you need to practice using *descendent selectors*. This project will help you do both. Nesting lists means that you place a complete list inside another list. Descendent selectors are selectors that set a style on a certain element *only* if it is a descendent of another particular element. You will complete this project in two parts. First, you will create an HTML document with a three-level nested list, and, second, you will create a separate style sheet and link your document to it.

Step-by-Step

1. Create an HTML document and save it as nested_list.htm.

2. Use the <ol> element to create an ordered (numbered) list. Do *not* use the type attribute to specify a numbering scheme. You will do this on your style sheet.

3. Add two list items in between the <ol> tags. Put whatever content you like into the list items. For this illustration, they will simply be named "Outline Point One" and "Outline Point Two."

4. Now comes the trickiest part of nesting lists. Add a second set of <ol> tags inside the <li> tags for Outline Point One. The <ol> tags should be placed *after* the list item's contents, but *before* the list item's closing tag: <li> Contents **<ol></ol>** </li>.

5. Inside your second set of <ol> tags, insert two or three sets of <li> tags. Name these whatever you want. This illustration names them "Sub-point One" and so on.

Hint

Things can get confusing quickly when you get to the third level of a nested list. You may find it helpful to align the various tags vertically in order to help you remember which tag goes with which list. See the code listing at the end of the project for an illustration.

6. Inside each set of list item tags you just added, insert *another* set of <ol> or <ul> tags. For the sake of variety, this project is using a bulleted list, <ul> for the third level, and the points are named "Note One" and "Note Two."

7. Perform Steps 3 through 6 again for Outline Point Two.

Tip

An easy way to do this is by highlighting the code, copying it to the clipboard, then pasting a new copy of the entire outline into your code. This procedure also reduces the chances of errors creeping into the outline.

8. Save the page and display it in a browser. It should look like Figure 10-5.

9. Create a plain text document in a text editor and save it as outline.css.

10. Add a style rule that sets a white background for the entire page.

11. Set the font for the ol selector to bold.

12. Write a style rule that causes the first level of your outline to display in uppercase Roman numerals (upper-roman).

13. Write a style rule for the second level of your outline that causes it to display in an uppercase alphabet (upper-alpha). You will need to use a descendent selector to make this work. The selector should be ol ol.

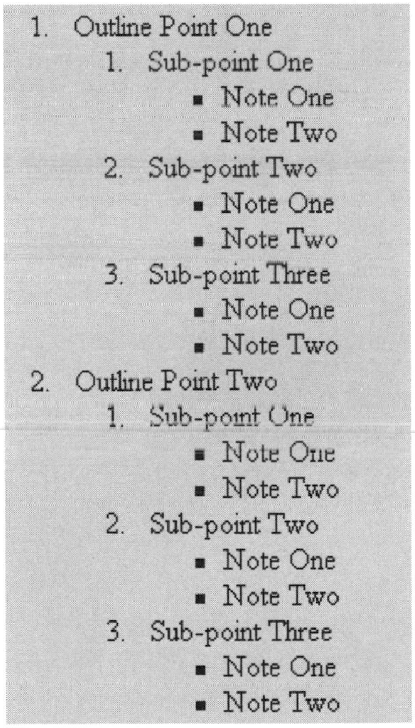

```
1.  Outline Point One
        1.  Sub-point One
                ■ Note One
                ■ Note Two
        2.  Sub-point Two
                ■ Note One
                ■ Note Two
        3.  Sub-point Three
                ■ Note One
                ■ Note Two
2.  Outline Point Two
        1.  Sub-point One
                ■ Note One
                ■ Note Two
        2.  Sub-point Two
                ■ Note One
                ■ Note Two
        3.  Sub-point Three
                ■ Note One
                ■ Note Two
```

10

Figure 10-5   An unstyled HTML outline

14. Add a style rule for the third level of your outline. If you use an ordered list, set it to decimal. Your selector will need to be ol ol ol. If you use an unordered list, set it to circle. Another alternative would be to supply your own graphical bullet. You can use any of the following selectors: ol ol ul, ol ul, or ul. This is because the unordered list is not used anywhere else in this document. Thus, you don't have to use a descendent selector for it. However, the advantage of using a descendent selector is that it does give you a slightly higher *specificity* for that particular style. (For a refresher on specificity rules, see Module 5.)

15. Save the style sheet and close it.

16. Open your HTML document (nested_list.htm) again and add a link to the style sheet inside the <head> portion of the page.

17. Save the document and open it in your browser. It should resemble Figure 10-6.

nested_list.htm

```
<html><head><title>Nested Lists</title>
<link rel="stylesheet" type="text/css" href="outline.css"/>
</head>
<body>
<ol>
<li>Outline Point One
    <ol><li>Sub-point One
        <ul><li>Note One</li>
            <li>Note Two</li></ul>
      </li>
        <li>Sub-point Two
         <ul><li>Note One</li>
            <li>Note Two</li></ul>
        </li>
        <li>Sub-point Three
        <ul><li>Note One</li>
            <li>Note Two</li></ul>
        </li>
    </ol>
</li>
<li>Outline Point Two
    <ol><li>Sub-point One
        <ul><li>Note One</li>
            <li>Note Two</li></ul>
        </li>
        <li>Sub-point Two
        <ul><li>Note One</li>
```

```
                    <li>Note Two</li></ul>
        </li>
         <li>Sub-point Three
        <ul><li>Note One</li>
            <li>Note Two</li></ul>
        </li>
        </ol>
    </li>
</ol>
</body></html>
```

outline.css

```
body    {background-color: white;}
ol      {font-weight: bold;
         list-style-type: upper-roman;}
ol ol   {list-style-type: upper-alpha;}
ul      {list-style-image: url(blackstar.gif);}
```

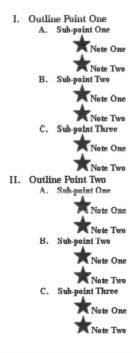

| **Figure 10-6** | CSS styles applied to outline |

Project Summary

This project gave you a chance to work with nested lists and with descendent selectors. With nesting lists you can create fairly complex outline structures for your pages. Using CSS to set the list style types, you can control the numbering or bullet system for your outlines, either on a site-wide, outline, or individual item basis. The list-style properties enable you to take one of the more elementary aspects of HTML and tailor it to your needs. As you will see in Module 14, using "generated content" you can make your lists even more sophisticated.

✓ Mastery Check

1. The display property enables you to change the fundamental _____ of any HTML element.

2. Write a style rule that adds a "marker" before a level-three heading.

   _____

   _____

3. List the four original (CSS 1) values for the display property.

   _____

   _____

4. What property/value combination would you use if you wanted to prevent a browser from adding its own line breaks to your text?

   _____

   _____

5. Write a style rule for the fourth level of an ordered list (outline) that will set the display to lowercase Roman numerals and will cause the item numbers to display inside the list item's box.

   _____

   _____

Part 3

Designing with CSS

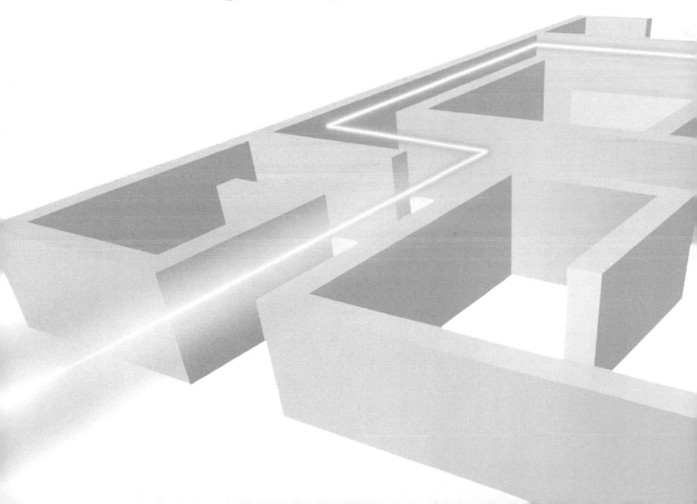

Module 11

The Visual Model

The Goals of this Module

- Understand the Visual Model
- Learn About Box Generation
- Work with the Float and Clear Properties
- Understand Positioning Schemes
- Work with Relative and Absolute Positioning

If you've been working through this book module-by-module, by now you should have developed a fairly good command of the basics of Cascading Style Sheets. You know the difference between selectors, properties, and values. You know what a declaration is and how it differs from a style rule. You are familiar with linked, embedded, and inline style sheets. Also, you have worked with various properties, and have developed an understanding of the basic CSS toolbox. However, you may be wondering how all of these things come together to enable you to create page layouts with CSS. Although you can create very nice page layouts using just the properties you have learned about thus far, more sophisticated layouts can be created by using the properties identified with the *visual model*.

Understand the Visual Model

Normally, when people think of Web pages they think of the kind of pages you view on a computer monitor. In other words, they think in terms of a *visual* medium. Although the Web is now moving into many different types of media, its roots go back to a visual presentation. In CSS, this is known as the *visual model*. If you want to use CSS to design Web pages in the traditional sense of the word, you must learn how to work with the visual model. A key part of the visual model is the concept of *box generation*.

Box Generation

In the CSS visual model, every element is assumed to generate a box in which its contents are placed. You can manipulate the size, appearance, and position of the box by adding *padding*, *borders*, and *margins*. (To review the box properties, see Module 9.) As the following illustration demonstrates, *padding* adds space inside the box, *borders* are drawn around the outside of the box, and *margins* govern the space around the box.

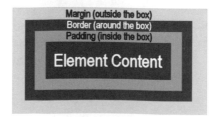

By learning how to control the positioning of boxes, you can create sophisticated page layouts and designs. If you have worked with a desktop publishing program, greeting card software, or even a word processor, you are probably familiar with the idea of arranging text and image boxes on a page. CSS layout works in much the same way. However, you need to learn how the various boxes on a page relate to one another before you learn how to position them.

Containing Blocks

Every box is contained within another box, usually referred to as the *containing block*. The position, width, and other aspects of most boxes will be determined by the size and position of the containing block. The "master" containing block on a Web page is the root element. The root element is the element from which all the other elements on the page descend. All of the other elements on the page are considered to be inside this *initial containing block*. As the following illustration shows, the width of each of the boxes is the same as the containing block (in this case, the entire window).

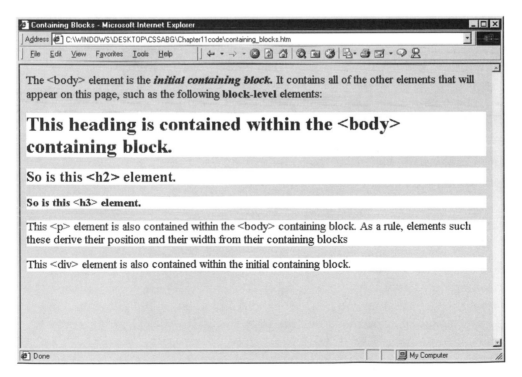

11

Tip _____

In an HTML document the actual "root" element is the <html> element. However, for design purposes you should consider the root to be the <body> element.

Block, Inline, and Anonymous Boxes

The first step in understanding how boxes on a page may be positioned is to gain an awareness of the different kinds of boxes you may encounter on a page. For the most part, these boxes are based on the types of elements they contain, that is, either block or inline. However, a third type of box—called an "anonymous" box—is also included to cover content that does not fit neatly into either of the two other types. The types of boxes that you will find on a page are

- **Block Boxes**   Block-level elements, such as <div>, <h#>, <p>, and so on, generate block boxes to contain their content. According to the W3C, "Block level elements generate a *principal block box* that only contains *block boxes*." Block boxes are organized vertically, each succeeding box placed beneath the previous one.

- **Inline Boxes**   Inline boxes are generated by inline elements, such as <span>, <img />, <e>, <u>, and so forth. Their contents are presented in "line-boxes," as opposed to a complete block on a page. These boxes will cover only inline content, rather than setting apart a complete block on a page.

- **Anonymous Boxes**   Content in a block box that is not enclosed in a block-level element is nevertheless regarded as if it were surrounded by its own box. This is called an "anonymous" box.

Although the relationships between these three box types may seem confusing, the principle is simple. Block elements "block off" a portion of the page; inline elements generate inline boxes that cover only the content to which they apply. Any block or inline content that is not "covered" by a specific box is assumed to be in an "anonymous" box. The following illustration and code demonstrate the relationship between the different kinds of containing boxes:

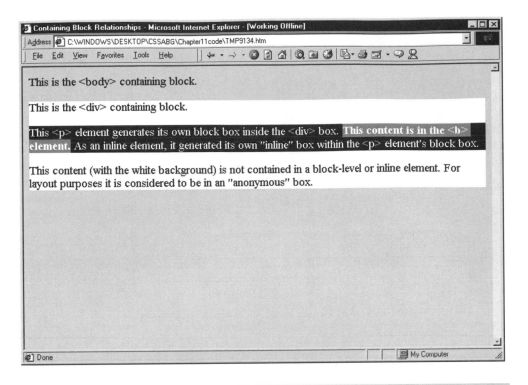

```
<html>
<head>
<title>Containing Block Relationships</title>
<style>
body        {font-size: 1.2em;}
div         {background-color: white;}
p           {background-color: black;
             color: white;}
b           {background-color: cyan;}</style></head>
<body>
This is the &lt;body&gt; containing block.<br /><br />

<div>This is the &lt;div&gt; containing block.

<p>This &lt;p&gt; element generates its own block box
inside the &lt;div&gt; box.

<b>This content is in the &lt;b&gt; element.</b>
```

11

```
As an inline element, it generated its own
&quot;inline&quot; box within the &lt;p&gt; element's
block box.</p>

This content (with the white background)
is not contained in a block-level or inline element.
For layout purposes it is considered to be in an
&quot;anonymous&quot; box.
</div>
</body></html>
```

Notice how the block-level elements, <div> and <p>, each create a containing box that sets aside a complete portion of the page, while the inline element, <b>, generates a box that extends only as far as that element's contents. For example, in the preceding illustration, a line is enclosed in the bold text, <b>, element. Since the <b> element is an inline element, its box extends only as far as the actual contents. The content at the very top and bottom of the div element box is not contained in either an inline or block element. Thus, it is considered to be in an anonymous box.

Note

To make it easier to see the boxes, the background-color for the <div> element has been set to white. The <p> element is white text on a black background. The <b> element has been set to white text on a cyan background. The background for <body> is displaying Internet Explorer's default background (approx. rgb(75%,75%,75%)).

1-Minute Drill

● What are the three types of boxes you might see on a page?

● What is the *initial containing block* of an HTML document?

● What is the true "root" element of an HTML document?

● Block, inline, and anonymous boxes
● The <body> element
● The <html> element

Ask the Expert

Question: Why do I have to spend so much time learning about boxes? All I want to do is figure out how to do a page layout.

Answer: Think of it this way. In ancient times (before computers, word processors, and CSS), if you wanted to lay out a brochure, or perhaps a newsletter, you would write your content, create your headlines, choose your photos and logos, and so on. Then, you would develop your layout by cutting and pasting snippets of text, images, and headlines on to a larger sheet of paper. By rearranging these various "blocks," you could experiment with different layouts until you found the one you liked the best. Once you were pleased with your layout, you would photograph it to create printing plates. In essence, you are doing the same thing with CSS when you work with "boxes." It's just that the boxes are "virtual" boxes. You won't have pieces of paper in your hand to rearrange; however, by learning and using CSS positioning properties, you can rearrange the various blocks on your page just as surely as you could if they were all printed out on little pieces of paper.

Box Dimensions

The actual size of a box depends on a number of different factors. As you have already learned, padding, borders, and margins can affect a box's size. However, if all of these are left at their default value of "zero," a box will take on the width of its containing block. For example, if you have an <h2> element that is the child of the <body> element, then the <h2> box should be as wide as the browser window, as in the following illustration:

However, try inserting a <div> element onto the page and setting its margins so that it does not take up the full browser window (say, 20% left and right).

Then, put a <p> element inside the <div>. The <p> element's box should be the same width as that of the <div>, as the following illustration demonstrates.

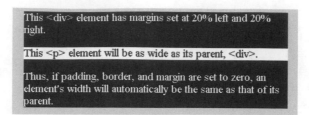

A quirk of Netscape 4 is that it treats block boxes as if they were inline, ending the boxes with their content, instead of extending them to the width of the parent. Keep this in mind as you begin to work with boxes in CSS. As you can see in the following illustration, the layout looks *very* different.

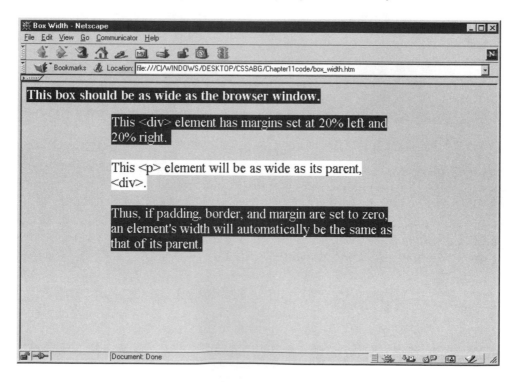

```
<html><head><title>Box Width</title>
<style>
body    {font-size: 1.2em; background-color: silver;}
h3      {background-color: blue; color: white;}
div     {margin-left: 20%;
         margin-right: 20%;
         background-color: blue;
         color: white;}
p       {color: blue; background-color: white;}</style>
</head>
<body>
<h3>This box should be as wide as the browser window.</h3>

<div>This &lt;div&gt; element has margins set at 20% left
    and 20% right.
<p>This &lt;p&gt; element will be as wide as its parent,
   &lt;div&gt;.</p>

Thus, if padding, border, and margin are set to zero,
an element's width will automatically
be the same as that of its parent.
</div></body></html>
```

Tip

Browsers are supposed to compute and adjust a box's width based on a formula that combines the values of seven properties into a total that equals the width of the parent element (containing box). The formula is: *margin-left + border-left + padding-left + width + padding-right + border-right + margin-right = width of parent element*.

While a box's width is determined by its containing block, its height will generally be determined by its contents. Notice in the preceding illustration how the box adjusts vertically to accommodate its contents. If the box contains a *replaced element* (an image for example), the box takes on the size and width of the replaced contents. For example, if a box contains an image that has dimensions of 200 pixels by 400 pixels, the box will take on those dimensions. The following illustration shows three elements: <h3>, <img />, and <p>. The background color for each has been set to white. Notice how the <h3> and

11

\<p\> elements show a background that extends completely across the browser window, while the \<img /\> element shows no background at all. This is because the \<img /\> element is an inline replaced element, and its "box" automatically adjusts to the image's dimensions.

If you do not want the browser to automatically set the dimensions of a box, there are some properties you can use to set them yourself.

Hint

A *replaced element* is an element that is actually "replaced" by some other content. For example, the \<img /\> element is a replaced element because it basically serves as the placeholder for a graphical image that will be inserted in the document. Another replaced element is the \<object\> element. Keep in mind that for a replaced element to take on the width and height of its content *before* the rest of the page loads, you must supply those values, either with HTML's width and height attributes or with CSS's width and height properties. If you don't do this, the page will take longer to load.

The Width and Height Properties

It is possible to specify the width and height a box should have by using the width and height properties. These properties function in much the same way as HTML's width and height attributes. For instance, if you've worked with HTML, you know that when you include an image on a page, it is important to specify its width and height in pixels. Thus, the HTML code for inserting a 200x300 image on a page would look something like this: **<img href="practice.gif" width="200" height="300" alt="Practice"/>**. This enables the browser to reserve the proper amount of space for that image as it loads the page. In HTML, these attributes also enable you to "scale" an image to a larger or smaller size. For example, if you didn't want your image to take up so much space, you might set the width and height attributes to width="100" and height="150". With CSS, the width and height properties allow you to do the same with boxes.

Actually, scaling images with CSS is easier than it is with HTML. If you are using CSS to resize an image, you only need to provide one value, either width or height. The browser will automatically set the other value proportionally. Thus, with CSS you need never have an image that appears out of proportion because it was improperly scaled.

Tip

It's still not a good idea to scale images with HTML or CSS. You'll have better performance (quicker downloads) if you actually resize the image in an image editing program such as PaintShop Pro or Adobe PhotoShop.

Values

Because the height and width properties are normally set by the browser according to the standards mentioned in the preceding section, it is generally not necessary to specify the height or width for a box. You will tend to use these properties mostly for setting image sizes or in special cases where you are using text with the "float" property. The height and width properties take the following values:

● **Length** (in, cm, mm, px, pt, pc)

● **Percentage** (of the containing box)

● **Auto** (browser-determined)

11

Hint

If you use percentages in setting widths and heights, keep in mind that the percentage is based on the width of the containing box (parent element), not of the browser window.

Syntax

The width and height properties can be applied to both block-level and replaced elements, such as images and "objects." Also, because the initial containing block cannot be positioned or resized, you cannot use the width or height properties with the "body" selector. However, all of the following style rules would be acceptable:

```
img.logo        {width: 10%;}
p               {height: 15px;}
h1              {width: 33%; height: 2.5em;}
#425x200        {width: 425px; height: 200px;}
```

Keep in mind that you cannot use negative percentage values with the width or height properties, either. Table 11-1 lists some other characteristics of these properties.

1-Minute Drill

● What is the formula for calculating a box's width?

● What generally determines a box's height?

● What is different about the box generated for an image?

The min-width and max-width Properties (CSS 2)

If you want to prevent browsers from automatically resizing boxes, you can use the *min-width* and *max-width* properties. As their names imply, these properties

---

● margin-left + border-left + padding-left + width + padding-right + border-right + margin-right = width of the parent element
● The box's content
● The box takes on the dimensions of the image

Do they inherit?	Default value	Browser support	Work with
Yes	Auto	Width: inconsistent Height: strong (except for Netscape 4)	Block-level and replaced elements

Table 11-1   Characteristics of the width and height properties

are designed to set minimum and/or maximum widths for boxes. Like the width
and height properties, these properties accept length and percentage values. If no
value is specified, then a default value of "none" is applied. The most important
characteristic of these properties to note is that almost no current browsers
support them. Table 11-2 lists some other key characteristics of the min-width
and max-width properties.

The Min-Height and Max-Height Properties (CSS 2)

Again, as their names imply, these properties enable you to set minimum
and/or maximum height values for boxes. They will accept length and
percentage values and have a default value of none. If you use a percentage
value, it is measured in relation to the parent element. For example, if you
have a div block that measures 100 pixels in height, and you set a "p" selector
to have a maximum height of 25%, the maximum height will be 25 pixels. As
with the min-width and max-width properties, these properties are poorly
supported. Table 11-3 lists other key characteristics of the min-height and
max-height properties:

Do they inherit?	Default value	Browser support	Works with
No	None	Poor	Block-level and replaced elements

Table 11-2   Characteristics of the min-width and max-width properties

11

Do they inherit?	Default value	Browser support	Works with
No	None	Poor	Block-level and replaced elements

Table 11-3 Characteristics of the min-height and max-height Properties

Simple Layout with Float and Clear (CSS 1)

One of the easiest ways to create layouts by manipulating boxes is with the *float* and *clear* properties. These properties, which were part of the CSS 1 specification, enable you to move boxes sideways and control how other boxes wrap around them. As you begin to work with float and clear, you may find that they remind you of HTML's "align" attribute.

The Float Property

In HTML, it is possible with the "align" attribute to cause an image to move to the right or left of a Web page, causing text to wrap to one side of the image. CSS 1 took that concept, which previously had applied only to images, and applied it across the board. With the float property, it is possible to arrange any of the boxes on a page so that they will float to one side of the page, with content wrapping to the other side. One obvious use of the float property is with images. However, the float property can also be used to create "sidebars," side navigation bars, even double-column layouts.

Float will accept only keyword values of "left," "right," or its default value of "none." Thus, the syntax for float is straightforward. If you want to cause a selector's box to float to the left, with content wrapping to the right, simply specify the selector and add the declaration, "float: left;". For a right-side float, the declaration would be, "float: right;". As the following illustration demonstrates, the float property can create some interesting results:

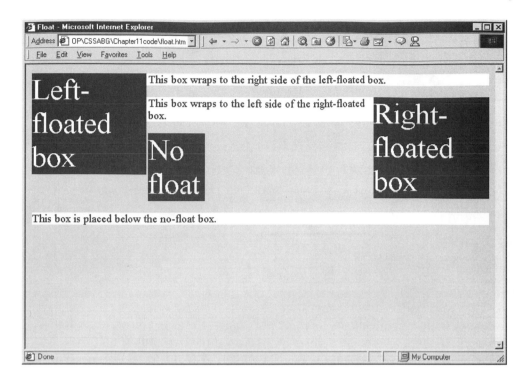

```
<html><head><title>Float</title>
<style>
.lgtxt      {font-size: 3em;
             background-color: black;
             color: white;
             float: left;
             width: 25%;}
.lgtxt2     {font-size: 3em;
             background-color: black;
             color: white;
             float: right;
             width: 25%;}
.lgtxt3     {font-size: 3em;
             background-color: black;
             color: white;
             float: none;
```

```
                  width: 25%;}
p              {background-color: white;
               font-size: 1.1em;}</style></head>
<body>
<p class="lgtxt">Left-floated box</p>

<p>This box wraps to the right side of
    the left-floated box.</p>

<p class="lgtxt2">Right-floated box</p>

<p>This box wraps to the left side of
    the right-floated box.</p>

<p class="lgtxt3">No float</p>

<p>This box is placed below the no-float box.</p>
</body></html>
```

Notice how the various floats interact with each other. As you try to follow the interaction of the different boxes in the example, remember that the elements are all presented on the page in the order that they occur in the HTML code. Their positioning is determined by the rules that govern floats (See "Ask the Expert"). Table 11-4 lists some other important characteristics of the float property.

Does it inherit?	Default value	Browser support	Works with
No	None	Inconsistent	Any elements except positioned elements and generated content.

Table 11-4   Characteristics of the Float Property

Ask the Expert

Question: What are the rules that govern the behavior of a floated box?

Answer: The rules get pretty complicated, but stated as simply as possible, they are

- The left side of a left-floated box may not be positioned past the left side of its containing block (parent element).

- If a left-floated box is preceded by other left-floated boxes, it should be positioned either to the right or below the box immediately preceding it.

- A left-floated box's right side may not overlap any right-floated boxes.

- The top of a floated box may not be higher than its containing block (parent element).

- The top of a floated box may not be higher than the tops of any floating boxes preceding it.

- The top of a floated box may not be higher than the tops of any other boxes occurring earlier in the page's source.

- A left-floated box's right side may not extend past the right side of its containing block.

- A floated box must go as high on the page as possible.

- Left-floating boxes are to be positioned as far to the left as possible. Right-floating boxes should be positioned as far to the right as possible. A higher position on the page is to be preferred over a position further to the left or right.

11

The Clear Property

As you work with the float property, you may find times when you want to float an element's box to one side or another, but you want to prevent other boxes from wrapping around the floated box. You use the clear property to accomplish this. As you might expect, the clear property accepts the same values as float: "left," "right," and "none." To see the impact of the clear property on a layout, try making one change in the code for the previous illustration. Add the declaration "clear: right;" to the "p" selector. When you save it and display it in your browser, it should look like this:

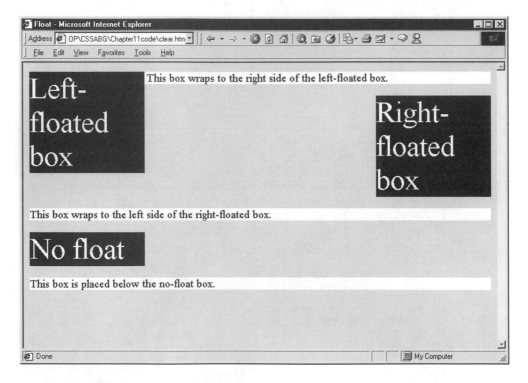

The middle paragraph block now drops down below the "right-floated" box, because it (the paragraph block) has a value of "clear: right." In other words, the "clear: right;" declaration will not permit floated content on the right side of that paragraph. Thus, the paragraph is repositioned below the right-floated box. Table 11-5 lists some other important characteristics of the clear property.

Does it inherit?	Default value	Browser support	Works with
No	None	Inconsistent	All except positioned elements and generated content

Table 11-5   Characteristics of the clear Property

Project 11-1: Create a Simple Layout with Float and Clear

The float and clear properties are undoubtedly the easiest means by which you can affect the positions of boxes on your page. While you may not have as precise control as you would with absolute and relative positioning (covered in the next section of this module), you also don't have to learn very much about positioning schemes. Since the browser applies the rules governing floated and clear boxes, most of the actual positioning is out of your hands. In this exercise, you will use the float and clear properties to manipulate one image and four paragraphs.

Step-by-Step

1. Create an HTML document and save it as float_and_clear.htm.

2. Find an image you would like to use (or download the one used in this project from Osborne's Web site: **www.osborne.com**) and insert it into your HTML code using the <img /> element. You can set the dimensions to whatever you'd like. The width and height attributes for the image used in Figure 10-1 are set to 125 and 181 pixels, respectively.

3. Create four separate paragraphs using the <p> element. Put whatever text you want into these paragraphs or copy from the code that follows these steps.

4. In the <head> portion of the page, add a set of <style> tags.

5. Write a style rule that sets the body text to display as bold face.

6. Make the paragraph boxes easier to see by setting their background colors to something different than your browser's default page background. Set the backgrounds to "white" if you are using Internet Explorer or to "cyan" if you are using Netscape or Opera.

11

7. Save the page, and display it in a browser. It should resemble Figure 11-1.

8. Set the font size for the entire document to 1.1 ems.

9. Set the float property for the image to a value of "left."

10. Create a class and name it "sidebar." Set the float property for the sidebar class to "right." Also, set its background color to blue, the text color to white, the width to 25%, and the font to 1em.

11. Apply the "sidebar" class to the *second* paragraph by using the class="sidebar" attribute inside that paragraph's opening <p> tag.

12. Create another class and name it "caption." Set the clear property of the caption class to "left."

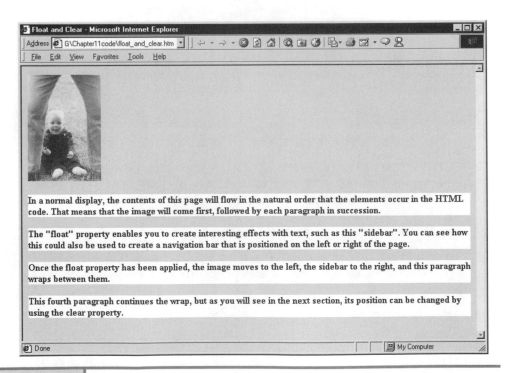

Figure 11-1   An image and four paragraphs

13. Apply the "caption" class to the *fourth* paragraph by using the class="caption" attribute inside that paragraph's opening <p> tag.

14. Make the paragraph boxes (except for the sidebar) disappear by either removing the background-color attribute from the "p" selector or by setting the body background color to match the paragraphs. Save your page and view it in a browser. It should resemble Figure 11-2.

Project Summary

This layout, created only with float and clear, is simple and uncomplicated. Of course, you could do more to change the appearance of the page by manipulating margins and padding and even by adding borders. In fact, you

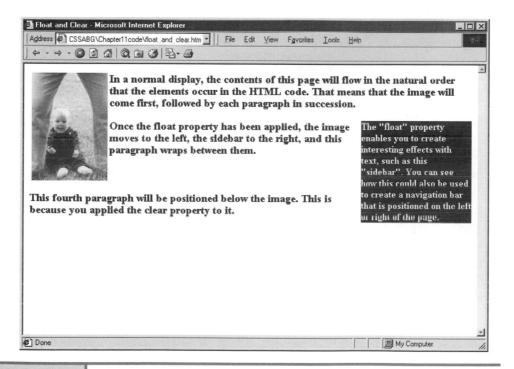

Figure 11-2   A simple layout created with float and clear

may want to go back into this page and experiment a bit. Try adding a right margin to the image or a left margin to the sidebar, and vice-versa. As you play with the different properties and manipulate the positions and sizes of boxes, you can begin to get a feel for how you might use these properties in creating attractive layouts for Web pages.

```html
<html><head><title>Float and Clear</title>
<style>
body       {font-weight: bold; background-color: white;}
img        {float: left;}
p          {background-color: white; font-size: 1.1em;}
.sidebar   {background-color: blue;
            color: white;
            width: 25%;
            font-size: 1em;
            float: right;}
.caption   {clear: left;}
p          {background-color: white}
</style></head>
<body>
<img src="cjp250x361.jpg" width="125"
     height="181" alt="CJ" />
<p>In a normal display, the contents of this page will flow
   in the natural order that the elements occur in the HTML
   code. That means that the image will come first,
   followed by each paragraph in succession.</p>

<p class="sidebar">The &quot;float&quot; property enables
   you to create interesting effects with text, such as
   this &quot;sidebar&quot;. You can see how this could
   also be used to create a navigation bar that is
   positioned on the left or right of the page.</p>

<p>Once the float property has been applied, the image
   moves to the left, the sidebar to the right, and this
   paragraph wraps between them.</p>

<p class="caption">This fourth paragraph will be
   positioned below the image. This is because you
   applied the clear property to it.</p>
</body></html>
```

Element Positioning (CSS 1)

Although the float and clear properties give you the ability to control the positions of various elements on the page, it is a far cry from being able to move the boxes around as if they were small snippets of paper. Instead, the float and clear properties give you sort of an "if-then" type of layout ability. *If* you do *this* with one box, *then* the other box will do *this*. However, if you want to be able to directly position elements on a page *anywhere you want them*, then you need to understand CSS positioning schemes and the properties that are used to make them work.

Positioning Schemes

There are four positioning schemes that you can take advantage of when you are working with CSS—at least in theory. The problem with the various positioning schemes, as with anything else in CSS, is always one of browser support. Thus, while you have four positioning approaches to choose from, weak browser support reduces your options to three at best. The CSS positioning schemes are the following: static, absolute, relative, and fixed positioning.

Static Positioning

Static positioning is the easiest scheme to begin with because you are already familiar with it, although perhaps not by that name. It could best be described by the statement "Go with the flow." Static positioning simply follows the natural flow of the document, allowing elements to be positioned according to the position they hold in the source code. While the positions of element boxes may be altered slightly by margins, padding, borders, and the float or clear properties, the boxes still follow a basic succession from the top of the page down.

Absolute Positioning

Absolute positioning is the scheme that best approximates the old "cut and paste" layout mentioned earlier in this module. With absolute positioning, you can move and position element boxes anywhere on the page or anywhere within their parent boxes. You can even overlap boxes and create a "layered" effect if you want. (For more on how to do this, check out Module 12.)

Although absolute positioning may sound like a difficult concept, it's really quite simple. Suppose you set a position of top: 25% and left: 40% for an element. You are simply specifying the location of the *top-left corner* of an element's box in relation to the top-left corner of its containing block (parent element). Thus, absolute positioning is "absolute" because you are determining—without any other influencing factors—the position of a box within its containing block. In this case, your point of reference is the containing block's top-left corner. As the following illustration shows, the heading is completely taken out of the normal flow of the document and actually overlaps the paragraph that "follows" it in the HTML code:

```
<html><head><title>Absolute Positioning</title>
<style>
h1       {background-color: black;
          color: white;
          position: absolute;
          top: 25%;
          left: 40%;}
p        {background-color: white;
          color: black;
          font-size: 1.5em;}</style></head>
<body>
<h1>This heading has been positioned
    down 25% and across 40%.</h1>
<p>This paragraph has been left in its natural position.
   This paragraph has been left in its natural position.
   This paragraph has been left in its natural position.
   This paragraph has been left in its natural position.
   This paragraph has been left in its natural position.
   This paragraph has been left in its natural position.
</p>
</body></html>
```

Relative Positioning

Perhaps where people learning CSS most often become confused is in understanding relative positioning and how it relates to absolute positioning.

Again, it's really not that difficult. As with absolute positioning, you are specifying the location of the top-left corner of an element's box. However, this time your point of reference is different. A box is relatively positioned when you specify its location *in relation to where it would normally occur on the page*. Remember "static" positioning? Elements are positioned according to the normal flow of the document. With relative positioning, you are moving those elements around, starting from where they would normally occur. For example, in the following illustration you will see the first heading and paragraph are positioned "statically" or, in other words, where they would normally go. The second heading also is in its natural place on the page; however, the second paragraph has been given a position value of "relative," a top value of -25px, and a left value of 50px. Notice how the paragraph has moved up and to the right and how it now slightly overlaps the heading.

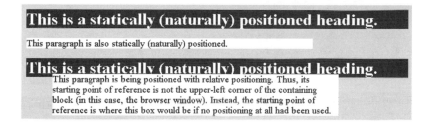

This is because relative positioning uses the element's natural position as a starting point. To see the difference, type in the code that follows and change the position value to "absolute." Now the second paragraph will be at the very top of the page. This is because absolute positioning uses the upper-left corner as its point of reference.

```
<html><head><title>Relative Positioning</title>
<style>
h1                {background-color: black;
                   color: white;}
p                 {background-color: white;
                   font-size: 1.1em;
                   margin-right: 25;}
p.relative        {background-color: white;
                   font-size: 1.1em;
                   margin-right: 25%;
                   position: relative;
                   top: -25px;
                   left: 50px;}</style></head>
```

```
<body>
<h1>This is a statically (naturally)
    positioned heading.</h1>
<p>This paragraph is also statically
    (naturally) positioned.</p>
<h1>This is a statically (naturally)
    positioned heading.</h1>
<p class="relative">This paragraph is being
positioned with relative positioning.
Thus, its starting point of reference is not
the upper-left corner of the containing block
(in this case, the browser window). Instead, the
starting point of reference is where this box would
be if no positioning at all had been used.</p>
</body></html>
```

Tip

Although a top-left reference point has been spoken of, it is also possible to work from other points of reference, such as top-right, bottom-left, and so on. However, as you are learning to work with absolute and relative positioning, it is easier to begin working from a single reference point. Then, as you grow accustomed to how positioning works, you can increase the ways in which you apply it.

Fixed Positioning

A fourth positioning scheme is known as *fixed positioning*. This type of positioning allows you to specify an element's location *in the browser window*. In addition, that location is identified as "fixed." In other words, while the rest of the page's content scrolls, that box remains where it is. This type of positioning creates a similar effect to what you can do with frames. You can have a logo or, ideally, a navigation bar that remains at the top or side of a page all the time, while other content comes and goes. Unfortunately, at the time of this writing, the fixed positioning scheme is virtually unsupported by the browsers. Thus, you'll have to wait a while before you can make use of it.

Tip

The easiest way to avoid browser support problems with positioning properties is to use the <div> and <span> elements when you want to position element boxes.

1-Minute Drill

● What is the default or "normal" positioning scheme?

● What is the point of reference for absolute positioning?

● What is the point of reference for relative positioning?

The Position Property

Once you have a handle on the different approaches to positioning boxes on a page, your next step is learn the properties that control positioning. To control a box's position on a page, you need two different types of properties. First, you need to use the "position" property to specify which positioning scheme should be applied to the box. Next you need to specify the "coordinates" you want applied to the box by means of the top, bottom, left, and right properties.

As you might expect, the position property accepts keyword values of "static," "absolute," "relative," and "fixed." The default value is "static," and the syntax is straightforward. You can apply the position property to any element by merely adding the declaration, "position: *value*." Table 11-6 supplies some other key characteristics of the position property.

Does it inherit?	Default value	Browser support	Works with
No	Static	Inconsistent Cross-browser support is strongest for the \<div\> and \<span\> elements.	All elements

Table 11-6 Characteristics of the position Property

11

● Static
● The containing block
● The position that the element would normally hold

The Top, Right, Bottom, and Left Properties

The position property in and of itself is not sufficient to position an element, because it has no means for specifying a location. For that, you need to use the top, right, bottom, and left properties. These properties may be used to specify a location based on the particular frame of reference that the position property has identified. Top, right, bottom, and left all accept either length (in, cm, mm, px, pt, pc) measurements or percentage measurements.

The syntax for these properties is simple, as long as you keep your positioning scheme and reference points in mind. For example, if you are working with absolute positioning and want to move an "h1" heading's box down 10 pixels from the top and 30% from the left side of the screen (assuming that the <body> element is the "parent" element), then you would write the style rule this way:

```
h1   {position: absolute;
       top: 10px;
       left: 30%;}
```

Table 11-7 lists other important characteristics of the top, right, bottom, and left properties.

Project 11-2: Playing with Blocks

Absolute and relative positioning are not difficult to work with, once you have had the chance to experiment with them. In this project you will create and position several colored blocks or boxes, just to get a feel for working with positioning. It's also fun to experiment and see what you can do with positioning as well as apply some of the other things you learned in this module.

Do they inherit?	Default value	Browser support	Work with
No	Zero	Inconsistent Cross-browser support is strongest for the <div> and <span> elements.	All elements

Table 11-7   Characteristics of the top, right, bottom, and left properties

Step-by-Step

1. Create an HTML document and save it as absolute_and_relative.htm.

2. Create five ID selectors and name them: redbox, greenbox, bluebox, yellowbox, and cyanbox. Remember that an ID selector must have the crosshatch character, # (the pound sign), preceding the name, as in: #redbox.

3. Assign each of the ID selectors a height and width of 100 pixels.

4. Set the background color for each of the boxes to match its name. For example, the background color for #redbox should be red, for #greenbox green, and so on.

Note

For Figures 11-3 through 11-5 in this project, #greenbox was given a background color of "lime" to make it stand out better in the grayscale illustrations.

5. Set the text color for each box to a contrasting color, so the text will stand out. It doesn't matter which color you use, as long as it is visible against the colored background.

6. In the <body> portion of your HTML document, add five sets of <div> elements, and assign each an ID corresponding to one of the ones created in Step 2. For example, one should be <div id="redbox"> </div>.

7. In between each set of <div> tags, add some content. In Figure 11-3, the contents simply reflect the box's color. You can add whatever content you would like.

8. Save the page and display it in your browser. It should resemble Figure 11-3. This is the "static" positioning of these elements.

9. Modify the style rules for each of the boxes by adding the position property, with a value set to "relative."

10. Position the boxes by using the top, right, bottom, and left properties with different combinations of values. Try using lengths, percentages, and combinations of both, along with different property combinations. Be sure to note how the various boxes reposition when you set the "coordinates" with these properties.

11

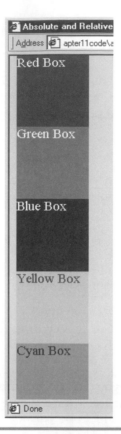

Figure 11-3   Five different-colored boxes in a "static" arrangement

11. Save the page and view it in your browser. The values listed in the code that follows this project produced the results in Figure 11-4.

12. Experiment with the boxes by changing the value of the position property from "relative" to "absolute." The results of that change from the original settings are reflected in Figure 11-5. Two boxes have moved completely off the screen, one is halfway off, and the remaining two have moved closer to the top of the screen. This is because the frame of reference has now changed from the elements' static positions to borders of the containing block. The same values have radically different effects. Alter the values to bring the boxes all back onto the page.

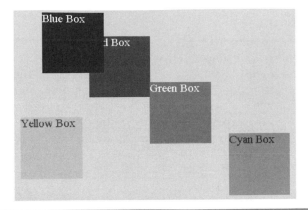

Figure 11-4 Relatively positioned boxes

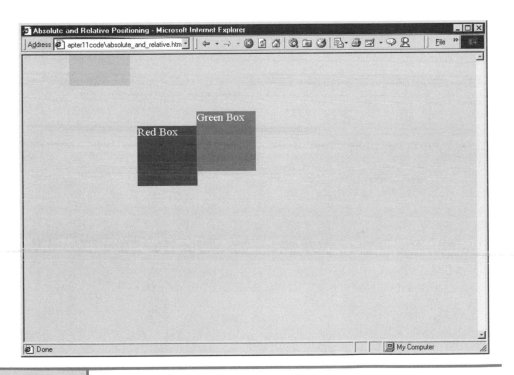

Figure 11-5 Absolutely positioned boxes

11

Project Summary

This project allows you to learn about positioning through experimentation. Since you are not really trying to create any particular kind of layout, you are free to experiment and see what results you get. Try experimenting further with the positioning properties by trying to position a box in each corner of the screen and one in the center. You might also try to create a layout in which you stack or overlap the boxes. Try positioning the boxes in a stair-step arrangement. As you begin to become comfortable positioning boxes, you will be taking a long step toward being able to design page layouts with CSS.

☑Mastery Check

1. Write a style rule for the "img" selector that will cause other elements to "wrap" down the left side of the image.

   _____

   _____

2. Write a style rule for the <div> element that will set its dimensions at 250 pixels by 250 pixels, give it a background color of navy and text color of yellow, and position it with absolute positioning so that the box's upper-left corner is in the center of the page.

   _____

   _____

3. Use the float property to write style rules that will position three boxes side by side on the page, beginning at the left side. Use ID selectors to name the boxes "box1," "box2," and "box3."

   _____

   _____

4. The browser window is the point of reference for the _____ positioning scheme.

5. What is relative positioning relative *to*?

   _____

   _____

Module 12

CSS Visual Effects

The Goals of this Module

- Understand the overflow Property
- Understand the clip Property
- Work with Visibility
- Apply the z-index Property
- Understand How Dynamic HTML Works

In Module 11 you learned how to use the float and clear properties to control content flow, how to position elements on a page with the position property, and how to specify the width and height of an element. Although these are useful properties, their very use can create some sticky design problems. What do you do if you have made a box too small for its contents? If elements overlap, is it possible to control which one is on top? If so, how do you do it? The properties that control CSS visual effects enable you to solve these problems; they also can open up for you the world of Dynamic HTML.

Understand Overflow and Clip

If you use the width and height properties to specify the size of an element, you could very easily face a situation where the contents of one of that element's "children" cannot fit in its box. When this occurs, what happens to the contents? The overflow and clip properties enable you to tell a browser how to handle such an overflow. These two properties can be somewhat complicated and difficult to work with, so you might need to work through this section a bit more slowly than normal.

Note

Realistically, you probably won't use the overflow and clip properties very often. If you find them too difficult, you might want to skip over this section and go on to the visibility and z-index properties

The Overflow Property

Browsers normally set an element's width and height automatically. However, with the width and height properties, it is possible for you to override the browser's "judgment" as to how much space various elements should take up on a page. As a rule, it's best to allow the browser to control elements' sizes, but if you are designing a layout that uses positioned elements, you will probably find it necessary to specify the sizes of your elements. For example, you may want to have a navigation bar on the left side of the page, or perhaps a letterhead type heading at the top. Or, maybe you want to create the kind of structured layout normally associated with tables. In cases such as these, you would use "width" and "height" to influence element size. However, as Figure 12-1 shows, you may find that your content overflows the box in which you have placed it:

Tip

One time you *always* want to use the width and height properties is with images or other "replaced content." If you don't, the browser will take longer to load your pages because it will have to "figure out" the dimensions of your images before it can create the page layout.

Obviously, if your content is spilling all over the page, your layout will suffer. With the overflow property, you have several options for controlling how this content is displayed.

Values

The overflow property accepts four keyword values: *visible, hidden, scroll,* and *auto.* These values will enable you to tell browsers if they should allow the content to spill over, if they should "hide" the content, or if they should set up a scrolling mechanism, similar to what you might see with frames.

If you set an element's overflow value to "visible," the content will remain on the screen and, at least theoretically, should overflow its containing block, as in Figure 12-1. In actuality, browsers that support this property tend to render the "visible" value by extending the containing block, rather than by allowing

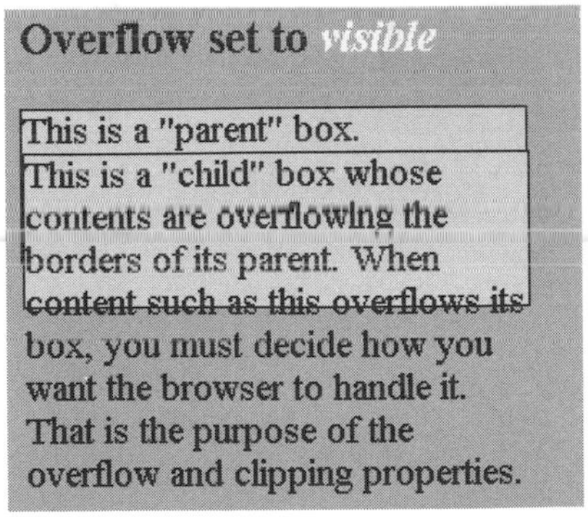

Overflow set to *visible*

This is a "parent" box.
This is a "child" box whose contents are overflowing the borders of its parent. When content such as this overflows its box, you must decide how you want the browser to handle it. That is the purpose of the overflow and clipping properties.

Figure 12-1   A box whose contents are overflowing its borders

12

for a true overflow. The following illustration shows how Internet Explorer 5.5 renders the boxes from Figure 12-1:

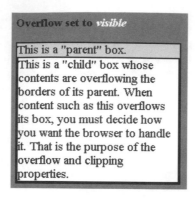

As you can see, the element's containing block has been extended to allow the contents to be completely visible. On the other hand, if you want overflowing contents to remain hidden, you would use the "hidden" value.

A value of "hidden" will force the containing block to remain at the size you specified with the width and height properties. Any overflowing content will be "clipped" (hidden), and no means of scrolling or viewing those contents will be provided. The following illustration demonstrates how the box's content is cut off at the borders of its parent element (containing block).

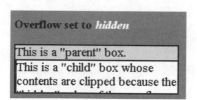

If you set the overflow value to "scroll," you will create a mini window, similar to what you could create with Internet Explorer's *inline frame,* <iframe>, element. In this case, the browser will keep the parent box at its specified size, but it will also add vertical and/or horizontal scroll bars as needed. This will allow your visitors to view all of the box's content by using the scroll bars, as the following screen shot illustrates:

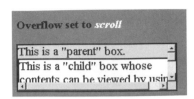

A fourth option you can choose is "auto," which allows the browser to choose how to handle content that overflows its box. The CSS 2 Specification does not determine exactly how the "auto" value should be applied, but rather leaves it up to the user-agent (browser). However, it does specify that the browser should supply scroll bars so that all of the content may be viewed. The following illustration shows how IE 5.5 renders the "auto" value.

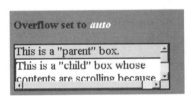

Note

The code for the previous four illustrations has been included here, in case you want to try reproducing them on your own browser. As Netscape 4.7's support of the overflow property is weak, you will have the best results with either IE 5+ or Netscape 6.

```
<html><head><title>Overflow Test Page</title>
<style>
body      {font-size: 1.2em;
           background-color: rgb(60%,60%,60%);}
h3 i      {color: white;}
div       {overflow: visible;
           width: 250px;
           height: 75px;
           background-color: silver;
           border: solid thin black;}
div.1b    {background-color: white;}
div.2     {overflow: hidden;
           width: 250px;
           height: 75px;
           border: solid thin black;}
```

12

```
div.2b      {background-color: white;}
div.3       {overflow: scroll;
             width: 250px;
             height: 75px;
             border: solid thin black;}
div.3b      {background-color: white;}
div.4       {overflow: auto;
             height: 75px;
             width: 250px;
             border: solid thin black;}
div.4b      {background-color: white;}
</style></head>
<body>
<h3>Overflow set to <i>visible</i></h3>
<div>This is a "parent" box.
<div class="1b">This is a "child" box whose
contents are overflowing the borders of its parent.
When content such as this overflows its box, you must
decide how you want the browser to handle it. That is
the purpose of the overflow and clipping properties.</div>
</div>
<hr />
<h3>Overflow set to <i>hidden</i></h3>
<div class="2">This is a "parent" box.
<div class="2b">This is a "child" box whose
contents are clipped because the &quot;hidden&quot;
value of the overflow property was applied.</div>
</div>
<hr />
<h3>Overflow set to <i>scroll</i></h3>
<div class="3">This is a "parent" box.
<div class="3b">This is a "child" box whose
contents can be viewed by using the scroll bars
created by the &quot;scroll&quot; value for
the overflow property.</div>
</div>
<hr />
<h3>Overflow set to <i>auto</i></h3>
<div class="4">This is a "parent" box.
<div class="4b">This is a "child" box whose
contents are scrolling because the overflow
property has been set to &quot;auto&quot;.</div>
</div>
</body></html>
```

Ask the Expert

Question: What conditions would create a situation where content overflows its box?

Answer: The CSS 2 specification lists at least five things that could create an overflow:

- You have specified that a line cannot be wrapped or broken. Thus it could conceivably be too long for its containing block.

- The "width" property for the child element is wider than that of the parent.

- The "height" property for the containing block is less than the height of its contents.

- The child element is positioned absolutely, thus placing it in a position where its contents might spill over the edges of its containing block.

- The box has negative margins.

Syntax

The overflow property can only be used with block-level or replaced elements, and it should be applied to the parent element (containing block). For example, if you will check the preceding code listing, you will notice that the overflow property is applied to parent elements (div, div.2, div.3, div.4), not the child elements (div.1b, div.2b, div.3b, div.4b). Thus, the following style rules would be acceptable applications of the overflow property:

```
div       {overflow: visible;}
img       {overflow: hidden;}
p         {overflow: scroll;}
.auto     {overflow: auto;}
#si23     {overflow: hidden;}
```

12

Tip

Remember that a *block-level* element is one that marks off a division on a page (<p>, <h#>, <div>, and so on). A *replaced* element is an element that acts as a placeholder for something else (<img>, <object>, and so on).

Although the overflow property is a great concept, it unfortunately is not supported by most older browsers. In fact, only Internet Explorer 5+ and Netscape 6 support it. Thus, unless you are certain your visitors will be using these browsers, you probably will not want to make much use of it. However, in time, when it is better supported, overflow will be a very useful tool. Table 12-1 lists some other important characteristics of the overflow property.

1-Minute Drill

● What are the possible values for the overflow property?

● What will a value of "hidden" do with overflowing content?

The Clip Property

After seeing overflow in action, you may be wondering what can be done about the content that disappears when a value of "hidden" is chosen. The clip property was developed to give you some control over how a browser displays (or doesn't display) such contents. The concept behind the clip property is that you can specify a shape and supply "coordinates" that will tell the browser how much of the clipped content should be visible. In other words, you draw an imaginary rectangle, and the content inside the rectangle would be kept visible, while content outside the rectangle is rendered invisible. Although this may seem confusing at first, it's really not very difficult.

Does it inherit?	Default value	Browser support	Works with
No	Visible	Weak (Only IE 5 and Netscape 6 support)	Block-level and replaced elements

Table 12-1 Characteristics of the overflow Property

● Overflow will accept values of: visible, hidden, scroll, and auto
● It will cause the content to be "clipped," rendering the overflow invisible

Note

In future versions of CSS, the W3C plans to make ways of specifying different shapes for clipped content, but as of this writing, the only shape that will work is a rectangle.

For example the illustration that follows shows a paragraph that is spilling over the borders of its containing box. Since the default value of the overflow property is "visible," the contents can be seen:

The content of this paragraph will overflow its containing box. The clip property can be used to determine how much of the content is visible, *and* how it displays. Clip can also be used for cropping images, but you're really better off using an image-editing program.

However, if the value of overflow is changed to "hidden," then the contents that will not fit into the containing block are rendered invisible:

The content of this par; will overflow its conta box. The clip property used to determine how of the content is visibl how it displays. Clip c; be used for cropping in

12

By applying the clip property, you can control how much content is rendered invisible, either reducing it further or expanding it so that more content is revealed. As the following illustration demonstrates, it is possible to reduce the "window" through which the content is viewed. If you have set the overflow property to "hidden," then that is all the content that will be visible. On the other hand, if you have set overflow to "scroll" or "auto," a scroll bar should be drawn to enable your visitor to scroll through the hidden contents.

Tip

To experiment with overflow and clipping, try copying the following code and then changing the values of the overflow and clip properties. You will need to have Internet Explorer 5 or Netscape 6 to properly view your results.

```
<html><head><title>The Clip Property</title>
<style>
body      {background-color: silver;
           font-size: 1.3em;}
div       {background-color: cyan;
            width: 200px;
            height: 200px;
            border: thin solid black;
            position: absolute;
            top: 5%;
            left: 5%;
            overflow: hidden;}
p         {width: 250px;
            height: 250px;
            border: thin solid black;
            position: absolute;
            top: 5%;
            left: 5%;
            clip: rect(50px 170px 150px 20px);}</style>
</head>
<body>
<div>
<p>The content of this paragraph will
overflow its containing box. The clip
property can be used to determine
how much of the content is visible,
```

```
<i>and</i> how it displays. Clip can
also be used for cropping images, but
you're really better off using an
image-editing program.</p>
</div>
</body></html>
```

Values

Although the concept behind the clip property is simple, its application can be a bit tricky. Clip requires that you specify a shape and supply coordinates that define the shape's outer edges. Since the only shape that will currently work is rectangle, then the values for clip would be written like this: rect(*value value value value*). The "values" inside the parentheses represent the top, right, bottom, and left edges of the rectangle. You can use any length measurements for values (in, cm, mm, pt, pc, px, em, ex), or you can use the keyword "auto." A value of "auto" leaves that side of the rectangle unchanged. Negative values are acceptable, but you cannot use percentage values.

Syntax

There are several tricky aspects to using the clip property. As with other properties, the four values are always applied in clockwise order: top, right, bottom, left. However, unlike other properties, you cannot specify a single value that the browser will apply to all four sides of the rectangle. You must specify a value for each of the four sides. If you want to leave one or more sides unchanged, use "auto." Thus, a clip value that adjusts only the left side of a rectangle might be written: rect(auto auto auto 20px).

Another interesting quirk of the clip property is that the values are all figured from the *top* and *left*. Thus if you try to set a five-pixel clip around the outside of the preceding illustration by adding values of 5px for each of the four sides, you will be unsuccessful. As a matter of fact, the contents will disappear entirely. For example, with a 200-pixel-square box, the values used to create a ten-pixel clip would be: rect(10px 190px 190px 10px). This is because the right and bottom values must move all the way across and down the box, respectively, to create the clip window.

The following style rules would all be legitimate applications of the clip property:

```
div        {clip: rect(auto 3in 3in auto);}
p          {clip: rect(auto auto auto 2em);}
blockquote {clip: rect(30px 100px 100px auto);}
```

12

Hint

It is permissible to mix and match length measurements with the clip property. In other words, you can use ems for one value, pixels for another, inches for another, and centimeters for the fourth.

Characteristics

The clip property, in theory at least, should be able to work with any property that has an overflow value set to something other than "visible." However, in practice it appears that the properties to which clip is applied must also be absolutely positioned. (See Module 11 for more on absolute positioning). Although clip is an interesting concept, it is tricky to use and, until browser support becomes stronger, will probably not be one of the more important tools in your CSS toolbox. Table 12-2 lists some other characteristics of the clip property.

1-Minute Drill

● What does the clip property enable you to do?

● How should a declaration with the clip property be written?

Does it inherit?	Default value	Browser support	Works with
No	Auto	Weak (Only IE 5 and Netscape 6 support)	Block-level and replaced elements that are absolutely positioned and with an overflow value *other than* "visible."

Table 12-2 Characteristics of the clip Property

● Clip enables you to control how much clipped content is displayed by a browser
● A clip declaration should be written: rect(top-value right-value bottom-value left-value)

Control Visibility and Layering

Among the most interesting of the visual effects properties are *visibility* and
z-index. The visibility property enables you to switch elements "off," rendering
them invisible without affecting the overall layout of the page. Z-index controls
the order in which overlapping elements are stacked or layered. These two
properties are important components of *dynamic HTML (DHTML)*, a "souped-up"
version of HTML that uses CSS and JavaScript (or another scripting language)
to allow the content of Web pages to change in response to actions of the user.

The Visibility Property

The visibility property might remind you of another property that has the
potential of rendering elements invisible: the *display* property. Although these
two elements both render elements invisible, there is a huge difference between
the two. If you make an element invisible with the display property by setting
the value to "display: none;" the browser does not generate a "box" for that
element. In other words, the element is treated as if it did not exist at all, and
the page layout is drawn without reserving any space for it. In essence, using
a declaration of "display: none;" is the same as removing the element from the
page. However, if you make an element invisible with the visibility property,
the element and its contents merely become *transparent*. In this case, the browser
still creates a box for it, and space on the page is reserved for it. In fact, the
space reserved will be exactly the same as it would be if the element were visible.
For example, as the following illustration shows, all three of the headings on
the sample HTML page are visible:

This headline is visible.

This headline will be hidden.

This headline is also visible.

12

However, you can see in the next illustration, changing the middle heading's visibility property to hidden causes that headline to disappear while leaving the rest of the layout unaffected.

This headline is visible.

This headline is also visible.

Note

Visibility is easy to work with. Just type in the following code, then change the values for the visibility property from visible to hidden, or vice-versa, and watch how the display changes. (Remember to save your page before trying to display it.)

```
<html><head><title>Visibility</title>
<style>
h1       {visibility: visible;}
.a       {visibility: hidden;}
.b       {visibility: visible;}
</style></head>
<body>
<h1>This headline is visible.</h1>
<h1 class="a">This headline will be hidden.</h1>
<h1 class="b">This headline is also visible.</h1>
</body></html>
```

Values
The visibility property accepts keyword values of "visible," "hidden," or "collapse." A value of "visible" obviously leaves the element unchanged and visible, while "hidden" causes the element, its contents, and its borders (if it has any) to become transparent. A value of "collapse" is used in special situations, to cause table rows or columns to disappear without affecting the overall layout of the table.

Syntax
The default value for visibility is "inherit," because an element will inherit the visibility of its parent; however, for all practical purposes, the default value should be understood as "visible." Visibility can be used with any element, and the syntax is straightforward. Thus, all of the following style rules are valid applications of the visibility property:

```
h1          {visibility: hidden;}
p.menu      {visibility: hidden;}
div         {visibility: visible;}
span        {visibility: hidden;}
#231        {visibility: collapse;}
.special    {visibility: visible;}
```

Characteristics

The visibility property finds its greatest usefulness when it is used in conjunction with a scripting language such as JavaScript or VBScript. With these languages it is possible to cause elements to appear and disappear by changing their visibility properties in response to a user action. For example, you might write a script that causes a menu to appear on a mouseover or a click event. A business site might have several pictures of its owners or managers that are normally invisible, but appear "dynamically" when someone "mouses over" the person's name. Also, since visibility enjoys strong browser support, you can use this property with little worry about compatibility problems. Table 12-3 lists some key characteristics of the visibility property.

1-Minute Drill

● How is "visibility: hidden;" different from "display: none;"?

● To what does the "collapse" value of the visibility property apply?

Does it inherit?	Default value	Browser support	Works with
Yes	Inherit (visible)	Strong	All elements

Table 12-3   Characteristics of the visibility Property

12

● "Visibility: hidden;" merely makes the box and its contents transparent, leaving the rest of the page layout unaffected. "Display: none;" actually turns off the box generation and the browser "reflows" the page as if the box were not there.

● The "collapse" value applies to table rows and columns.

The z-Index Property

You may have noticed when you were working with absolute and relative positioning, that it is possible to cause various page elements to overlap one another. At first glance, this may appear to be mostly an annoyance; however, by creatively arranging and layering elements, you can put together some very attractive designs. The z-index property is a useful tool in that it allows you to specify a "stacking order" for the elements on your page. By changing an element's z-index, you can bring it from the bottom of a stack to the top or vice-versa. You can also rearrange entire stacks with this simple property.

Values and Syntax

The values and syntax for the z-index property are very easy to master: z-index either takes a value of "auto" (the default value) or you assign it a number. Thus, the declaration: "z-index: 5" would assign a value of 5 to whatever

Ask the Expert

Question: Z-index is a strange name. It would be more intuitive if it were named "stacking-order," or something similar. What does "z-index" mean anyway?

Answer: Perhaps "z-index" isn't the most straightforward name that could have been given to this property, but it really is appropriate—once you understand the term's origin. When you are working with coordinates on a page, the letter x represents the vertical axis and the letter y represents the horizontal axis. That works fine as long as Web pages are only two-dimensional. However, when you layer or stack elements with CSS, you are—in theory at least—working in three dimensions: across the screen (horizontal), up and down the screen (vertical), and *out toward the user*. Thus, the letter z represents that third "virtual" dimension where elements are stacked one upon another toward the user. If the elements actually had mass, the stack would be rising up off the screen. That's why the stacking order is called the "z-index." It represents an index of where an element should be placed on the z axis.

element it is assigned. The primary factor you need to keep in mind is that the higher the number value, the higher in the stacking order an element is placed. In other words, elements are numbered from bottom to top. For example, if you are working with a series of ten elements and have assigned them z-index values of 1 through 10, the element with a z-index of 1 will be at the bottom of the stack. The element with a z-index of 10 will be at the top of the stack, that is, the most visible position. The following style rules are all valid examples of the z-index property:

```
div      {z-index: 5;}
.menu    {z-index: 2;}
#nav     {z-index: 137;}
```

Tip

Remember that the higher the number you give as a z-index the higher in the stack a particular box will appear. To assure that an element will be on top, it is permissible to give it a higher number than any of the others. For example, if you have a stack of five boxes and you want to make sure that one is always on top, you could give it a z-index of 10, 15, or even 100.

Characteristics

There are two important things to remember about the z-index property. First, it works only with *positioned* elements. In other words, you cannot merely apply this property at random on a page. You must use it with elements to which you have already applied either absolute, relative, or fixed positioning. Second, to realize its full potential, z-index requires the use of a scripting language such as JavaScript or VBScript. Otherwise, about all you can use it for is to set a static order for the overlapping elements on your page. However, as you'll see later in this module, by writing some simple scripts that work with the z-index property, you can bring your pages to life. Other important characteristics of the z-index property are listed in Table 12-4:

12

Does it inherit?	Default value	Browser support	Works with
No	Auto	Strong	Positioned elements

Table 12-4   Characteristics of the z-index Property

Understand Dynamic HTML

One frustration designers have had with HTML virtually from the inception of the World Wide Web is that HTML can create only "static" pages. However, in a world where computer graphics and visual effects are the norm, for most designers static Web pages just won't do. Several different approaches have been developed to bring "life" to Web pages, such as GIF animations, JavaScript, Java applets, and Flash animation. One creative way of "animating" Web pages that makes use of CSS is known as Dynamic HTML.

Dynamic HTML is one of those terms you may have heard or read about, but didn't really understand. In fact, its name is somewhat misleading. From reading the name, *Dynamic HTML*, you might infer that this is a special version of HTML that is somehow able to do more than "regular" HTML. While Dynamic HTML is indeed able to do more, it is not really a different version of HTML. In reality Dynamic HTML is made up of four components: HTML, CSS, JavaScript (or another scripting language), and the Document Object Model (DOM).

Animations are nice, but as a rule they are not interactive. The purpose of DHTML is to enable designers to create pages that are able to respond to the actions of a user by changing *dynamically* when an *event* occurs on a page. That event may be when your visitors move a mouse cursor over a certain part of your page (onMouseOver) or when the cursor is moved off of a certain place (onMouseOut). Other events include click events (onClick) and presses of a particular key (onKeyPress). These interactive responses are created with the four "ingredients" of DHTML.

HTML is obviously the first and most important component. With HTML you create the basic structure that makes up your page. However, as has already been noted, HTML is static in and of itself, so you need more than HTML to enable your pages to "react" to your visitors. As you have learned in the last few modules, CSS gives you the ability to control the positioning, visibility, and even stacking order of elements. By combining HTML with CSS, you have the potential for creating the interactivity that is characteristic of DHTML. Here is where scripting languages and the DOM come in.

Hint

HTML is not strictly "static" if you consider that hypertext links are a pretty awesome interactive feature themselves.

Scripting languages such as JavaScript, Jscript, or VBScript are the means for "programming" your Web pages to respond to your visitors. For example, when you "mouseover" an icon on a Web page and a hidden menu suddenly pops up, it is very likely that a scripting language was used to program that response. It is the scripting language that puts the *D* in DHTML. With a scripting language, you can write instructions that can actually change the content and style of a page as a user interacts with it. The concept that makes this possible is the Document Object Model (DOM).

Tip

Don't be discouraged if you're not a programmer. There are many "pre-written" scripts available on the Web, ready for you to use. Often they can be downloaded with instructions for including them on your page. You may have to tinker with your page a bit to get everything to work properly, but these scripts are a great resource for those who don't have the time or inclination to learn how to do Web page scripting.

The Document Object Model is the fourth component of dynamic HTML. It is essentially a way of making a document more "concrete," so that it is easier to apply Web page scripting to any part of the page. In other words, instead of thinking of an HTML document as hundreds of lines of code, with the DOM you learn to think of the document in objective rather than abstract terms. By learning to view a page as a collection of "objects," you can write scripts that will manipulate those objects.

If the concept of objects still seems fuzzy, try thinking of it this way: Suppose you just bought a newly constructed house and are planning where to put your furniture, how you're going to decorate it, what colors to use for your appliances, and so on. Are you going to sit down with the blueprints and make your plans from them? Not likely. Blueprints are abstract. It's hard to imagine how your favorite sofa and home entertainment system are going to look solely on the basis of some abstract documents. You are much more likely to take a walk through the house, go into the living room, kitchen, bedrooms, and so on.

If you've got a good imagination, you might create the HOM (House Object Model). Then, you would think of the house as a series of "objects," including the "house" object, the "living room" object, the "kitchen" object, the "bedroom" object, and so on. As you plan for your furniture, you would even take it a step

12

further; in the "kitchen" object, you'd want a "refrigerator" object, a "stove" object, and so forth. Each of those objects will have *properties* (characteristics), such as color, size, type (gas or electric oven), and so forth. Are you getting the idea?

Using JavaScript on your imaginary house object, you could become quite specific in your thinking and planning. If you wanted to specify a color for your refrigerator, you might write something like "house.kitchen.refrigerator.color = peach." This is essentially how the Document Object Model works; however, instead of rooms in a house, you're dealing with parts of a document. Thus, you might use objects to set a background color for a page by writing a script that has a line such as this: "document.style.backgroundColor = green." However, you could also write a script that causes the background color to change when you mouseover a headline or click on a link. That's when HTML becomes "dynamic."

Dynamic HTML has great potential; unfortunately, because it requires that you be fairly conversant with web page scripting, it is not as easy to use. There are, however, a number of good resources you can take advantage of if you want to experiment with DHTML and learn how to use it. Table 12-5 lists some Web sites you may wish to visit for more information on DHTML:

Web Site	URL	Resources
DHTML Shock	www.dhtmlshock.com	Articles, tutorials, free scripts
DevX	www.devx.com	DHTML help, discussions, free sample code
Webmonkey	www.webmonkey.com	Good tutorials
Dynamic HTML Guru	www.htmlguru.com	Tutorials, DHTML news, demos
DHTML School	www.w3schools.com/dhtml	Tutorials, excellent DOM reference source

Table 12-5   DHTML Resources

Project 12-1: Create a Dynamic Web Page

To give you an idea of the potential for creating interactive Web pages with Dynamic HTML, you are going to construct a page with six different-colored blocks that have been positioned to overlap with "absolute" positioning. Then, you will write a simple JavaScript that will cause each of the blocks to move to the top of the stack upon a "mouseover." When you remove the cursor, the block will return to its normal place in the stack. Even if you've never worked with JavaScript before, you shouldn't find this particular project too difficult, since the script has been deliberately kept simple. Just keep in mind that since JavaScript is case-sensitive, you will need to make sure that your code matches the sample code given at the end of the project.

Note

In the interest of keeping this project relatively uncomplicated, it has been written for only one type of browser. You will need Internet Explorer 4 or higher for this project to work properly. It will not work in Netscape or Opera.

Step-by-Step

1. Create an HTML document and save it as zindex_demo.htm

2. Add a set of <style> tags inside the <head> portion of the page.

3. Add the body selector between the style tags.

4. Create 6 ID selectors, naming them (in this order) "red," "green," "blue," "yellow," "cyan," and "white."

5. Set the background color for the body selector to silver or gray and the font size to 1.2 ems.

6. Set the background color of each ID selector to match its name. That is, the "#red" selector should have its background color set to "red," and so on. Set the text color to "white" for the first three properties, and "black" for the last three.

7. Set the width and height properties for each selector to 100 pixels wide by 100 pixels high.

8. Add a thin, solid, black border to each selector.

9. Align the text in each property to center.

12

10. In the <body> portion of the page, use the <div> element with the ID attribute to create a box for each of the ID selectors you created. In between the <div> tags, write the name of the background color. For example, the code for the red box should look like this: **<div id="red">Red</div>**.

11. Save the page and view it in Internet Explorer. You should see a succession of colored boxes on the left side of the browser window. You will have to scroll to bring the sixth box into view. Your results should resemble Figure 12-2.

12. Now you will use absolute positioning to "layer" the boxes. Go back to the six ID selectors and add the position attribute to each, with its value set to "absolute."

13. For the first ID selector, set the top property to 5% and the left property to 5%. The second selector should be set to top = 10% and left = 10%. For each additional selector, add 5% to the value of the top and left properties.

Figure 12-2 | Boxes Stacked in Their "Natural" Positions

14. Save the page and view it in Internet Explorer. Your boxes should now be stacked diagonally from the upper left toward the center of the page, as in Figure 12-3.

15. Now you will use JavaScript with the z-index property to make your boxes "come alive." Set the stacking order for each of the boxes by adding the z-index property to each of the ID selectors. The value you give each box will determine its position in the stack. The easiest way to do this is to simply assign each selector a number corresponding to its current position. Thus, the first box (red) will be given a z-index of "1," green will be "2," and so on.

Caution

In the next few steps, you will be working with JavaScript. Be sure that your script matches *exactly* (including case) the script given in the code listing. Otherwise, you will receive error messages.

16. Add a set of <script> tags inside the <head> portion of the page. The opening tag should look like this: <script type="text/javascript">. The closing tag will look like this: </script>.

17. In this step you will create a function that will change the z-index value of the red box, causing it to be brought to the top of the stack. Your function should look like this: function redUp() {red.style.zIndex = 7;}.

18. Now you will create a function that returns the red box to its original place. Your code should look like this: function redDown() {red.style.zIndex = 1;}.

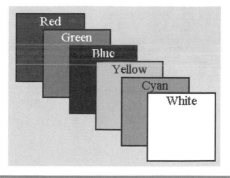

12

Figure 12-3 | Boxes layered using absolute positioning

19. Create similar functions for the green, blue, yellow, and cyan boxes. On the "up" function, the z-index should be set to "7" because that will bring it to the top of the stack (since there are six boxes in the stack). On the "down" function, set the z-index to its original value. Since the white box is already on top, it is not necessary to create a function for it. If you get stuck, refer to the complete code at the end of this project.

20. All that remains is to insert event handlers into your HTML that will "call" the functions and create the "dynamic" response. For this project, you will use the onMouseOver event handler to cause a box's z-index to be changed when the mouse cursor passes over that box. To cause this to happen, all you need to do is to add: onMouseOver="redUp()" to the opening <div> tag for the red box. The tag should look like this: <div id="red" onMouseOver="redUp()">. Add a similar event handler to each of the other boxes, making sure you refer to the proper function (that is, for the green box, the function will be "greenUp()," and so on.

21. If you stop at this point, your boxes will remain in their new positions after they are moved. To cause them to return to their original spots, use the onMouseOut event handler with the down functions. For example, the opening tag for the red box should now look like this:

    <div id="red" onMouseOver="redUp()" onMouseOut="redDown()

22. Save your page and view it in Internet Explorer. When you move the mouse over any of the boxes (except white), the box should come to the top of the stack. Moving the mouse off the box should return the box to its original place. Your results should resemble Figure 12-4.

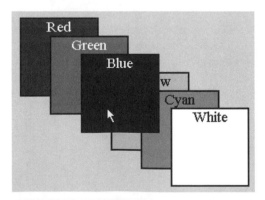

Figure 12-4 Blue Box Jumps to the Top with onMouseOver

23. If you receive an error message, the culprit is probably a typo in your script or in the event handlers. Cross-check your code with the sample code to help debug it.

```
<html><head><title>Dynamic HTML Demo</title>
<script type="text/javascript">
function redUp() {red.style.zIndex = 7;}
function redDown() {red.style.zIndex = 1;}
function greenUp() {green.style.zIndex = 7;}
function greenDown() {green.style.zIndex = 2;}
function blueUp() {blue.style.zIndex = 7;}
function blueDown() {blue.style.zIndex = 3;}
function yellowUp() {yellow.style.zIndex = 7;}
function yellowDown() {yellow.style.zIndex = 4;}
function cyanUp() {cyan.style.zIndex = 7;}
function cyanDown() {cyan.style.zIndex = 5;}
</script>

<style>
body      {background-color: silver;
           font-size: 1.2em;}
#red      {background-color: red;
           color: white;
           width: 100px;
           height: 100px;
           border: thin solid black;
           text-align: center;
           position: absolute;
           top: 5%;
           left: 5%;
           z-index: 1;}
#green    {background-color: lime;
           color: white;
           width: 100px;
           height: 100px;
           border: thin solid black;
           text-align: center;
           position: absolute;
           top: 10%;
           left: 10%;
           z-index: 2;}
#blue     {background-color: blue;
           color: white;
           width: 100px;
```

```
               height: 100px;
               border: thin solid black;
               text-align: center;
               position: absolute;
               top: 15%;
               left: 15%;
               z-index: 3;}
#yellow   {background-color: yellow;
               color: black;
               width: 100px;
               height: 100px;
               border: thin solid black;
               text-align: center;
               position: absolute;
               top: 20%;
               left: 20%;
               z-index: 4;}
#cyan     {background-color: cyan;
               color: black;
               width: 100px;
               height: 100px;
               border: thin solid black;
               text-align: center;
               position: absolute;
               top: 25%;
               left: 25%;
               z-index: 5}
#white    {background-color: white;
               color: black;
               width: 100px;
               height: 100px;
               border: thin solid black;
               text-align: center;
               position: absolute;
               top: 30%;
               left: 30%;
               z-index: 6;}</style> </head>
<body>
<div id="red" onMouseOver="redUp()"
     onMouseOut="redDown()">Red</div>

<div id="green" onMouseOver="greenUp()"
     onMouseOut="greenDown()">Green</div>
```

```
<div id="blue" onMouseOver="blueUp()"
    onMouseOut="blueDown()">Blue</div>

<div id="yellow" onMouseOver="yellowUp()"
    onMouseOut="yellowDown()">Yellow</div>

<div id="cyan" onMouseOver="cyanUp()"
    onMouseOut="cyanDown()">Cyan</div>

<div id="white">White</div>
</body></html>
```

Project Summary

This project gives you just a taste of what can be done when you combine
HTML, CSS, a scripting language, and the DOM to create dynamic HTML.
Obviously DHTML can be much more complex than what you have done
in this project, but you can see the potential. If you want to explore the
possibilities of DHTML, your next step should be to learn how to work with a
scripting language such as JavaScript. A good place to start is Osborne's book,
JavaScript: A Beginner's Guide, by John Pollock. It will get you off to a good start.
For more on DHTML and the DOM, try visiting the W3C's site: **www.w3.org**.

12

☑ *Mastery Check*

1. List the four key components of DHTML.

_____

_____

2. According to its z-index, which of the following selectors will be on top of the stack? on the bottom? in the middle?

div {z-index: 28;}
#123 {z-index: 4;}
purple {z-index: 16;}

_____

_____

3. What values could you use with the "overflow" property if you wanted your visitors to be able to view the "hidden" content.

_____

_____

4. You have a 300x300 pixel box, to which you have applied the overflow property. Write a declaration with the clipping property that will give you a 15-pixel margin around the clipped contents.

_____

_____

5. If you want to make an element's "box" disappear *without* affecting the overall layout of the page, which property/value combination should you use?

   A. display: none;

   B. overflow: hidden;

   C. visibility: hidden;

   D. visibility: none;

Module 13

CSS and Site Design

The Goals of this Module

- Learn General Web Design Principles
- Understand How to Develop a Web Site
- Create a Page Layout with CSS
- Organize a Stylesheet
- Learn How to Validate your HTML and CSS
- Design for Cross-Browser Compatibility

Now that you have the "tools" in hand to create Web pages with CSS, you're *almost* ready to use it in designing your Web site. However, before you sit down and start coding that new site, you may find it helpful to take some time learning principles for good Web design. You see, although CSS provides you with cutting edge ability to influence the appearance of your Web site, it is just as possible to create lousy Web pages with CSS as it is with HTML. So before you code, here are some things you may want to keep in mind.

Understand Good Web Design

CSS is a great tool. By applying good design principles, you can create beautiful layouts and attractive pages. You can also create incredibly ugly pages with CSS. In other words, design tools are no better than the ability of the person who is using them. If you ignore principles of good design, then you will produce poorly done pages, whether you use HTML, CSS, DreamWeaver, FrontPage, or any other Web authoring tool. There's nothing about Cascading Style Sheets that will magically endow you with a good sense of design. In fact, it's probably easier to create poor Web pages with CSS because you have so many more options at your disposal. Thus, some time invested in learning about good Web design will be well spent.

Web Site Planning

In addition to gaining a grasp of general Web design principles, it's a good idea to know how to create a Web site that is well organized. All too often, Web sites are created haphazardly, with new pages and content added according to the author's whims. Whether you are simply putting up a personal site or you're trying to start an online business, you will do well to take the time to lay out your site carefully. As you do, consider the following steps:

- **Develop a purpose statement**   Why are you going to all the trouble to put up a Web site? What do you want your visitors to do, get, find, buy, discover, experience, or learn at your site? Is your site personal, business, non-profit, informational, or a combination of two or more of these? A clear understanding of why your site exists will be invaluable in the process of developing it.

- **Analyze your target audience**   Who will be visiting your site? Will your audience be a specific-issue group, such as amateur astronomers, or are you targeting a broader cross-section of people (book lovers, for example)?

What age group are you targeting? If the site will be designed for children, you are likely to take a much different approach than you would with a site targeted at senior citizens.

● **Plan your content**   Using the two previous steps as guidelines, determine what kind of content you will need to have on your site. Will you need a response form or a guestbook? Will some kind of multimedia be needed? Do you need a searchable catalog? What kind of images do you need?

● **Storyboard your site**   A *storyboard* is a layout of your site and its pages. You can either sketch it out as a flow chart or use something like index cards to create a layout. As the following illustration shows, a good storyboard can help you visualize your site, plan your navigation links, and organize your material in the most efficient manner possible.

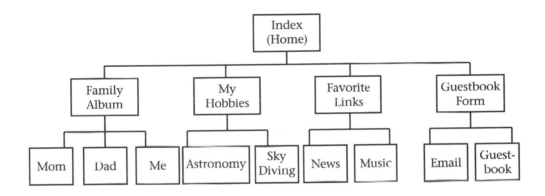

Web Site Design

If you are creating a Web site "just for the fun of it," then design principles are perhaps not a major consideration for you. However, if you are putting up a site for any other reason and you want to attract an increasing (or at least regular) audience to your site, then you should keep in mind some general principles that will enable your Web "presence" to have its strongest possible impact.

Navigation Should Be Clear and Understandable

Imagine going to a public library to look for a book someone said you just *had* to read. Upon arriving, you discover that the library offers no means of navigation. There are no computer terminals, no categories on the shelves, and you can't even find a card catalogue. When you go up to the main desk and ask the librarian where to find the book, you are told, "It's out there somewhere." As you turn and survey a library of 300,000 volumes, you decide it's not worth the trouble and leave for the nearest bookstore.

Granted, the illustration is an exaggeration. It's extremely doubtful you would ever have 300,000 pages on your site, but the point is that poorly designed navigation will cripple your site quicker than almost anything else. Have you ever visited a site where you couldn't find your way around because the navigation system wasn't easy to follow? Did you stay long? Probably not. Neither will your visitors. If your visitors cannot find what they are looking for with relative ease, they will leave.

To create a good navigation system for your site, keep the following principles in mind:

● *Always* **have a set of text-based links somewhere on the page**   That way, if people visit your site with a text-based or non-visual browser, they will still be able to find their way around.

● *Always* **put some form of navigation on every page**   If someone comes to your site via a search engine, often they will hit one the pages in the interior of your site. If you don't have a navigation system on the page, they will find themselves "stranded" there. Give them the means to find their way to your main page at least. Ideally, the navigation system for the entire site should be on every page.

● *Always* **make graphical navigation clear**   Nothing is more frustrating than visiting a site and finding nothing but pictures to navigate with. It's even worse if your visitors have to guess what the pictures mean. If the meaning of the images is not intuitive, add a textual description to clarify.

● *Always* **provide a site map**   A site map is a single page that shows the overall layout of your site and provides links to the key pages. Many of your visitors can orient themselves to your site and its contents with a site map, and they can more quickly find exactly what they want.

Limit Your Use of Animation

Animation seems to capture the imagination of many beginning Web authors, and who can blame them? There is indeed something captivating about being able to create animations and put them on your own site. Even if you don't have the software to make your own animations, there is plenty available on the Web, free of charge. Unfortunately, a lot of Web authors find animation *so* fun to use that they pepper their pages with animations of every kind. You'll find blinking text, scrolling status bars, animated e-mail icons, 3-D rotating logos, and more. Generally, these pages become an assault on the eyes, and the average visitor is more than glad to flee. A recurring, albeit somewhat clichéd, principle when dealing with Web pages is "Less is more." One high quality, well-placed animation will do much more than ten cheaply done ones that are scattered over your page. If you plan on adding animations to your page, keep in mind the following principles:

● **Animation should not be an end in itself**   Don't use animation for animation's sake. An animation should serve a purpose. Generally, it should draw a visitor's attention to a particular portion of the page. If you don't have a good reason for using animation, don't use it.

● **Limit the number of animations on a page**   Too many animated graphics competing with each other become a distraction, pulling the visitor's eye in multiple directions at once. Choose (or create) your animations carefully, and limit them to one or, at most, two on a page.

● **Avoid endless looping**   Endless repetition is at best boring and, at worst, annoying. After a GIF animation has cycled several times, it will have served its purpose. If you are creating your own animations, set them to loop four or five times, then stop. Your visitors will bless you for it.

● **Resist the temptation to use <blink> or <marquee>**   Netscape's <blink> element will cause text to blink on and off endlessly, while IE's <marquee> scrolls text across the screen. Both are annoying. Don't use them. Please.

1-Minute Drill

● Why should every page on your Web site have some form of navigation aid?

● Why should animations be kept to a minimum?

● To avoid stranding visitors who don't enter your site through the home page
● Too many animations compete with one another for a viewer's attention, and become distracting

Choose Colors Carefully

Altogether separate from a discussion on so-called "Web-safe" colors is the matter of choosing aesthetically pleasing colors. As with animation, it is undeniably fascinating to be able to type in a few letters and numbers and come up with one of 16.7 million possible colors. It's kind of like finger-painting without the mess. The problem arises when a Web designer decides to use combinations of colors that clash or are hard on the eyes. Feel free to have all the fun you want, experimenting with different colors and color combinations. However, when you choose colors for your site, choose color combinations that will enhance your presentation, rather than detract from it. Here are a few suggestions:

- **Limit the number of colors you use**   Just because you can choose from among nearly 17 million colors doesn't mean you must try them all on one page. Yet, you no doubt have seen pages where the authors have tried to squeeze as many colors in as they can, adding animated "rainbow" horizontal rules as "icing on the cake." Reduce your selections on a page to a background color and two, or maybe three, foreground (font) colors. It will make the page much more attractive.

- **Avoid strong contrasts**   In other words, don't use a navy background with bright yellow letters, or a scarlet red background with black letters. It's hard on the eyes. Try to find color combinations that will look attractive without being garish.

- **Avoid weak contrasts**   This is, of course, the opposite problem to the previous one. If your background and foreground colors are *too* similar, text can be very difficult to read. This can cause as much eye strain as too much contrast. Table 13-1 provides some color resources you may wish to take advantage of when choosing colors for your Web site.

Tip

For a refresher on the issue of Web-safe colors, see Module 8.

Resource	Description	URL	Cost
Web-Safe Colorizer	An online program that allows you to compare background and foreground colors	www.richinstyle.com	Free online
Web Designer's Color Tool	Inexpensive shareware program that allows you to set background, text, and link colors	www.cybercatt.com/WDCT	Shareware
Color Schemer	Choose one base color, and the software suggests an entire scheme.	www.colorschemer.com	Shareware or free online version
Net Color	In addition to setting background, text, and link colors, this program allows you to display up to three images as well.	www.gourami.com	Shareware

Table 13-1   Color Software for Web Designers

Give Attention to Composition

A good layout artist spends a great deal of time planning the composition of a brochure or magazine layout. Nothing is placed haphazardly or randomly, and the overall composition is designed to be both attractive and functional. Unfortunately, many Web sites are designed with a "shotgun" approach to layout. The page authors throw in just about everything they can think of, often creating cluttered pages that are difficult to decipher. On the other hand, a well-designed page will be crafted in such a way that every part of the page—even the white space—contributes to the overall layout.

Hint

There is a difference in what the term "white space" means when it is applied to layouts as opposed to CSS. In CSS, "white space" refers to the extra spaces in lines of code, which are normally condensed by browsers to a single space. The white-space property tells a browser how to handle those extra spaces. However, in layouts, "white space" is blank space on the page. In the hands of a skilled designer, white space can be used to make a page easier to read by directing a viewer's eye to the most important parts of the page.

When planning your layout, keep in mind the following principles:

- **Keep your pages uncluttered**   Again, "less is more" when planning a layout. Have you ever visited a page that is cluttered with various banner ads and icons, all competing for attention with the main content of the page? Try comparing it with a well-designed site where only relevant content is on the page. The latter is much more pleasing to the eye.

- **Use white space to your advantage**   Don't give in to the temptation to fill every pixel on a page with content. Better to have more pages with less content on each than one page with everything "crammed" in.

- **Avoid vertical and horizontal scrolling**   Design your layout to minimize the need for scrolling (particularly horizontal scrolling). It may be difficult to avoid vertical scrolling, but when a page is too wide for the screen, it detracts from the overall layout. Think of how irritating it would be to watch a television program where the picture did not fit on the screen. You probably wouldn't watch very long. Your visitors will probably not stay very long either, if you make them work to read your pages.

- **Design for fast download time**   Since most people still access the Web with "old fashioned" modems, rather than with cable, DSL, or satellite access, you need to keep your page sizes small. Too many images or a single image that is too large can slow down your page download to the point where you could lose your visitors before the page ever loads. If you keep the total size of individual pages down to about 50K, your visitors will bless you.

Tip

For more information on how to design good Web sites, check out *Web Usability and Navigation: A Beginner's Guide*, by Merlyn Holmes.

1-Minute Drill

- Why should you avoid strong and weak color contrasts?
- What does "white space" mean in design?
- What does "white space" mean in CSS?

- They are difficult to read and can cause eye strain
- In design, white space is space on the page without text or graphics
- In CSS (or computer coding) white space refers to extra spaces between characters

Project 13-1 Plan a Web Site

This project will take some time if you follow all the steps, but it will give you the opportunity to plan out a sample Web site. Even if you don't want to actually create a real site right now, you might develop an imaginary site or a personal site, just for the experience. As you work through the planning steps, you will learn how to develop a well-organized and easily navigated site.

Step-by-Step

1. Decide on a site that you would like to create. It can either be imaginary, or you can use this exercise to begin planning a real Web site. In a notebook or on your computer, write a purpose statement for the site. Why does it exist? What is it intended to accomplish? What will your visitors do, get, find, buy, experience, discover, or learn on the site?

2. Analyze your target audience. Who do you want to attract to your site? Write down a description of the kind of visitors that you hope to get.

3. List the content you will offer. Is your site a bookstore? Are you a non-profit organization? Is it a family album site? What are you going to want to put on the site.

4. What "bells and whistles" will you need to have on your site? Guestbook? Catalog? Order form? Do you need audio or video? Why? Should you have a Flash intro page? Why? Will people be downloading things from your site?

5. Based on your answers to the previous questions take some 3x5 cards and, using one card for each page, develop a storyboard for your Web site. On the lined sides of the cards, list a title for the page and describe the contents. On the cards' blank sides sketch out a simple layout. Experiment with different possible arrangements for your storyboard.

6. Create an HTML document for each of the pages you have designed on the storyboard and link them together according to the layout you developed with the storyboard. Prepare each page to be linked to an external style sheet by adding the following element to the <head> portion of each page:

```
<link rel="stylesheet" type="text/css" href="mysite.css" />
```

7. Put your planned content into the various pages. If you are doing a site just for practice, then you may wish to simply import some text files to act as filler text.

13

Project Summary

The more time you invest in planning your site, the easier it will be to create, maintain, and develop. The simple steps that you just worked through will enable you to design your Web site and experiment with different kinds of layouts *before* you start coding. Remember, it is much more difficult to make large scale changes after you have coded a site, created links, and so on,. When it's all on paper or 3x5 cards, you can work with it until you are satisfied that you have come up with the best design possible.

Design with Stylesheets

How do you design with stylesheets? That all depends. If you are developing a large site and you want as broad an influence as possible, then you may want to create a "base" stylesheet that sets style rules for all of the HTML elements. This can be a rather tedious process, though, unless you make use of someone else's base stylesheet. The advantage to this approach is that, once you are done, you have a "master" stylesheet that can be reproduced and altered to fit your needs with future pages or sites.

Tip

Visit the RichInStyle Web site for a nice example of a base style sheet you can use. The URL is **www.richinstyle.com**.

On the other hand, if you are merely wanting to use CSS to design your page layouts, and you don't necessarily need to influence *every* HTML element, then you can do just as well by creating a less extensive stylesheet. Remember, every browser has its own stylesheet built in. Thus, if you choose to set styles for only a limited number of elements, you are choosing to allow the browser to apply its default stylesheet for the rest. As long as you are careful in your design, and test your pages, this approach will most likely suit your needs. However, whether you are creating an extensive "base" stylesheet or doing "spot" styling, your results will be better if you keep your stylesheets "lean and legible."

Creating "Lean" Stylesheets

"Fat" stylesheets are stylesheets that are loaded down with unnecessary or repetitive style rules. These take longer to download, slowing down the entire page loading process. Plus, they represent wasted time and effort on your part. To keep your stylesheets "lean," consider some of the following practices:

Don't Write Style Declarations that Merely Set Default Values

For example, you could write a style declaration that sets a value of "text-decoration: none;" for all of your selectors. However, this is not really necessary, since that's already the default value. Adding that kind of declaration is essentially a waste of time and space. For example,

```
p  {text-decoration: none;}
```

is a useless rule because the default value for text-decoration is "none." In other words, no text decoration will be added to the "p" selector anyway. Thus, you don't need to specify a value of "none." Where the preceding rule *would* be useful is if you were writing a stylesheet for an HTML document that already existed, and you wanted to remove some underlining without having to rewrite the HTML. For example, suppose you're asked to do a stylesheet for a Web site that had many paragraphs emphasized by underlined text (using the <u> element). The site owner wants all those underlines removed. You could remove all of the underlines at once with a style rule that reads

```
u {text-decoration: none;}
```

A simple rule of thumb would be that you don't need to apply values such as "normal" or "none" unless you are trying to remove a style that already exists.

Don't Write Repetitive Style Rules

It is possible to write separate identical style rules for selectors. However, if a number of selectors will all share the same styles, it's a more efficient use of your time to write one rule for all of those selectors. Remember, all you need to do is to separate the selectors by commas. Instead of

```
h1 {font-size: 2em;}
h2 {font-size: 2em;}
h3 {font-size: 2em;}
```

use

```
h1, h2, h3 {font-size: 2em;}
```

13

Don't Write Piecemeal Rules

This might be stating the obvious, but don't write multiple style rules for a single selector. This is most likely to happen if you go back in to modify a stylesheet and you add new rules rather than modify existing ones. In other words, don't write

```
h1 {margin: 1.1em;}
h1 {font-size: 2.5em;}
h1 {background-color: white;}
```

when you can write

```
h1 {margin: 1.1em;
    font-size: 2.5em;
    background-color: white;}
```

Use Shorthand Properties When Possible

Whenever possible, reduce the number of declarations you have to write by making use of shorthand properties. For example if you wanted to set a border for the h1 selector, you could write it this way:

```
h1 {border-style: solid;
    border-width: thin;
    border-color: red;}
```

On the other hand, your stylesheet will be "leaner" if you use the border shorthand property:

```
h1 {border: solid thin red;}
```

Caution

Because some of the shorthand properties are not as well supported by the browsers, be sure to test your pages to make sure your styles display properly.

Creating "Legible" Stylesheets

Whether you are writing HTML, JavaScript, or CSS, it's always a good practice to use whatever means are available to make your code as legible as possible. If you have to go back into a stylesheet eight or nine months down the road and modify it, you might be surprised at how much you have forgotten. As a result, you will have to waste time deciphering your own stylesheet before you can work with it. In addition, if others ever have to work with or modify one of your stylesheets, you want to make it as easy as possible for them to understand what you are doing. Creating legible stylesheets is largely a matter of common sense—and common courtesy.

Use Comment Lines Frequently

Comment lines are vital in any type of coding. They allow you to add notations that explain certain details of your code, but the comments themselves are not displayed by the browser. It is easy to add comments to your HTML or CSS, but each "language" requires a different type of comment tag. For HTML, a set of comment tags looks like this:

```
<!-- This is an HTML comment line. -->
```

Anything enclosed between these HTML comment tags will not be displayed. On the other hand, a CSS comment line would look like this:

```
/* This is a CSS comment line. */
```

As with the HTML comment tags, these tags will prevent a browser from displaying any lines in your stylesheet that are enclosed between them.

Use Descriptive Names with IDs and Classes

If you have to read through your stylesheet down the line and come to a class selector that looks like "p.special," you might have a hard time remembering what that particular class actually does. Or, if you find an ID selector that reads: "div#104ab," you might be scratching your head for a while, trying to decipher it. Always use names that will retain their meaning for you and that will be relatively easy to understand for anyone else who reads your stylesheet. The best way to do this is to use class and ID names that are descriptive of what their function will be in the HTML document. For example, a special class related to logos might be named ".logo," or styles for a navigation bar could be ".navbar."

Organize your Style Rules by Selector Type

Another common sense policy for creating legible stylesheets is to organize your style rules according to the types of selector. A long stylesheet can quickly become difficult to understand if the selectors have not been organized. A suggested order might be:

- Simple Type (Element) Selectors
- Contextual (Descendent) Selectors
- Class Selectors
- ID Selectors

13

- Pseudo-Class Selectors
- Pseudo-Element Selectors
- Child Selectors
- First Child Selectors
- Adjacent Selectors
- Attribute Selectors

As you may have noticed from the preceding list, a large number of advanced selectors have been added to the CSS 2 specification. These selectors will be covered in Module 14.

Tip

Try separating each of the different groups of selectors with a comment line that will serve as a descriptive heading (for example, /*Type Selectors*/,).

Project 13-2 Experiment with CSS Layouts

In Project 13-1, you developed a concept for a Web site and, perhaps, created some basic Web pages. In this project, you will create a stylesheet that will give your Web site a distinctive look. This stylesheet layout will be relatively simple. However, as you work with it, you may wish to experiment with more complex approaches.

Step-by-Step

1. Create an HTML document and save it as index.htm. Also, create a blank text document and save it as siteStyle.css.

2. Add a link to your stylesheet file in the <head> portion of the HTML document.

3. Add a level one heading (<h1>) to the page, giving the page an appropriate title. For example, you might place a "Welcome to My Web Site" type heading, or the name of a business or organization. Don't worry about alignment right now.

4. Below the heading, add a slogan and enclose it in the <div> element. Also, add the following attribute to the opening <div> tag: class="slogan".

5. Use the <div> element to enclose the address, phone number, and other contact information. The opening <div> tag should also have the class="address" attribute.

6. Add an image with the <img /> element (don't forget to set its width and height) and add a description with the "alt" attribute.

7. Add some text to each of the pages, either by cutting and pasting it from some of your own documents or by using lorem.txt. Be sure to enclose each paragraph in the <p> element. The opening <p> tag should have the class="bodytxt" attribute.

Note

Lorem.txt can be downloaded from Osborne's Web site (**www.osborne.com**) along with the rest of the code from this book.

8. Create a set of links to other pages, and perhaps an e-mail link. These don't necessarily have to be linked to real pages; however, it would be good practice to actually create several other pages and link to them.

9. Enclose all of the links in a single set of <div> tags. The opening <div> tag should have the class="navbar" attribute.

10. When you are finished, save index.htm and display it in your browser of choice. It should look something like the following illustration:

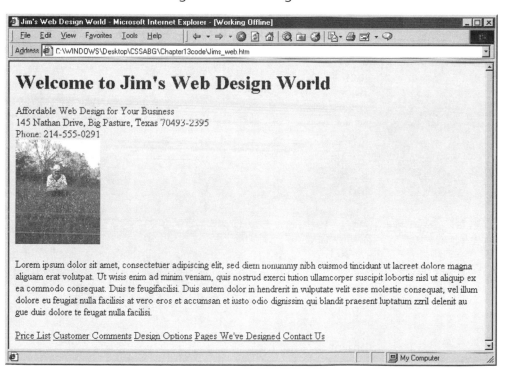

```
index.htm
<html><head><title>Jim's Web Design World</title>
<link rel="stylesheet" type="text/css"
```

```
        href="siteStyle.css" />
<style> </style></head>
<body>
<h1>Welcome to Jim's Web Design World</h1>
<div class="slogan">Affordable Web Design
    for Your Business</div>
<div class="address">145 Nathan Drive<br />
Big Pasture, Texas<br />
Phone: 214-555-0291</div>
<img src="jhp274x339.jpg" alt="Jim's Web Design World"
    width="137" height="169" />
<p class="bodytxt">Lorem ipsum dolor sit amet, consectetuer
adipiscing elit, sed diem nonummy nibh euismod tincidunt ut
lacreet dolore magna aliguam erat volutpat. Ut wisis
enim ad minim veniam, quis nostrud exerci tution
ullamcorper suscipit lobortis nisl ut aliquip ex ea
commodo consequat. Duis te feugifacilisi. Duis autem
dolor in hendrerit in vulputate velit esse molestie
consequat, vel illum dolore eu feugiat nulla facilisis
at vero eros et accumsan et iusto odio dignissim qui
blandit praesent luptatum zzril delenit au gue duis
dolore te feugat nulla facilisi.</p>
<div class="navbar">
<a href="page2.htm">Price List</a>
<a href="page3.htm">Customer Comments</a>
<a href="page4.htm">Design Options</a>
<a href="page5.htm">Pages We've Designed</a>
<a href="mailto:me@myemail.com">Contact Us</a>
</div>
</body>
</html>
```

11. Now that you have constructed a basic page that looks acceptable (albeit somewhat bland) without a stylesheet, begin to develop your layout by writing style rules for your siteStyle.css stylesheet. Start by adding a comment line that reads "Type Selectors." Next, write a style rule for the body selector, selecting a background color and a foreground (text) color. Set the margins to 0em for the top and bottom and 30 pixels for the left and right. Finally write a declaration that will set the font to Arial or sans-serif.

12. For the h1 selector, set a top margin of 75 pixels and a bottom margin of -1 pixel.

13. Write a style rule for the img selector, setting the float to left and adding a right margin of 30 pixels.

14. Add a comment line that reads "Class Selectors."

15. Create a class selector named "div.address," then set the font size to .80 ems and align the text to the right.

16. Create a class selector named "div.navbar." Set the text alignment to center and add a 30 pixel margin to the top.

17. Create a class selector named "div.slogan," then give it a top border that is solid, thin, and set to the same color as your foreground (text) color. Also, set the font weight to bold, the font style to italic, and align the text to the right.

18. Create a class selector named "p.bodytxt" and set its line height to 1.75 ems.

19. Add a comment line that reads "Pseudo Classes."

20. For the a:link, a:visited, and a:active selectors, set the background color, text color, and font family to the same as your settings for the body selector.

21. For the a:hover selector, switch the background and text color settings.

22. Save your stylesheet, then load index.htm into your browser. The following illustration was done on Internet Explorer 5.5; however, the page will display with only minor variations in Netscape 4.7 and Opera 5.

13

Project Summary

As you worked with this project, you learned how to write a lean, well-organized stylesheet to add style to a simple HTML page. Of course, it is possible to create more complex layouts with CSS. However, the more complicated your layouts become, the more problematic is the issue of browser compatibility. The next section of this module will cover browser compatibility and how to develop "crash-proof" pages.

```
siteStyle.css
/* Type Selectors */
body      {background-color: rgb(100%,89%,76%);
           color: rgb(60%,20%,0%);
           margin: 0em 30px;
           font-family: Arial, sans-serif;}

h1        {margin-top: 75px;
           margin-bottom: -1px;}

img       {float: left;
           margin-right: 30px;}

/*Class Selectors */

div.address {font-size: .80em;
             text-align: right;}

div.navbar  {text-align: center;
             margin-top: 30px;}

div.slogan  {border-top: solid thin rgb(60%,20%,0%);
             font-weight: bold;
             font-style: italic;
             text-align: right;}

p.bodytxt   {line-height: 1.75em;}

/* Pseudo Classes */

a:link, a:visited, a:active
              {background-color: rgb(100%,89%,76%);
               color: rgb(60%,20%,0%);
               font-family: Arial, sans-serif;}

a:hover       {background-color: rgb(60%,20%,0%);
               color: rgb(100%,89%,76%);}
```

Develop "Crash-Proof" Pages

When a Web page "crashes" because of style problems, it doesn't necessarily mean that the user's browser locks up (although that could conceivably happen). It generally means that the page itself becomes unusable or its layout becomes so jumbled as to render it illegible. Any number of factors can cause this, although with CSS it is likely to be a layout that is too dependent on weakly supported or "buggy" stylesheet properties. When viewed in a non-visual browser or one that does not support CSS, the layout collapses. Another possibility is failure to take into account the issue of cross-browser support, even if the page layouts are not overly dependent on CSS. However, one problem that is often overlooked is poorly written HTML.

Because poorly written HTML can cause problems with CSS, the first step in creating "crash-proof" pages is to make sure that your Web documents are both "well formed" and "valid." A document that is syntactically correct (written properly) is considered *well formed*; a document that conforms to a *document type definition* (DTD) is considered *valid*. At the very least, you want your HTML documents to be well formed. Ideally, they should be valid. While that may sound confusing, it's not all that difficult.

Well-Formed HTML Documents

A *well-formed* HTML document is one that is "grammatically correct." In other words, it is properly written, and all errors of syntax have been removed. If you've worked with HTML, you probably have an idea of what that means. However, if you are new to HTML, or haven't studied the changes in HTML that have come along since the adoption of XHTML as the official standard, you may find a review helpful. You should be aware that the move toward the stricter standards of XHTML and XML has changed the rules for writing HTML.

All Elements Must Have Both Opening and Closing Tags

In earlier versions of HTML, it was possible to leave closing tags off of certain elements (<p>, <li>, and so on). For example, even though the paragraph element has both opening and closing tags, <p> </p>, you could create a paragraph using only the opening <p> tag, and it would display properly. Now, for a document to be considered well formed, you should write opening and closing tags for every element.

13

```
<p>This used to be acceptable, but is now incorrect.
<p>Always use opening and closing tags.</p>
```

Empty Elements Must Be Written with a Closing Slash

An *empty element* is an element that does not contain any content and does not require a closing tag. For example, the "horizontal rule," <hr />, element is an empty element (
 is another). It used to be permissible to write such an element as if it were merely an opening tag: <hr>. Now it is necessary to add the "closing slash" to an empty element's tag, thus identifying it as an "empty element."

```
Incorrect:   <img src="pix.gif">
Correct:     <img src="pix.gif" />
```

Hint

The <img> element is technically not an "empty" element, but rather a "replaced" element. However, since it takes no closing tag, it should be written the same way you would write an empty element.

Elements Should Be Properly "Nested"

With properly nested elements, you should not have any tags overlapping in your document. If you have tags that are overlapping, it can confuse the browser that is "parsing" (reading) the document. Elements that are properly contained within one another are referred to as "nested."

```
Incorrect:   <a> <b> </a> </b>
Correct:     <a> <b> </b> </a>
```

The Document Should Have One "Root" Element

A well-formed document should have one root element that contains all the other elements. With HTML, browsers are generally forgiving enough to overlook the omission of the <html> element. If you don't believe it, just create a plain text page without any HTML markup at all. Then, write a headline like this: <h1>Test</h1>, but leave out all of the other HTML elements you would normally include. Save the file with an .htm extension and display it in a browser. The heading element will display just as you would expect it to. However, even though it is possible to display an HTML page without its root <html> element, in order to have a well-formed document, you must include it as well as the closing </html> tag.

Values Should Be Enclosed in Quotation Marks

Again, in the early days of HTML, it was acceptable to apply values to attributes without enclosing them in quotes. For your document to be well formed, you must now enclose *all* values in quotation marks.

```
Incorrect:    <hr width=25% />
Correct:      <hr width="25%" />
```

Elements Should Be Written in Lower Case

HTML is not case-sensitive However, XHTML is based on XML, which *is* case-sensitive. Thus, it now has become important to be consistent in how you write your elements. In the past, it didn't really matter whether you wrote <body>, <BODY>, or <Body>. Strictly speaking, you can still use whichever case you want, as long as you're consistent. However, it is generally recommended that you write element tags and their attributes/values in lowercase.

```
Incorrect: <P>Don't mix upper and lower case.</p>
Correct:   <p>It's safest to stick with lower case.</p>
```

The preceding characteristics are what make up a well-formed HTML document. However, it is possible for a document to be well formed without being valid.

Valid HTML Documents

A *valid* HTML document is one that conforms to a particular document type definition (DTD). Think of a DTD as a blueprint or standard for how HTML should be written, down to the smallest detail. Validating an HTML document simply means that it has been compared to this external standard, and it "measures up." A valid document is not just grammatically correct: it uses only those HTML elements and attributes that are found in the DTD.

Tip

You don't have to memorize or learn a DTD to validate your HTML. As you will see, there are validating programs that will take care of that for you. All you need to know are the basic characteristics of the DTD you want your page to conform to.

Since there are different versions of HTML, there are a number of document type definitions your document could possibly be validated against. For example, you might have a document that is considered valid when compared to the standard for HTML 3.2, but that fails when compared to the HTML 4.01 standard. To apply the current HTML specification, there are three DTDs you can use:

● **HTML 4.01 Strict**   The W3C currently defines this as "all the elements and attributes that have not been deprecated, and that do not appear in frameset documents."

13

- **HTML 4.01 Transitional**   This is currently defined as "everything in the strict DTD plus deprecated elements and attributes (most of which concern visual presentation)."

- **HTML 4.01 Frameset**   The W3C describes the frameset DTD as "everything in the transitional DTD, plus frames as well."

Writing Valid HTML

If you're getting worried, writing valid HTML is not nearly as difficult as it sounds. In fact, you need to keep in mind only two things. First, you need to decide which DTD you want your documents to conform to. Most likely, you are writing pages that would be considered "HTML 4.01 Transitional." All that means is that you are using the elements and attributes that have been adopted as part of HTML up to the present, *including* those deprecated elements and attributes such as <font>, bgcolor, align, and so on. Incidentally, this would *not* include proprietary elements such as Netscape's <blink> or IE's <marquee>. If you want to have a valid document, you need to avoid elements such as these.

Hint

If you are writing for the "HTML 4.01 Strict" DTD, it means you refrain from using *any* of the deprecated elements and attributes and that your pages derive their style only from stylesheets.

The second thing a valid HTML document needs is to have a statement at the beginning that identifies what standard the page conforms to. It is somewhat similar to writing at the top of the page "This is an HTML 4.01 transitional document." Of course, the statement must be written so that a browser can understand it. Thus, for the "HTML 4.01 Transitional" DTD, you would put this *document type declaration* at the very top of the page (even before the opening <html> tag):

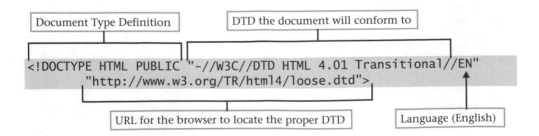

To use the "Strict" or "Frameset" DTDs, you would merely change the name in the top line of the preceding tag to whichever applied. Then you would also change "loose.dtd" to either "strict.dtd" or "frameset.dtd."

Tip

Don't confuse a document type *declaration* with a document type *definition*. The declaration is the statement at the top of an HTML page that "declares" what standard the document conforms to. The document type *definition* is the actual standard.

"Validating" Your HTML

You've written your page and put the proper document type declaration—how do you "validate" your page? The easiest way is to make use of the W3C's HTML validator. If your site is already online, you simply enter the URL of the page you want to validate, and select the standard (DTD) by which you want to evaluate it. On the other hand, if you want to validate pages that you have not yet placed online, the validator has an "upload" option that will allow you to upload the page to their server for validation.

The actual validation process generally only takes a few seconds, after which you will receive a "report." If your page does not "validate," the report will give you a detailed list of the areas where you need to make changes. For example, if you tried to validate a document against the "strict" standard, and the validator found an occurrence of the <font> element, you would receive a prompt displaying the exact line of code where the error was found.

Valid CSS

A third and final aspect of developing "crash proof" pages is making sure that your stylesheets have been validated. A valid stylesheet is not compared against a document type definition, but against the CSS specification. Stylesheet validation not only checks your syntax for semicolons between declarations, closing brackets for style rules, and so on, it also makes sure you have covered the "bases" in your stylesheet design. For example, if you submit a stylesheet to a validator, and you have used the "background-color" property to set a background, the validator will also check to make sure you specified the "color" property for the foreground. If you haven't, it will remind you to. In essence, validating your HTML and CSS is the same thing programmers do when they "debug" code.

13

A good validating program will do all the hard work for you, and, again, the W3C offers one free of charge. In fact, you can actually download the W3C's CSS validator and keep it on your own computer so that you don't have to go online every time you want to validate a stylesheet. Of course, you can also use the validator without downloading it, in much the same way as you would use the HTML validator.

Tip

The Web Design Group has a good HTML and CSS validator available on its Web Site, **www.htmlhelp.com**. It's a great resource that's worth checking out. To use the W3C's validator, go to **www.w3.org**.

1-Minute Drill

● What is a "well-formed" HTML document?

● What is a "valid" document?

Design for Cross-Browser Compatibility

Your last, and possibly greatest, challenge in preparing your stylesheets and pages for the Web to design for cross-browser compatibility. Cross-browser compatibility does not mean you try to create a page that is *identical* in every browser. A fact of life in working with Web pages is that they will look different when displayed on different browsers. If you want a page to look exactly the same wherever it is displayed, you need to be working with print media. Your goal in cross-browser compatibility is to fine-tune your pages and stylesheets so that your pages look *good* in whichever browser displays them.

Compatibility Options

So how *do* you design stylesheets that will look good on your users' browsers? Unfortunately, there's no simple answer to that question. A lot depends on your knowledge of your audience. For example, if you are on a corporate Intranet,

---

● A well-formed document is one that uses correct HTML syntax.
● A valid document is one that conforms to a particular document type definition.

and you know that all of the people who view your site will be using Netscape 4.7, then you don't have to worry about the compatibility issue at all. Just design your stylesheets so that your pages look good in Netscape 4.7. On the other hand, if your pages are on an Internet server, and you will have people looking at your pages with different browsers, you need to make some decisions.

Use the W3C's Core Stylesheets

Perhaps the easiest way to use stylesheets without having to worry about compatibility is by linking your pages to one of the W3C's core stylesheets. These stylesheets are available free-of-charge, and all you need to do to use them is link to them. The advantage with these is that you can begin to use stylesheets on your site without having to design them yourself. The obvious disadvantage is that you are boxed in to someone else's design. However, remember that you can make adjustments to the stylesheet by using embedded or inline styles, making sure that your selectors have a high specificity.

Note

If you're fuzzy on what "speciflcity" is review Module 5.
All you need to do is insert a <link /> element with the URL for the stylesheet you would like to apply, like this:

```
<link rel="stylesheet" type="text/css"
      href="http://www.w3.org/StyleSheets/Core/Chocolate />
```

If you want to try linking to the W3C core stylesheets, Table 13-2 lists the eight different styles available and the URL you would use to link to each.

Style	URL
Chocolate	http://www.w3.org/StyleSheets/Core/Chocolate
Midnight	http://www.w3.org/StyleSheets/Core/Midnight
Modernist	http://www.w3.org/StyleSheets/Core/Modernist
Oldstyle	http://www.w3.org/StyleSheets/Core/Oldstyle
Steely	http://www.w3.org/StyleSheets/Core/Steely
Swiss	http://www.w3.org/StyleSheets/Core/Swiss
Traditional	http://www.w3.org/StyleSheets/Core/Traditional
Ultramarine	http://www.w3.org/StyleSheets/Core/Ultramarine

Table 13-2   W3C Core Stylesheets

13

Hint

To "sample" these stylesheets, just create a simple HTML document with a few headings and some text. In the head portion of the page, include the link as shown in the previous section. Then save the page and go online. Open your favorite browser and load the page. It will automatically apply the stylesheet. To try a different stylesheet, just open the page in NotePad or another text editor and change the name of the stylesheet in the link. Save it again and reload it in your browser. Now it will display the new style.

Ignore the Compatibility Issue

Another option is that you could just ignore the compatibility issue altogether. You could just design for whatever browser you use and not worry about other users. If you are just doing a personal site and don't really care about generating increased traffic, you may find this a viable option. However, if you are designing a site for a business or organization, or if you want to attract an increasing audience, then ignoring a portion of your visitors is not very good practice.

Limit Your Use of Properties

Another option you might consider would be limiting your use of properties to those that are supported by both Internet Explorer and Netscape. By familiarizing yourself with the strengths and weaknesses of the different browsers and avoiding those properties that are not well supported, you can create a style sheet that looks good across the board. Useful resources for this option are the many "browser compatibility" charts available both in books and online. However, because writing a single stylesheet requires you to limit your use of properties that are unsupported in *either* IE or Netscape, you may find this approach more restrictive than you'd like.

Write Multiple Stylesheets

If you want to make certain that your stylesheets are compatible with the largest possible audience, *and* you don't want to limit yourself unnecessarily, then your best option is to write a separate stylesheet for each browser. This could be troublesome if you tried to write a stylesheet for every possible browser out there, but that's not really necessary. Begin by writing a style sheet for IE 5. Then, when you have the styles displaying the way you want them to, save that style sheet and make two other copies of it. Next, making use of compatibility charts and CSS test programs, adjust the other two style sheets, testing them in Netscape 4 and IE 4 until you have corrected the buggy and unsupported properties. Once you have refined your alternate style sheets, save them with names that will identify the browsers for which they were designed, for example, mysite_IE4.css.

The next step is to use a scripting language such as JavaScript to write a browser detection script. When a page loads, this script will check to see what browser is being used, then it will serve up the proper stylesheet. If you know how to write JavaScript or VBScript, doing this is a very easy task. If you are not familiar with these languages (and prefer not to learn them), you still have options. Browse almost any Internet search engine for "browser detection scripts," and you will find plenty of pre-written scripts you can merely cut and paste into your pages. You may have to "tweak" the scripts by putting in the correct filenames for your stylesheets, among other things, but most of the scripts will come with instructions on how to do this. Table 13-3 lists some sources for browser detection scripts.

Compatibility Resources

A key element in designing good stylesheets is in learning to take advantage of the wealth of resources available online. There are a number of excellent sites that offer browser compatibility charts, test pages, bug charts and suggested workarounds, and much more. One advantage of the online resources is that most are updated regularly, so you can be relatively certain your information is current. Although there are more CSS resources than space to list them all here, Table 13-4 lists several of the best:

Web site	URL
RichInStyle	http://www.richinstyle.com/free/detection.html
The Complete Webmaster	http://www.abiglime.com/webmaster/articles/jscript/012899.htm
JavaScript City	http://www.javascriptcity.com/scripts/detect1.htm

Table 13-3 | Sources for Browser Detection Scripts

13

Resource	URL	Description
WebReview.com's CSS Reference Guide	www.webreview.com /style	Includes Eric A. Meyer's excellent browser compatibility charts.
CSS Pointers Group	http://css.nu	Excellent collection of CSS articles and resources.
Web Design Group	www.htmlhelp.com	CSS reference charts, validators, and much more.
The Web Standards Project	www.webstandards.org	Has a CSS page with links to many helpful resources.
RichInStyle.com	www.richinstyle.com	Browser test pages, compatibility charts, CSS and HTML tutorials.
WestCiv.com	www.westciv.com	Online guide to CSS, tutorials, Style Master (style sheet software).
W3C's CSS Page	www.w3.org/style/css	CSS specification, browsers, authoring tools, validator, test suite, and more.

Table 13-4   Online CSS Resource Pages

☑ *Mastery Check*

1. Every page on your site should have some form of:

    A. DTD

    B. Navigation system

    C. Image

    D. CSS

2. What is a storyboard?

_____

_____

3. What is the difference between a *document type definition* and a *document type declaration*?

_____

_____

4. What is the difference between a *well-formed* and a *valid* document?

_____

_____

5. Correct the following HTML code so that it is well formed and add a document type declaration that validates it against the HTML 4.01 strict DTD.

```
<html>
<h1>This is a heading</h1>
<p>This is paragraph one.
<img href=mypicture.jpg width=100 height=100 alt=Me!>
This is paragraph two.
<p><font face="Arial">Paragraph three.</p></font>
```

13

Module 14

Advanced CSS

The Goals of this Module

- Compare CSS 1 and CSS 2
- Work with Advanced Selectors
- Understand Generated Content
- Understand Aural Style Sheets
- Survey User Interface Properties
- Understand Paged Media
- Understand Font Specification Properties

Throughout this book, you have read references to CSS 1 and CSS 2. What's the difference between the two? CSS began as a simple means of applying style to Web pages—separating structure from presentation. As such, its syntax was fairly straightforward, even intuitive. If you have a basic understanding of HTML elements, attributes, and values, it is only a small step to working with CSS selectors, properties, and values. CSS is described by the W3C as "a simple mechanism for adding style (e.g. fonts, colors, spacing) to Web documents." However, in the years since CSS was first introduced, it has been developed into much more than a mechanism for telling a browser what font to use or for specifying fonts and colors. With the CSS 2 specification, you can create stylesheets for aural (audio) browsers, for paged (print, handheld) media, and much more. Unfortunately, these added capabilities came at a price. CSS has become considerably more complex than it was at its inception. In this module you will learn about some of the more advanced aspects of CSS 2.

Understand CSS 2

Although CSS 2 includes an expanded range of both selectors and properties, the easiest way to spot the distinction between CSS 1 and 2 is by comparing the basic categories the properties fall into. By observing how the two specifications are organized, it is possible to understand the general focus of each.

Tip

If you want to make the comparison for yourself, simply go to the W3C's Web site (**www.w3.org**) and then click on the link for CSS. You will go to another page that will provide you with links to the CSS Specifications. Follow those links, and compare the table of contents for CSS 1 and 2. You will easily see the difference between the two.

CSS 1 Property Categories

The major categories of CSS 1 properties are

- Font Properties
- Text Properties
- Color and Background Properties

- Box Properties

- Classification Properties

As you can see, the preceding categories are focused primarily on visual presentation issues: fonts, text, colors, background images, margins, and so on. However, when you compare the table of contents for the CSS 2 specification, you will observe a very different set of categories. As a matter of fact, although all the properties from CSS 1 are included in the new specification, some of the property categories have changed, new ones have been added, and at least one (classification properties) has been eliminated.

CSS 2 Models and Property Categories

As you survey the CSS 2 specification, you will find properties organized as:

- **Box and Visual Formatting Models**   Box properties have been renamed the box "model," and a visual formatting "model" has been added. The box model includes those properties that control margin, padding, and borders. The visual formatting model includes the properties that govern box positioning and page flow.

- **Visual Effects**   Visual effects properties include the overflow, clipping, and visibility properties.

- **Generated Content, Automatic Numbering, and Lists**   This category of properties (and of pseudo-elements) is used to control content that is automatically "generated" by the browser (for example, list bullets (markers) and automatic paragraph numbering).

- **Paged Media**   The paged media properties enable a Web author to specify styles for pages that will be printed or displayed in a "paged" display medium (for example, PDAs).

- **Colors and Backgrounds**   The color and background properties remain largely unchanged from CSS 1.

- **Fonts**   In addition to the CSS 1 font properties, CSS 2 includes a system for describing and/or downloading fonts to a user's system. This is an attempt to address the problem of using fonts in page layouts that your visitors might not have on their own systems.

14

● **Text**   The text properties are largely unchanged from CSS 1, except that the white-space property has been moved here from the classification properties. Also, the text-shadow property has been added.

● **The Table Model**   This is a special "model," designed to make it possible for a table's structure to match its visual presentation. This is a key issue for non-visual browsers, which often have difficulty interpreting HTML tables.

● **User Interface**   These properties enable you to influence the user's (your visitor's) interface. In other words, you can specify how cursors should appear, select colors that will match your visitor's system colors, and even outline certain portions of a page when they have your visitor's attention (focus).

● **Aural Style Sheets**   A key priority of CSS 2 is *accessibility*. The W3C wants to make the Web accessible to as many people as possible. Aural style sheets enable you to do that by offering a set of properties that tell speech synthesizers and audio browsers how to interpret your Web pages.

1-Minute Drill

● What are the five major categories of properties for CSS 1?

● What is a key priority of CSS 2?

Advanced CSS and the Beginner

As you compare the properties of CSS 1 and 2, it quickly becomes evident that CSS 2 goes far beyond simple Web pages. From a beginner's standpoint, the question obviously is, "How much of this do I need to know?" A second important question is, "How much of this can I use?" The answer to both questions is: "Not a lot."

How Much of CSS 2 Do I Need to Know?

On the one hand, it is important to have a basic grasp of CSS 2. After all, you're not going to be a beginner forever. There are aspects of CSS 2 that will be very

---

● Font, Text, Color/Background, Box, and Classification Properties
● Accessibility (making the Web as accessible to as many people as possible)

important to Web authors in the future. As the Web moves toward the goal of separating structure and presentation, you will find it increasingly helpful to know how to use absolute and relative positioning in creating your layouts. Also, as you will see in the next section, the advanced selectors introduced with the CSS 2 specification will be extremely helpful if, for example, you are asked to develop stylesheets for an existing Web site. Many of the new selectors make it possible for you to apply styles without having to rewrite the HTML code.

On the other hand, there are aspects of CSS 2 that many Web authors will never need to use. You may never have a need to create an aural style sheet or to design from the CSS table model. You may not be interested in including generated content or stylesheets for paged media. If you have developed a strong command of CSS 1 and understand the basics of CSS 2, you will be well equipped for designing with stylesheets.

How Much of CSS 2 Can I Use?

The unfortunate reality is that most current browsers don't even fully support CSS 1, let alone CSS 2. Although Netscape 6 has very strong CSS support, including an impressive amount of support for CSS 2 selectors and properties, the same cannot be said for the other browsers. Even Internet Explorer 5.5, which prior to Netscape 6 offered the strongest CSS support, is weak where much of CSS 2 is concerned. Likewise, Opera 5 supports a good portion of CSS 2, but not all of it. Thus, the more you use CSS 2, the more compatibility problems you will have to deal with. At present, you are better off sticking with CSS 1 for most of your style work. When you do use selectors and properties from CSS 2, try to stick with the ones that will not significantly impact your page design if they are displayed on a non-supporting browser.

Note

As of this writing, IE 6 was still in beta testing. Thus, the question of its support for CSS 2 remains open.

Understand Advanced Selectors

CSS 2 selectors build on the foundation laid by CSS 1, adding greater precision in some cases and totally new abilities in others. For example, the child and the adjacent sibling selectors are similar to descendent selectors, but additionally give you the ability to focus your selections much more tightly. On the other

14

hand, the new attribute selectors enable you to select elements in a whole new way: based on the presence or value of a particular HTML attribute. As browser support increases, all of these new selectors will be valuable additions to your CSS toolbox.

The Universal Selector

While most of the new selectors enable you to be more specific in your selections, this one enables you to be more general. If you want to apply a style across the board, you can do it easily with the *universal* selector. With this selector, you can apply style to all of the elements on a page with a single rule. The universal selector is represented by an asterisk (*) and functions as a wild-card or blanket selector. Table 14-1 lists the characteristics of the universal selector.

Advanced Descendent Selectors

Descendent selectors work by focusing on an element's position in the document "family tree." In CSS 1, these were called *contextual* selectors. CSS 2 adds some new descendent selectors that enable you to focus your selections very specifically. With the child and the adjacent sibling selectors, you can easily select very specific locations on the family tree.

Tip

If you're having trouble remembering the concept of the "document tree," see Module 5.

The Child Selector

This selector is similar to the descendent selector, but much more precise. With descendent selector, an element only needs to "descend" from another element to be affected by a style. It could be a grandchild or great grandchild, but the style would still apply. With the child selector, an element must be a *direct child*

Selector	Syntax	Function	Support
Universal	* {property: value;}	Selects all elements	Weak

Table 14-1   The Universal Selector

rather than merely a descendent. Consider the following style rules. The first rule is a descendent selector that will select any bold text element, <b>, that is a descendent of a <p> element.

```
p b {color: red;}
```

When this style rule is applied to the following line of code, the text inside the <b> tags will be red.

```
<p>This is the <i><b>best</b></i> day of my life!</p>
```

To change the preceding selector to a child selector, all you need to do is insert a "greater than" sign, (>) between the *p* and the *b*, as in the following rule:

```
p>b {color: red;}
```

If you apply this rule to the preceding line of code, you will see that the word "best" is no longer red. This is because the <b> element in that line is a "grandchild" of the <p> element. However, if you remove the <i> </i> tags, as in the following code, the style will be applied, because the <b> element is now a direct child of <p>. Table 14-2 lists the basic characteristics of the "child" selector.

```
<p>This is the <b>best</b> day of my life!</p>
```

Tip

You will need Netscape 6, Opera 5, or IE 5/Mac for most of the illustrations in this module to work properly.

Selector	Syntax	Function	Support
Child	a>b {property: value;}	Selects direct descendents (children)	Weak

Table 14-2   Characteristics of the Child Selector

14

Adjacent Sibling Selector

To continue the family analogy, the adjacent sibling selector keys in on elements that are siblings (both direct children of the same element) and applies style to the *second* element. However, there is one added requirement: the sibling elements must be *adjacent*. That is, the two elements must not be separated by any other elements. For instance, suppose you have a construction that looks like this:

```
<div>
<h1>This is a headline</h1>
<p>This is a paragraph</p>
</div>
```

The <h1> and <p> are both direct descendents of the <div> and thus are *siblings*. They are also *adjacent siblings* because no other elements come between them. However, if another element, say an <h2>, were introduced between those two, then the <h1> and <p> would still be considered siblings, but not adjacent siblings.

To create an adjacent sibling selector, you would use the "plus" sign (+) between the elements you are selecting, as in the following style rule:

```
h1+p    {font-style: italic;}
```

As the following illustration shows, when this rule is applied, a paragraph that immediately follows an <h1> element will be italicized, but other paragraphs will not.

Big News

*This is the **best** day of my life!*

Thank you!

```
<h1>Big News</h1>
<p>This is the <b>best</b> day of my life!</p>
<p>Thank you!</p>
```

Tip

Adjacent siblings can be separated by text or content, but not by other elements.

Selector	Syntax	Function	Support
Adjacent Sibling	A+b {property: value;}	Selects a direct descendent (b) that is also adjacent to another direct descendent (a)	Weak

Table 14-3   Characteristics of the Adjacent Sibling Selector

Attribute Selectors

In CSS 1, the id and .class selectors make use of HTML's "id" and "class" attributes. With these selectors, it is possible to create a certain class or id and apply it to any HTML element. Thus, for example, you could create a class named ".navbar" and use it to apply styles to any elements that you wanted to use in navigation bars. For the styles to be applied, an element would have to have the class="navbar" attribute inside the opening tag. Or, you could create an id named "#copyright" and apply it to a copyright line with the id="copyright" attribute.

Hint

Remember that an attribute in HTML is similar to a property in CSS. In other words, it refers to a characteristic of an element. For example an <img /> element should have the "width" and "height" attributes. These attributes refer to the image's width and height in pixels. Thus, you might find the following tag: <img width="50" height="100" /> in an HTML document.

Class and id selectors give the Web designer incredible freedom in applying styles to HTML elements; however, they have a key weakness. The "class" or "id" attribute must be present in the element you wish to stylize. That's fine if you are writing the HTML code yourself, but what if you have been asked to create a stylesheet for an existing site? Since the code for that site may not have the "class" and "id" attributes neatly written and organized for you, your only alternative would be to go into the HTML and painstakingly add them yourself. Thankfully, CSS 2 comes to the rescue with *attribute* selectors that enable you to select an element based on four different possibilities:

- If a particular attribute is present in that element

- If the element contains a particular attribute-value combination

14

- If a particular value is present among a group of "space-separated" values

- If a particular value is present among a group of "hyphen-separated" values

Note

"Space-separated" simply refers to multiple values, separated by a space. For example a "title" attribute with the value "Chapter One" has space-separated values. An attribute selector could key in on either "Chapter" or "One." A "hyphen-separated" value is separated from another value with a hyphen.

Although this list may seem somewhat daunting, chances are you will use only the first three attribute selectors. The fourth item in the list addresses some fairly specialized circumstances, and unless you are working on a site with multiple languages, you probably won't use that one. Table 14-4 lists the four types of attribute selectors and gives examples for each.

Pseudo-Classes and Pseudo-Elements

Remember that pseudo-classes and pseudo-elements address situations that are not necessarily a part of the HTML code. For instance, the :visited pseudo-class selects links that have been clicked on, or "visited." The advanced pseudo-classes

Selector	Syntax	Function	Support
Attribute	a[attribute] Example: p[align] Selects the <p> element when the "align" attribute is present	Selects an element (a) when a particular attribute [attribute] is present.	Weak
Attribute-value	a[attribute="value"] Example: p[align="center"] Selects the <p> element when the "align" attribute is present *along with* the value "center."	Selects an element when a particular attribute-value combination is present.	Weak

Table 14-4   Characteristics of Attribute Selectors

and pseudo-elements of CSS 2 make selection more specific, add dynamic interaction, and enable you to "generate" content.

The :first-child Pseudo-Class

The :first-child pseudo-class works something like a child selector, but it is even more specific. Returning to a family analogy, the :first-child pseudo-class would not only select one of your children, it would select your oldest (first) child. In CSS, this selector keys in on an element that occurs as the *first* child of another. For example, the following style rule,

```
p:first-child {background-color: green; color:white;}
```

will apply the style only to first paragraph in the following code:

```
<div>
<p>This paragraph should have a green background.</p>
<p>This paragraph should be normal.</p>
</div>
```

Note

Except for :hover, the examples in this section will work only in Netscape 6. Hover is supported by current browsers, but only for the <a>, element.

The :hover Pseudo-Class

As of this writing, the :hover pseudo-class only works with the anchor (link) element, but its effect is impressive. If you apply the :hover pseudo-class to a link, you can change the appearance of the link when a mouseOver occurs. Normally, this type of effect requires multiple images and a scripting language, but with CSS it's a snap. For example, if you add the following style rule to any HTML document,

```
a:hover {background-color: yellow;}
```

a yellow background will show up behind any link when you move the cursor over it.

The :focus Pseudo-Class

When a portion of your page has the "user's focus," (usually keyboard input), the :focus pseudo class comes into play. For example, if you put a form on your

14

page and you would like the form windows to change color when your visitor is entering data, you could write a rule such as this:

```
input:focus {background color: cyan;}
```

Try it on the following simple form:

```
<form>
<input>Name<br />
<input>Email<br />
<input>Address<br />
<input>City<br />
<input>State<br />
<input>Zip<br />
</form>
```

As you tab through the various fields, the field that has the focus (cursor) will change to cyan, while the others will be white.

The :before and :after Pseudo-Elements

Two new pseudo elements that are part of CSS 2 are the :before and :after pseudo elements. These are used along with generated content. *Generated content* is simply content that is not present as part of the page, but is generated by the browser. For example, in simple HTML the bullets and numbers that are added to unordered and ordered lists are generated content. You don't have to type them in; the browser supplies them. CSS 2 extends the reach of generated content far beyond simple lists. For example, throughout this book you have read numerous "tips," "hints," and "notes" that called your attention to important details referred to in the text. What if you wanted to do something like that in an HTML document? With the :before and :after pseudo-elements, it's easy. These pseudo-elements earned their names because they give you the ability to generate content "before" or "after" another element.

The following style rule creates a special class of paragraph, named "tips":

```
p.tips:before {content: "Tip: ";
               font-size:1.5em;
               color: blue;
               background-color: yellow;}
```

Now, if you add a special "tip" to your HTML code, you can give it a format that will make it stand out, *and* the browser will generate a special heading. Try using the following line of code in an HTML document, along with the preceding style rule. Table 14-5 lists the characteristics and syntax for the advanced pseudo-classes and pseudo-elements.

```
<p class="tips">This is a tip.</p>
```

Ask the Expert

Question: Why would I want to use generated content on a Web page?

Answer: Generated content (content that is not part of the original document) can be useful in many ways. As has already been mentioned, numbered and bulleted lists are common examples of generated content. When you create a numbered list in HTML, you don't need to add the numbers; the browser will do it for you. However, CSS 2 takes generated content even further. You can design style rules that will tell the browser to add captions to pictures, figure numbers to illustrations, even number the chapters (or paragraphs) of a document. Generated content can also take the form of quotation marks and other forms of punctuation that are dynamically generated by the browser.

Question: How does the browser know what kind of content to generate?

Answer: One way is through the use of the content property. If you will notice the previous example, the content to be generated is supplied with this property. Quotation marks can also be generated with the quotes property. Counters and automatic numbering are controlled with the counter-increment and counter-reset properties.

Question: Where can I learn more about generated content?

Answer: Check out the online tutorials at www.richinstyle.com and www.westciv.com.

14

Selector	Syntax	Function	Support
:first-child (pseudo-class)	a:first-child {property: value;} Example: p:first-child {font-style: italic;}	Selects an element (a) that is the *first* child of another element.	Netscape 6 only

Table 14-5 Characteristics of Advanced Pseudo-Classes and Pseudo-Elements

1-Minute Drill

- What selector could you use to apply style to all elements at once?
- The child and adjacent sibling selectors are _____ selectors.
- What selectors will cause content to be generated by the browser?

Project 14-1 Experiment with Advanced Selectors

The advanced selectors covered in the previous section are very useful tools for Web designers. Unfortunately, unless all your visitors will be using Netscape 6 or Opera 5, you really can't use these selectors now. However, it's a good idea to understand how they work. In this project, you will experiment with some of these selectors in applying style to an existing Web document

Step-by-Step

1. Find an existing HTML document that you want to experiment on. It can be one of your own Web pages, or you might try saving a page that you've come across on the Internet. The important thing is that the page be *already written*. You will be attempting to add styles to this page in much the same way you would if you were asked to work on an existing Web site. Keep in mind that you will need to use either Netscape 6 or Opera 5 to view this exercise. (For best results, use Netscape 6).

- The universal selector (*)
- Descendent
- The :before and :after pseudo-elements

2. Once you have found your page, open it in a text editor or an HTML editor. Take some time to study the code. You might find it easier to do this if you print out a copy of the code.

3. Open a blank page in a text editor and save it as advanced_selectors.css. This will be your stylesheet.

4. Add a link in the HTML document to this stylesheet, using the <link /> element. Remember to use the "type," "rel," and "href" attributes.

5. Since every HTML document is going to be different, you will need to experiment on the basis of your own document's family tree structure and attributes. For instance, try applying style with the child selector: a>b. Find an element that is a direct child of another element and write a style rule for it.

6. Find two "adjacent sibling" elements and apply a style with the adjacent sibling selector: a+b.

7. Add a style rule that keys in on the presence of a particular attribute, using the attribute selector: a[attribute].

8. Write a rule focusing in on a specific attribute-value combination that exists in the document. Use the attribute-value selector for this: a[attribute="value"].

9. Look through the document for some space-separated values. You can usually find these in the "alt" attribute that goes with most images. The "title" attribute is another good place to look. Write a style rule that will select on the basis of the words you find. The space-separated selector is your tool for this: a[attribute~="value"].

10. If you find any "hyphen-separated" values, write an attribute selector for one of those. The selector looks like this: a[attribute|="value"].

11. Use the :hover pseudo-class to add style to any links on a mouseOver. Your selector will look like this: a:hover. (Remember, this only works with the <a> element.)

12. If the page has a form, try applying the :focus pseudo-class to some of the form elements. Set them to a different background color when they have the keyboard "focus."

13. Try adding some generated content with the :before or :after pseudo-elements, perhaps before or after some <h1> elements on the page.

14

14. Try adding a style that will affect all the elements on the page by using the universal selector. The syntax would be * {property: value;}.

15. If you haven't already, save your changes and display the page in Netscape 6 or Opera 5.

Project Summary

This exercise gave you the opportunity to see how various advanced selectors work. It also gave you a feel for what it is like to try to modify the style of an existing page without changing the HTML code. It can be a bit tricky, but it is possible. It is unfortunate that these selectors are not well supported yet. Perhaps in a few years the browser manufacturers will have caught up with the development of CSS and will have strengthened their support of these useful Web design tools.

The following illustration demonstrates some of the advanced selectors. To reproduce the screen shot shown here, try copying the code that follows the illustration and saving it as an HTML file. Then, display it in Netscape 6 or Opera 5. You will need to supply your own images, or download the page created with this code (along with the other code from this book) from Osborne's Web site: **www.osborne.com**.

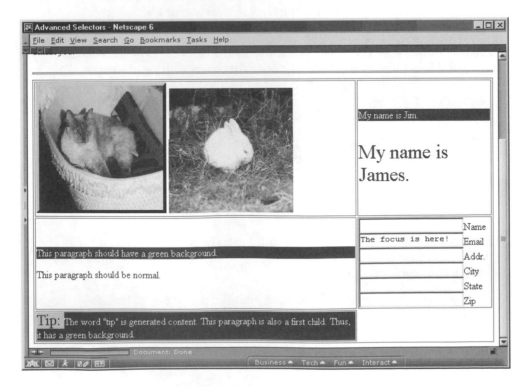

```
<html><head><title>Advanced Selectors</title>
<style>
*                    {color: blue;
                      background-color: white;}
h1+p                 {font-style: italic;}
div>b                {color: red;
                      background-color: white;}
img[alt~="Buttons"] {border: thick outset blue;}
p[title|="James"]    {font-size: 2em;
                      color: red;}
p:first-child        {background-color:
                      green; color:white;}
input:focus          {background-color: cyan;}
p.tips:before        {content: "Tip: ";
                      font-size:1.5em;
                      color: blue;
                      background-color: yellow;}
</style>
</head>
<body>
<div>This is the <b>best</b> day of my life!</div>
<hr />
<h1>Big News</h1>
<p>This is the <b>best</b> day of my life!</p>
<p>Thank you!</p>
<table border="1">
<tr><td>
<img src="boo.jpg"
    width="200" height="200"
    alt="My cat Buttons" />
<img src="bunbun.jpg"
    width="200" height="200"
    alt="Our rabbit Bunbun" />
</td><td>
<p>My name is Jim.</p>
<p title="James-H-Pence">My name is James.</p>
</td></tr>
<tr><td>
<div>
<p>This paragraph should have a green background.</p>
<p>This paragraph should be normal.</p>
</div>
</td><td>
<form>
<input>Name<br />
<input>Email<br />
<input>Addr.<br />
```

14

```
<input>City<br />
<input>State<br />
<input>Zip<br />
</form>
</td></tr>
<tr><td>
<p class="tips">This is a tip.</p>
</td></tr></table>
</body></html>
```

Advanced Properties

Some of the CSS 2 specification involved adding new properties to existing categories. For instance, the text-shadow property was added to the text properties, giving the designer the ability to create a "drop shadow" effect. However, the majority of the new properties added to CSS are in totally new categories. These properties add exciting new capabilities to CSS, such as aural (audio) style sheets, paged media, user interface design, and even custom font design. The two primary drawbacks with the new properties are that they are, as a rule, far more complicated to use than CSS 1 and are very poorly supported at this time. This section provides a survey of the advanced properties and some resources where you can learn more about them.

Aural Style Sheets

The World Wide Web used to be, for the most part, closed to those with visual impairment. With the advent of streaming audio, some of that has changed. However, there is still a great portion of the Web that is essentially inaccessible to those who can't see. With Braille and aural (audio) browsers, a whole new world is beginning to open up for the blind. Aural stylesheets can be helpful for those who have difficulty reading or who are just learning to read, among others. With that in mind, the CSS 2 specification includes a range of properties that govern how sound should be played over an audio browser or speech synthesizer. A few of these properties are:

- **Volume** Regulates the volume of the playback

- **Azimuth** Controls whether the sound appears to come from the left, center, or right

- **Speak** This property works something like the display property. It allows the designer to decide which text should be spoken and how the browser should speak it (normally or spelled out).

- **Speech-rate**   Allows you to control the speed at which text is spoken.

- **Richness**   Allows you to set the "tone" of the voice by a number value. The higher the value, the "richer" the voice. (A "rich" voice can be heard in a crowded room).

- **Cue**   The cue-before and cue-after properties will play a sound (ping, pop, and so on) before or after an element's content is played. This helps distinguish it from other elements.

- **Play-during**   The play-during property plays a background sound while the contents of an element are being rendered.

Aside from the unfamiliar properties, aural style sheet rules look like and function as do other rules. The syntax is the same; the properties and value units are different. For example, a simple aural style rule that will cause a speech synthesizer to render the text of an <h1> element might look like this:

```
h1      {voice-family: female;
         richness: 60;
         cue-before: url("bell.au");
         play-during: url("background.wav");}
```

Aural style sheets will increase accessibility to the World Wide Web, making it available to many people who previously could not benefit from it. If you are interested in learning more about aural style sheets, check out the CSS resources listed in Table 14-6, near the end of this module.

User Interface Properties

Many people like to customize their personal computer's environment. Perhaps you have created your own set of custom colors for your PC or Mac. Wouldn't it be nice if the Web pages you visit would tailor themselves to fit into your color scheme? With CSS 2, it is possible for a Web page designer to write a style sheet that will "read" the color settings you have on your own system and tailor the colors of the Web page to match them. This is one of the more interesting features of the user interface properties. These properties enable you to customize your visitor's "interface" (system) in several ways:

- **Cursor**   With the cursor property you can specify the type of cursor that should appear on the page, whether a crosshair, pointer, I-bar, hourglass, and so on.

- **Outline**   The outline properties enable you to place outlines around various elements on the page. Outlines are distinguished from borders in

14

that they take up no space, and they don't have to be rectangular. The outline properties are similar to the border properties in their syntax and values.

●   **User Preferences for Color**   Instead of a set of properties, the user color preferences represent a set of *values* that may be supplied wherever you want to specify a color. For example, if you want to set the background color of your page to match your user's desktop background, you could write a style rule that reads: body {background-color: Background;}.

●   **User Preferences for Fonts**   It is also possible to draw from your visitor's font preferences for some of your fonts. For example, to use the same font that your visitors use in their status bars, you could write a style rule something like this: p {font: status-bar;}.

User interface properties such as these will enable you to customize your pages to accommodate your visitors' environments. Unfortunately, most of these properties are currently supported only by IE 5 for Mac. The cursor property enjoys somewhat—but not much—better support.

Paged Media

Have you ever tried to print a page from a Web site? The results are usually less than ideal. Because a Web page is actually more like a "scroll," printers are at something of a loss when trying to make a hard copy. Page divisions are arbitrary and without respect to the layout of the content. Also, with the advent of handheld browsers and other "paged media," it is becoming more important to have a way of specifying where and how page breaks should occur.

CSS 2 addresses this problem by providing properties for paged media. These properties enable you to specify precisely where you want page breaks to occur, where you want page breaks to be avoided, margins and settings for left and right pages, and more.

How do the paged media properties work? The key is in understanding the term *paged media*. A normal Web page is considered to be *continuous media*, because it is like a scroll. As long as you keep adding content, the page gets longer and longer. By using the "at page" rule, @page, you can create a *page box*. This, in effect, instructs a browser to divide a single HTML document into multiple pages. You can specify the size of the page box to be 8½ by 11, the size of a computer screen, or any number of other possibilities. You can even specify the kinds of margins you want to have as well as insert crop marks if the page is to serve as copy for printing.

Ask the Expert

Question: What are "at" rules?

Answer: "At" rules mark off special rules for applying style. For example, in Module 2 you learned about the @import rule, which enables you to import a style sheet from another location or Web site. The @page rule specifies special styles for paged media. The @media rule can be used to specify special styles for other types of media (projection, Braille, handheld, aural, and so on). If you want to specify a particular character set, say for a different language, you can use the @charset rule. You can even set a rule that describes or gives download location for a font with the @font-face rule.

Question: How are @rules different from other style rules?

Answer: There's not a great deal of difference. In one sense, an "at" rule is just another type of selector. However, @rules are different in that they usually mark of a set of styles to be applied in special circumstances. Thus, rather than creating a lot of different style sheets, you could have a series of "at" rules that specify styles for different types of media, as in the following listing:

```
<style>
@page {property: value;}
@aural {property: value;}
@print {property: value;}
@braille {property: value;}
</style>
```

Font Specification Properties

One of the frustrations in designing with CSS is that your visitors may not have the same fonts on their systems as you have. Thus, you can create a beautiful layout with creative font choices, only to have your carefully chosen fonts replaced with a generic font. CSS 2 addresses this problem by providing font specification properties.

With font specification properties, you can literally give a browser the description of a font you wish to display. If that particular font is not resident

14

on the user's system, the browser can download the font you wish to use. It can also search for one that matches as nearly as possible your original choice, then modify it to fit your description.

For font description, you do not use properties and values, but rather *descriptors* and values. On one level, the descriptors are very similar to the standard font properties (font-family, font-style, font-variant, and so on). However, it is possible to provide extremely detailed descriptions of the kind of font you are looking for with descriptors such as *stemv*, *stemh*, *slope*, *cap-height*, and so on.

As with most of the other aspects of CSS 2 covered in this module, you will have to wait a while before you can make use of these properties, as the support for them is nonexistent as of this writing.

1-Minute Drill

● What is the difference between "paged media" and "continuous media"?

● What is an @rule?

● In font specification, instead of properties you use _____.

CSS 2 Resources

The complexity of much of CSS 2 puts it beyond the scope of a beginner's book such as this one. However, if you want to learn more about CSS 2, there are plenty of resources available, both online and in print. Table 14-6 provides a list of resources you may wish to take advantage of if you are interested in learning how to apply these advanced aspects of CSS 2 in your Web design.

● Paged media is dealt with as separate page "boxes," while continuous media functions like a scroll
● An @rule is a special type of selector that enables a designer to import data to a stylesheet and to set apart style rules for specific media types
● Descriptors

Book/Web Site	Publisher / URL
Cascading Style Sheets 2.0: A Programmer's Reference, by Eric A. Meyer	Osborne/McGraw-Hill, 2001
Cascading Style Sheets: Designing for the Web, Second Edition by Håkon Wium Lie and Bert Bos	Addison-Wesley, 1999
The CSS 2 Specification	www.w3.org
Webreview	www.webreview.com
Western CIvilisation	www.westciv.com
Rich in Style	www.richinstyle.com

Table 14-6   Sources of Information on CSS 2

14

☑ Mastery Check

1. What kind of selector would you use to apply a style only to the first paragraph element on a page?

   _____

   _____

2. What is the main limitation of the :hover pseudo-class?

   _____

   _____

3. When does the :focus pseudo-class select an element?

   _____

   _____

4. What would the following style rule select?
   img[alt~="Laurel"]

   _____

   _____

5. In an aural stylesheet, what would the "azimuth" property control?

   _____

   _____

6. Write a style rule that would add the word "Caution" before every <h1> element.

   _____

   _____

Part 4

Appendixes

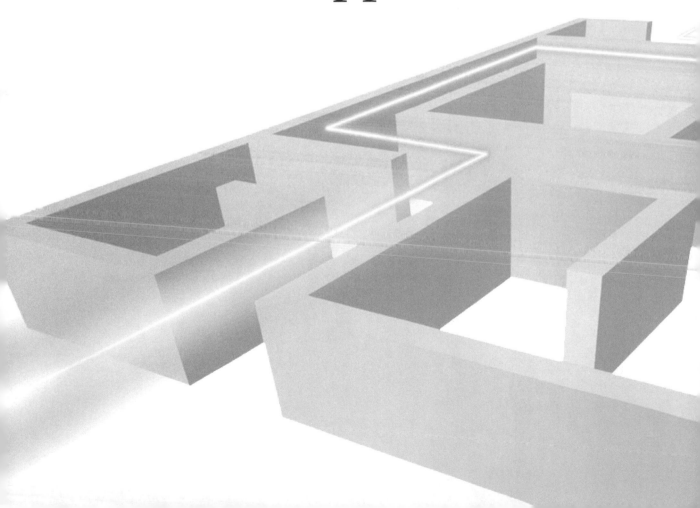

Appendix A

Answers to Mastery Checks

Module 1: HTML and CSS: Focus on the Similarities

1. According to the W3C, HTML markup should be used to define a Web page's:

    C. Structure

2. An HTML element functions like a:

    A. Container

3. In CSS, the concept of properties and values corresponds to HTML's:

    C. Attributes and values

4. CSS properties and values must always be separated by:

    B. A colon

5. Of the four types of stylesheets listed below, which one would have the priority over all the others?

    A. Inline

6. Which of the four style rules below is *correctly* written?

    C. <h1 style="color: red;">

Module 2: Understanding and Using Selectors

1. List the four major categories of selectors.

Type, Descendent, Attribute, and Pseudo

2. A selector that deals with situations not directly reflected in HTML code is called a _____-_____ or a _____-_____.

Pseudo-Class and Pseudo-Element

3. What things are wrong with the following style rule?

```
p.yellow+large  (background color:green;)
```

There is a plus sign between "yellow" and "large," there is a space between "background" and color," and the declaration is enclosed in parentheses instead of curly braces.

4. The <body> element is a _____ of the <html> element and a _____ of the <head> element.

Child, Sibling

5. Which of the following style rules is written correctly?

C is correctly written.

Module 3: Surveying CSS Properties

1. List the five basic categories of properties.

Text properties, font properties, color/background properties, box properties, and classification properties

2. To convert a block of text to "small caps," you would use:

Font-variant

3. Write a style rule for the <h1> element that sets the text color to red and the background color to white and adds a thin, inset, blue border.

```
h1        {color: red;
              background-color: white;
              border-style: inset;
              border-width: thin;
              border-color: blue;}
```

4. To change the bullet on an unordered list, what property would you use?

The list-style-type property.

5. Write a style rule that sets the default text for a page to a 12 point, blue font.

body   {color: blue; font-size: 12pt;}

Module 4: Applying Values

1. Which of the following measurement units would be best to use if you were designing a page to be printed on paper rather than viewed on a monitor?

Inches

2. There is an error in the following url value. Correct it.

body {background-image: url(mypicture.gif);}
The parentheses were incorrectly placed around the letters "url" rather than the actual url.

3. The color value #ff00cc corresponds to which of the following rgb values?

100%, 0%, 80%

4. If you want your pages to be scalable, you need to use _____ measurements.

Relative

5. True or false. An ex is the best choice for a measurement unit when you want to use relative measurements.

False (an em is the best choice)

6. True or false. Percentages are a form of absolute measurement.

False (percentages are relative measurements)

7. True or false. In additive color mixing, 100% of all the primary colors results in black.

False (white)

8. URI stands for _____ _____

_____

Uniform Resource Indicator

9. RGB stands for _____, _____, _____.

Red, Green, Blue

Module 5: Understanding Cascade and Inheritance

1. Define inheritance.

Inheritance is the mechanism by which the styles (properties) of a parent (ancestor) element are passed on to its children (descendents).

2. What is specificity?

Specificity is a means of calculating the amount of "weight" a browser will give a particular style rule, on the basis of the selectors that are used in the rule.

3. What is the cascade?

The cascade is a set of rules that determines the order in which multiple stylesheets and style rules are applied to an HTML document.

4. What happens when you add !important to a style declaration?

When you add !important to a style declaration, it is something like giving that declaration "VIP" status. It means that the browser will generally not allow it to be overridden by any other styles.

5. Calculate the specificity for the following selectors:

A.   ul li em.red #123 = 1-1-3

B.   table td i = 0-0-3

C.   body h1 #9394h = 1-0-2

6. According to the CSS specification, whose !important declaration should take priority?

The user's

7. If several identical selectors remain after the cascade is complete, how does the browser choose which style to apply?

The last style specified is the one that is used.

Module 6: Working with Font Properties

1. Which of the following is *not* a value of the font-style property?

small-caps

2. On the font-weight scale of 100-900, which value is considered "normal"?

400

3. List the five "generic" font types that CSS recognizes.

serif, sans-serif, monospace, cursive, and fantasy

4. List the different length measurements you can use to specify a value for font-size.

points, picas, inches, centimeters, millimeters, pixels, ems, and exes.

5. Of the previous value types, which is recommended for use on Web pages?

ems

Module 7: Work with Text Properties

1. Which property would you use to create an "overline" effect?

text-decoration

2. Which of these style rules is written incorrectly and why?

#first   {line-height: -2.2em;}
The line-height property does not accept negative values.

3. The text-align property should be used in place of what HTML attribute?

The align attribute

4. A percentage value used with text-indent is measured relative to which of the following:

The parent element

Module 8: Applying Color and Background Properties

1. Which of the following background-image declarations is *correctly* written?

{background-image: url(oldpix.jpg);}

2. To set the color for text, you use the _____ property.

color

3. Write a style rule for the <h1> element that will result in red text on a navy background.

h1 {color: red; background-color: navy;}

4. Which of the following style rules will cause an image to tile vertically, down the right side of the page?

body {background: white url(myimage.jpg) repeat-y right top;}

5. Using the background: property, write a style rule for the <body> element that will set a white background and place a single logo image that is fixed in the upper-right corner of the page. Use percentage values for the positioning.

body {background: white url(logo.gif) no-repeat 100% 0% fixed;}

Module 9: Using Box Properties

1. If four values are supplied for padding, margin, or border properties, in what order will browsers apply them?

Top, Right, Bottom, Left

2. Using shorthand properties, write a style rule for the <h3> element that will create a thick, red, grooved border on the top and bottom and a thin, solid, blue border on the right and left.

h3   {border-style: grooved solid;
        border-color: red blue;
        border-width: thick thin;}

3. Write the same style rule for a <p> element, using the individual (top, right, bottom, left) properties.

p {border-style-top: grooved;
    border-style-bottom: grooved;
    border-style-right: solid;
    border-style-left: solid;
    border-color-top: red;
    border-color-bottom: red;
    border-color-right: blue;
    border-color-left: blue;
    border-width-top: thick;
    border-width-bottom: thick;
    border-width-right: thin;
    border-width-left: thin;}

A

4. Using shorthand properties, write a style rule that adds 15 pixels of padding, 15 pixels of margin, and a thin yellow outset border to the <div> element.

```
div  {padding: 15px;
      margins: 15px;
      border: outset thin yellow;}
```

5. Using individual (top, right, bottom, left) properties, write a style rule for an <h2> element that applies 15% of padding to the top, 20 pixel margins on the right and left, and a thick green double border on the left and top sides.

```
h2    {padding-top: 15%;
       margin-left: 20px;
       margin-right: 20px;
       border-left-style: double;
       border-left-color: green;
       border-left-width: thick;
       border-top-style: double;
       border-top-color: green;
       border-top-width: thick;}
```

Module 10: Applying the Descriptive Properties

1. The display property enables you to change the fundamental _____ of any HTML element.

Behavior

2. Write a style rule that adds a "marker" before a level-three heading.

```
h3:before  {display: marker;
            content: url(image.gif);}
```

3. List the four original (CSS 1) values for the display property.

block, inline, list-item, none

4. What property/value combination would you use if you wanted to prevent a browser from adding its own line breaks to your text?

white-space: nowrap;

5. Write a style rule for the fourth level of an ordered list (outline) that will set the display to lowercase Roman numerals and will cause the item numbers to display inside the list item's "box."

```
ol ol ol ol {list-style: lower-roman inside;} or
ol ol ol ol {list-style-type: lower-roman;
             list-style-position: inside;}
```

Module 11: The Visual Model

1. Write a style rule for the img selector that will cause other elements to "wrap" down the left side of the image.

```
img {float: right;}
```

2. Write a style rule for the <div> element that will set its dimensions at 250 pixels by 250 pixels, give it a background color of navy and text color of yellow, and position it with absolute positioning so that the box's upper-left corner is in the center of the page.

```
div    {background-color: navy;
         color: yellow;
         height: 250px;
         width: 250px;
         position: absolute;
         top: 50%;
         left: 50%; }
```

3. Use the float property to write style rules that will position three boxes side by side on the page, beginning at the left side. Use id selectors to name the boxes: "box1," "box2," and "box3."

```
#box1 {float: left;}
#box2 {float: left;}
#box3 {float: left;}
```

4. The browser window is the point of reference for the _____ positioning scheme.

Fixed

5. What is relative positioning relative *to*?

The position an element would hold according to the normal (static) positioning scheme.

A

Module 12: CSS Visual Effects

1. List the four key components of DHTML

The four components of DHTML are HTML, CSS, a scripting language, and the DOM (Document Object Model).

2. According to its z-index, which of the following selectors will be on top of the stack? on the bottom? in the middle?

The div selector will be on top; #123 will be on bottom; .purple will be in the middle.

3. What values could you use with the overflow property if you wanted your visitors to be able to view the "hidden" content.

You would use "scroll," or "auto."

4. You have a 300 by 300 pixel box, to which you have applied the overflow property. Write a declaration with the clipping property that will give you a 15 pixel margin around the clipped contents.

clip: 15px 285px 285px 15px

5. If you want to make an element's "box" disappear *without* affecting the overall layout of the page, which property/value combination should you use?

visibility: hidden

Module 13: CSS and Site Design

1. Every page on your site should have some form of:

Navigation system

2. What is a storyboard?

A storyboard is a sketch or flow chart of your site, done on paper, 3x5 cards, or some other visual medium.

3. What is the difference between a *document type definition* and a *document type declaration*?

A *document type definition* (DTD) is the "blueprint" for various versions of HTML. Each version will have its own DTD. A *document type declaration* is a line in an HTML document that specifies which DTD the document is supposed to conform to.

4. What is the difference between a *well-formed* and a *valid* document?

A *well-formed* document is correctly written. A *valid* document conforms to a particular DTD.

5. Correct the following HTML code so that it is well formed and add a document type declaration that validates it against the HTML 4.01 strict DTD.

```
<!DOCTYPE HTML PUBLIC "-//W3C//DTD HTML 4.01 Strict//EN"
    "http://www.w3.org/TR/html4/strict.dtd">
<html>
<head><title>Page Title</title></head>
<body>
<h1>This is a heading.</h1>
<p>This is paragraph one.</p>
<img href="mypicture.jpg" width="100" height="100" alt="Me!" />
<p>This is paragraph two.</p>
<p>Paragraph three.</p> (The <font> element has been removed.)
</body>
</html>
```

Note
Boldfaced text indicates corrected elements.

Module 14: Advanced CSS

1. What kind of selector would you use to apply a style only to the first paragraph element on a page?

The :first-child pseudo-class.

2. What is the main limitation of the :hover pseudo-class?

Currently, it works only with the <a> element.

A

3. When does the :focus pseudo-class select an element?

It selects an element when the element has the keyboard (user's) "focus."

4. What would the following style rule select?

img[alt~="Laurel"]

It would select an image, <img />, element when the alt attribute contained the value "Laurel" among a space-separated group of values.

5. In an aural style sheet, what would the "azimuth" property control?

Azimuth would control the direction (left, right, center) that the sound appears to come from.

6. Write a style rule that would add the word "Caution" before every <h1> element.

h1:before {content: "Caution";}

Appendix B

CSS 1 Quick Reference

The following tables will provide you with a quick reference for the most commonly used and better supported CSS selectors and properties. Although this is primarily a CSS 1 reference, some selectors and properties from CSS 2 have been included. The first table lists different types of selectors. The tables that follow list the various CSS properties, organized by type, with examples of basic CSS syntax. The tables are generally organized with the most commonly used (and best-supported) selectors and properties listed first.

HTML Selectors

Selector	What it "selects"	Example
Type	HTML element	h1 Selects the h1 element
Multiple	Multiple HTML elements	h1, h2, h3 Selects all listed elements
Descendent (contextual)	A descendent element	h1 b selects: <h1><b></b></h1>
Class—.class	Any element with a matching class attribute	h1.xtra_large selects: <h1 class="xtra_large">
ID—#id	Any element with a matching id attribute	p#copyright selects: <p id="copyright">

Pseudo-Class Selectors

Pseudo-Class	What it "Selects"	Example
:link	Any element that is also an unvisited hypertext link	a:link {text-decoration: none;} removes link underlining
:active	Any element that is also an active hypertext link	a:active {color: red;} sets the active link color to red
:visited	Any element that is also a visited hypertext link	a:visited {color: green;} turns the color of visited links to green
:hover	Any element over which the mouse is currently "hovering"	a: hover {background-color: yellow;} gives the link a yellow background when a "mouseOver" occurs.

Pseudo-Element Selectors

Pseudo-Element	What it "Selects"	Example
:first-letter	The first letter of any element to which it is applied	p:first-letter {font-size: 2em;}
:first-line	The first line of any element to which it is applied	p:first-line {color: green;}

Font Properties

Property	Possible Values	Example
font-family	generic font names (serif, sans-serif, monospace, cursive, fantasy) or specific font names (Arial, Times New Roman, and so on)	h1 {font-family: serif;}
font-size	length, percentage, or keyword: larger, smaller, xx-small, x-small, small, medium, large, x-large, xx-large	p {font-size: 1.5em;}
font-style	normal, italic, oblique	p {font-style: italic;}
font-variant	normal, small-caps	span {font-variant: small-caps;}
font-weight	numerical: 100, 200, 300, 400, 500, 600, 700, 800, 900 keyword: normal, bold, bolder, lighter	p {font-weight: 700;}
font (shorthand)	font-style, font-variant, font-weight, font-size, line-height, font-family	p {font: italic bold 1.2em serif;}

Text Properties

Property	Possible Values	Example
word-spacing	length	p {word-spacing: 1em;}
letter-spacing	length	h1 {letter-spacing: .25ex;}
text-decoration	none, underline, overline, line-through, blink	a:link {text-decoration: none;}

Property	Possible Values	Example
vertical-align	length, percentage, keyword: baseline, super, sub, top, bottom, text-top, middle, text-bottom	img {vertical-align: super;}
text-align	left, right, center, justify	p {text-align: right;}
text-transform	none, uppercase, capitalize, lowercase	span {text-transform: capitalize;}
text-indent	length, percentage	p.indent {text-indent: 5%;}
line-height	length, percentage, number	h1 {line-height: 1.5em;}

Margin Properties

Property	Possible Values	Example
margin-top	length, percentage, auto	h1 {margin-top: 0.5em;}
margin-right	length, percentage, auto	h1 {margin-right: 15%;}
margin-bottom	length, percentage, auto	h1 {margin-bottom: .5em;}
margin-left	length, percentage, auto	h1 {margin-left: 12.5%}
margin	length, percentage, auto	h1 {margin: .5em;} or h1 {margin: .5em 15%;} (top/bottom, right/left) h1 {margin: .5em 15% .5em;} (top, right/left, bottom) h1 {margin: 1em 5% 1em 5%;} (top, right, bottom, left)

Padding Properties

Property	Possible Values	Example
padding-top	length, percentage	p {padding-top: 1mm;}
padding-right	length, percentage	div {padding-right: .5in;}
padding-bottom	length, percentage	h1 {padding-bottom: .3em;}
padding-left	length, percentage	h3 {padding-left: 20px;}

Property	Possible Values	Example
padding	length, percentage	p {padding: .5em;} or p {padding: .5em 20px;} (top/bottom, right/left) p {padding: .5in 15% .5in;} (top, right/left, bottom) p {padding: 1ex 5% 1em 5%;} (top, right, bottom, left)

Border Style Properties

Property	Possible Values	Example
border-top-style	hidden, dotted, dashed, solid, double, groove, ridge, inset, outset, none	div {border-top-style: dashed;}
border-right-style	(same as above)	p {border-right-style: solid;}
border-bottom-style	(same as above)	h1 {border-bottom-style: groove;}
border-left-style	(same as above)	img {border-left-style: inset;}
border-style (shorthand)	(same as above)	h1 {border-style: ridge;} or p {border-style: inset solid;} (top/bottom, right/left) h2 {border-style: dashed solid dashed;} (top, right/left, bottom) img {border-style: solid inset dashed outset;} (top, right, bottom, left)

Border Width Properties

Property	Possible Values	Example
border-top-width	thin, medium, thick, or length unit	h1 {border-top-width: thin;}
border-right-width	(same as above)	h2 {border-right-width: medium;}
border-bottom-width	(same as above)	img {border-bottom-width: thick;}
border-left-width	(same as above)	div {border-left-width: thin;}

Property	Possible Values	Example
border-width	(same as above)	p {border-width: thin;} or p.border {border-width: thin thick;} (top/bottom, right/left) div {border-width: thin thick medium;} (top, right/left, bottom) h1 {border-width: 3px 5px 2px 4px;} (top, right, bottom, left)

Border Color Properties

Property	Possible Values	Example
border-top-color	color (hex, short hex, RGB numeral, RGB percentage, keyword)	p {border-top-color: #ffcc00;}
border-right-color	(same as above)	div {border-right-color: #fc0;}
border-bottom-color	(same as above)	h1 {border-bottom-color: rgb(255, 255, 0);}
border-left-color	(same as above)	img {border-left-color: rgb(25%, 50%, 25%);}
border-color	(same as above)	p {border-color: red;} or p.border {border-color: red green;} (top/bottom, right/left) div {border-color: red green blue;} (top, right/left, bottom) h1 {border-color: red green blue yellow;} (top, right, bottom, left)

Border Properties

Property	Possible Values	Example
border-top	style, width, color	div {border-top: dashed thin yellow;}
border-right	(same as above)	p {border-right: solid thick red;}
border-bottom	(same as above)	h1 {border-bottom: inset medium blue;}
border-left	(same as above)	h3 {border-left: outset 1em green;}
border	(same as above)	h6 {border: inset thin yellow;}

Color / Background Properties

Property	Possible Values	Example
color	keywords: black, white, silver, gray, red, blue, green, yellow, fuscia, lime, navy, maroon, olive, teal, purple, aqua code: hexadecimal, shortened hex, RGB percentage values, RGB numerical values	p {color: red;}
background-color	keywords: black, white, silver, gray, red, blue, green, yellow, fuscia, lime, navy, maroon, olive, teal, purple, aqua code: hexadecimal, shortened hex, RGB percentage values, RGB numerical values	a:hover {background-color: navy;}
background-image	url	body {background-image: url(logo.gif);}
background-repeat	repeat, repeat-x, repeat-y, no-repeat	body {background-repeat: no-repeat;}
background-attachment	fixed, scroll	p {background-attachment: fixed;}
background-position	percentages, length, keyword: (top, center, bottom) (left, center, right)	body {background-position: top right;}
background	color, image, repeat, attachment, position	background: red url(mypics.gif) no-repeat fixed center center

Descriptive Properties

Property	Possible Values	Example
display	inline, block, list-item, none	h1 {display: inline;}
list-style-type	disc, circle, square, decimal, lower-roman, upper-roman, lower-alpha, upper alpha	ul {list-style-type: square;}
list-style-position	inside, outside	ol {list-style-position: inside;}
list-style-image	uri, none	ul {list-style-image: url(button.gif);}
list-style	style, position, image	ol {upper-roman outside;}
white-space	normal, pre, nowrap	p {white-space: pre;}

Positioning and Visual Effects Properties

Property	Possible Values	Example
width	length, percentage, auto	img {width: 245px;}
height	length, percentage, auto	img {height: 125px;}
float	left, right, none	img {float: right;}
clear	left, right, both, none	img {clear: both;}
position	static, relative, absolute, fixed	h1 {position: absolute;}
top*	length, percentage, auto	p { top: 10px;} (see note)
right*	length, percentage, auto	img {right: 5px;} (see note)
bottom*	length, percentage, auto	img {bottom: 5%;} (see note)
left*	length, percentage, auto	h1 {left: 25px;} (see note)
visibility	visible, hidden, collapse	h2 {visibility: hidden;}
z-index*	auto, numeral	img {z-index: 6;} (see note)
overflow*	visible, hidden, scroll, auto	p {overflow: scroll;}
clip*	shape/length, auto	p {clip: rect(5px 90px 90px 5px);}

Note

The properties marked with an asterisk (*) can be used only with positioned elements.

Index

E

F

INTERNATIONAL CONTACT INFORMATION

AUSTRALIA
McGraw-Hill Book Company Australia Pty. Ltd.
TEL +61-2-9417-9899
FAX +61-2-9417-5687
http://www.mcgraw-hill.com.au
books-it_sydney@mcgraw-hill.com

CANADA
McGraw-Hill Ryerson Ltd.
TEL +905-430-5000
FAX +905-430-5020
http://www.mcgrawhill.ca

GREECE, MIDDLE EAST,
NORTHERN AFRICA
McGraw-Hill Hellas
TEL +30-1-656-0990-3-4
FAX +30-1-654-5525

MEXICO (Also serving Latin America)
McGraw-Hill Interamericana Editores S.A. de C.V.
TEL +525-117-1583
FAX +525-117-1589
http://www.mcgraw-hill.com.mx
fernando_castellanos@mcgraw-hill.com

SINGAPORE (Serving Asia)
McGraw-Hill Book Company
TEL +65-863-1580
FAX +65-862-3354
http://www.mcgraw-hill.com.sg
mghasia@mcgraw-hill.com

SOUTH AFRICA
McGraw-Hill South Africa
TEL +27-11-622-7512
FAX +27-11-622-9045
robyn_swanepoel@mcgraw-hill.com

UNITED KINGDOM & EUROPE
(Excluding Southern Europe)
McGraw-Hill Education Europe
TEL +44-1-628-502500
FAX +44-1-628-770224
http://www.mcgraw-hill.co.uk
computing_neurope@mcgraw-hill.com

ALL OTHER INQUIRIES Contact:
Osborne/McGraw-Hill
TEL +1-510-549-6600
FAX +1-510-883-7600
http://www.osborne.com
omg_international@mcgraw-hill.com